SEMIOTEXT(E) ACTIVE AGENTS SERIES

Copyright © 2016 Robert Glück.

Published by Semiotext(e)
PO BOX 629, South Pasadena, CA 91031
www.semiotexte.com

Special thanks to Robert Dewhurst.

Cover: Jess, *The Mouse's Tale*, 1951–1954. Collage (gelatin silver prints, magazine reproductions, and gouache on paper). Copyright © 2015 by the Jess Collins Trust and reproduced by permission. Image courtesy of the San Francisco Museum of Modern Art.

Paintings by Frank Moore on pages 180, 183, 185, 187, and 189 are reproduced by permission from Sperone Westwater, New York. © Gesso Foundation.

Back Cover Photography: Xavier Permanyer Bel
Design: Hedi El Kholti

ISBN: 978-1-58435-175-7
Distributed by The MIT Press, Cambridge, Mass. and London, England
Printed in the United States of America

Communal Nude

Collected Essays

Robert Glück

Contents

FIVE: TALKS

for my friend Bruce Boone

ONE

A REAL FICTIONAL DEPTH

LONG NOTE ON NEW NARRATIVE

To talk about the beginnings of New Narrative, I have to talk about my friendship with Bruce Boone. We met in the early seventies through the San Francisco Art Institute's bulletin board: Ed and I wanted to move and Bruce and Burton wanted to move—would we all be happy living together? For some reason both couples dropped the idea and we remained in our respective flats for many years. But Bruce and I were poets and our obsession with Frank O'Hara forged a bond.

I was twenty-three or twenty-four. Bruce was seven years older. He was a wonderful teacher. He read to transform himself and to attain a correct understanding. Such understanding was urgently political.

Bruce had his eye on the future, a catastrophic upheaval he predicted with a certain grandeur, but it was my own present he helped me find. I read and wrote to invoke what seemed impossible—relation itself—in order to take part in a world that ceaselessly makes itself up, to "wake up" to the world, to recognize the world, to be convinced that the world exists, to take revenge on the world for not existing.

To talk about New Narrative, I must also talk about Language poetry, which was in its heroic period in the seventies. I treat diverse poets as one unit, a sort of flying wedge, because that's how we experienced them. It would be hard to overestimate the drama they brought to a Bay Area scene that limped through the seventies—with the powerful exception of feminist poets like Judy Grahn, and the excitement of poetry generated by new movements. Language poetry's Puritan rigor, delight in technical vocabularies, and professionalism were new to a generation of Bay Area poets whose influences included the Beats, Robert Duncan and Jack Spicer, the New York School (Bolinas was its western outpost), surrealism and psychedelic surrealism.

Suddenly people took sides, though at times these confrontations resembled a pastiche of the embattled positions of earlier avant-guards. Language poetry seemed very "straight male"—though what didn't? Barrett Watten's *Total Syntax*, for example, brilliantly established (as it dispatched) a lineage of fathers: Olson, Zukofsky, Pound, etc.

If I could have become a Language poet I would have; I craved the formalist fireworks, a purity that invented its own tenets. On the snowy mountaintop of progressive formalism, from the highest high road of modernist achievement, plenty of contempt seemed to be heaped on less rigorous endeavor. I had come to a dead end in the mid-seventies like the poetry scene itself. The problem was not theoretical—or it was: I could not go on until I figured out some way to understand where I was. I also craved the community the Language poets made for themselves.

The questions vexing Bruce and me and the kind of rigor we needed were only partly addressed by Language poetry, which, in the most general sense, we saw as an aesthetics built on an examination (by subtraction: of voice, of continuity) of the ways language generates meaning. The same could be said of other experimental work, especially the minimalisms, but Language poetry was our proximate example.

Warring camps drew battle lines between representation and nonrepresentation—retrospection makes the argument seem as arbitrary as Fancy vs. Imagination. But certainly the "logic of history" at that moment supported this division, along with the struggle to find a third position that would encompass the whole argument.

I experienced the poetry of disjunction as a luxurious idealism in which the speaking subject rejects the confines of representation and disappears in the largest freedom, that of language itself. My attraction to this freedom, and to the professionalism that purveyed it, made for a kind of class struggle within myself. Whole areas of my experience, especially gay experience, were not admitted to this utopia. The mainstream reflected a resoundingly coherent image of myself back to me—an image so unjust that it amounted to a tyranny that I could not turn my back on. We had been disastrously described by the mainstream—a naming whose most extreme (though not uncommon) expression was physical violence. Combating this injustice required at least a provisionally stable identity.

Meanwhile, gay identity was also in its heroic period—it had not yet settled into just another nationalism and it was new enough to know its own constructedness. In the urban mix, some great experiment was actually taking place, a genuine community where strangers and different classes and ethnicities rubbed more than shoulders. This community was not destroyed by commodity culture, which was destroying so many other communities; instead, it was founded in commodity culture. We had to talk about it. Bruce and I turned to each other to see if we could come up with a better representation—not in order to satisfy movement pieties or to be political, but in order to be. We (eventually we were gay, lesbian, and working-class writers) could not let narration go.

(I wonder if other readers register the extent to which the body of Language poetry is collage, pastiche, and the poetry of the "already said." A phrase can be, in the first place, an example of itself, of phrases generally, and that doubleness creates in this reader an ongoing sensation of déjà vu. Phrases, sentences, ring with a feeling of déjà vu, like the sentences of Raymond Roussel. That is my deepest relation to Language poetry, a poetry that deepens the sense of the arbitrary because it hollows out language through a multiplication of contexts. I am made aware, almost intolerably, of the infinite valences.)

I'm confined to hindsight, so I write as though Bruce and I were following a plan instead of stumbling and groping toward a writing that could join other literatures of the present. We could have found narrative models in, say, Clark Coolidge's prose, so perhaps narrative practice relates outward to the actual community whose story is being told. We could have located self-reference and awareness of artifice in, say, the novels of Ronald Firbank. So again, our quest for a language that knows itself relates outward to a community speaking to itself dissonantly.

We were fellow travelers of Language poetry and the innovative feminist poetry of that time: our lives and reading led us toward a hybrid aesthetic, something impure. We (say, Bruce Boone, Camille Roy, Kevin Killian, Dodie Bellamy, Mike Amnasan, Francesca Rosa, myself, and to include the dead, Steve Abbott and Sam D'Allesandro) are still fellow travelers of the poetries that evolved since the late seventies, when writers talked about "nonnarrative." One could untangle that knot forever, or build an aesthetic on the ways language conveys silence, chaos, undifferentiated existence, and erects countless horizons of meaning.

How to be a theory-based writer?—one question. How to represent my experience as a gay man?—another question, just as pressing. These questions led to readers and communities almost completely ignorant of each other. Too fragmented for a gay audience? Too much sex and "voice" for a literary audience? (One gay editor of an experimental press observed in his rejection that for me homosexuality is an *idée fixe*—I wonder what heterosexuality is to heterosexuals?) I embodied these incommensurates so I had to ask this question: How can I convey urgent social meanings while opening or subverting the possibilities of meaning itself? That question has deviled and vexed Bay Area writing for twenty-five years. What kind of representation least deforms its subject? Can language be aware of itself (as object, as system, as commodity, as abstraction) yet take part in the forces that generate the present? Where in writing does engagement become authentic? One response, the politics of form, apparently does not answer the question completely.

One afternoon in 1976, Bruce remarked on the questions to the reader I'd been throwing into poems and stories. They were theatrical and they seemed to him to pressure and even sometimes to reverse the positions of reader and writer. Reader–writer dynamics seemed like a way into the problems that preoccupied us, a toe in the water.

From our poems and stories, Bruce abstracted "text-meta-text": a story keeps a running commentary on itself from the present. The commentary, taking the form of a meditation or a second story, supplies a succession of frames. That is, the more you fragment a story, the more it becomes an example of narration itself—narration displaying its devices—while at the same time (as I wrote in 1981) the metatext "asks questions, asks for critical response, makes claims on the reader, elicits comments. In any case, text-metatext takes its form from the dialectical cleft between real life and life as it wants to be."[1]

We did not want to break the back of representation or to "punish" it for lying, but to elaborate narration on as many different planes as we could, which seemed consistent with the lives we led. Writing can't will away power relations and commodity life; instead, writing must explore its relation to power and recognize that group practice resides inside the commodity. Bruce wrote, "When evaluating image in American culture, isn't it a commodity whether anyone likes it or not? You make your additions and subtractions from that point on."[2]

In 1978, Bruce and I launched the Black Star Series and published my *Family Poems* and his *My Walk with Bob*, a lovely book.[3] In "Remarks on Narrative"—the afterword to *Family Poems*—Bruce wrote, "As has now been apparent for some time, the poetry of the '70s seems generally to have reached a point of stagnation, increasing a kind of refinement of technique and available forms, without yet being able to profit greatly from the vigor, energy and accessibility that mark so much of the new Movement writing of gays, women and Third World writers, among others. Ultimately this impasse of poetry reflects conditions in society itself."[4]

We appreciated the comedy of mounting an offensive ("A critique of the new trends toward conceptualization, linguistic abstraction and process poetry") with those slenderest volumes.[5] My poems and stories were set "in the family," not so antipsychological as they might have been given that we assumed any blow to interiority was a step forward for mankind.

We contended with the Language poets while seeking their attention in the forums they erected for themselves. We published articles in *Poetics Journal* and *L=A=N=G=U=A=G=E*, and spoke in talk series and forums—a mere trickle in the torrent of their critical work. If Language Poetry was a dead end, what a fertile one it proved to be!

New Narrative was in place by the time Hoddypoll published Bruce's novel *Century of Clouds* in 1980 and Donald Allen's Four Seasons Foundation published my *Elements of a Coffee Service* in 1982. We were thinking about autobiography. By autobiography, we meant daydreams, nightdreams, the act of writing, the relationship to the reader, the meeting of flesh and culture; the self as collaboration, the self as disintegration, the gaps, inconsistencies, and distortions of the self; the enjambments of power, family, history, and language. Bruce and I brought high and low between the covers of a book, mingling essay, lyric, and story. Our publishing reflected those different modes: stories from *Elements* appeared in gay anthologies, porn magazines, *Social Text*, and *Soup*; Bruce wrote about Georges Bataille for *The Advocate*.

I wanted to write with a total continuity and total disjunction since I experienced the world (and myself) as continuous and infinity divided. That was my ambition for writing. Why should a work of literature be organized by one pattern of engagement? Why should a "position" be maintained regarding the size of the gaps between units of meaning? To describe how the world is organized may be the same as organizing the world. I wanted the pleasures and politics of the fragment and the pleasures and politics of story, gossip, fable, and case history; the randomness of chance and a sense of inevitability; sincerity while using appropriation and pastiche. When Barrett Watten said about *Jack the Modernist*, "You have your cake and eat it too," I took it as a great compliment, as if my intention spoke through the book.

During the seventies, Bruce was working on his PhD at UC Berkeley. His dissertation was a structuralist and gay reading of O'Hara—that is, O'Hara and community—a version of which was published in the first issue of *Social Text* in 1979. He joined the Marxism and Theory Group at St. Cloud, which gave birth to that journal. Bruce also wrote critical articles, especially tracking the "gay band" of the Berkeley Renaissance.[6] We were aspiring to an ideal of learning derived as much from Spicer and Duncan as from our contemporaries. Bruce introduced me to most of the critics who would make a foundation for New Narrative writing.

Here are a few of them:

In *The Theory of the Novel*, Georg Lukács maintains that the novel contains—that is, holds together—incommensurates. The epic and novel are the community telling itself its story, a story whose integration becomes increasingly hard to achieve. *Theory of the Novel* leads to ideas of collaboration and community that are not naïve—that is, to narrative that questions itself. It redistributes relations of power and springs the writer from the box of psychology, since he becomes that part of a community that tells itself its story. I wrote "Caricature," a talk given at 80 Langton in 1983, mostly using Lukács's book, locating instances of conservative and progressive communities speaking to themselves: "If the community is a given, so are its types."[7]

In his essay, "Ideological State Apparatuses," Louis Althusser refigures the concept of base/superstructure, breaking down the distinction between public and private, and bringing to light ideological systems that had been invisible by virtue of their pervasiveness. In *Structural Anthropology*, Claude Levi-Strauss wrote that myth is "an imaginary resolution of a real contradiction."[8] In *The Political Unconscious*, Frederic Jameson transposed Levi-Strauss's description of myth onto narration. By 1980, literary naturalism was easily deprived of its transparency, but this formula also deprives all fantasy of transparency, including the fantasy of personality. If a personality is not different from a book, in both cases one could favor the "real contradiction" side of the formula. That is, if personality is a fiction (a political fiction!) then it is a story of contradiction in common with other stories—it occurs on the same plane of experience. This "formula" sets a novel and a personality as two equals on the stage of history, and supports a new version of autobiography that rejects the distinction between "fact" and "fiction."

Althusser comes with a lot of baggage. For example, he divided science from ideology, and ideology from theory. Frankly, Bruce and I pillaged critical theory for concepts that gave us access to our experience. In retrospect, it might be better simply to "go with" cultural studies. To the endless chain of equal cultural manifestations (a song by R.E.M., the Diet of Worms, Rousseau's *Confessions*), we add another equals sign, attaching the self as yet another thing the culture "dreamed up."

Georges Bataille was central to our project. He finds a counter-economy of rupture and excess that includes art, sex, war, religious sacrifice, sports events, ruptured subjectivity, the disso-lution of bodily integuments—"expenditure" of all kinds. Bataille showed us how a gay bathhouse and a church could fulfill the same function in their respective communities.

In writing about sex, desire, and the body, New Narrative approached performance art, where self is put at risk by naming names, becoming naked, making the irreversible happen—the book becomes social practice that is lived. The theme of obses-sive romance did double duty, destabling the self and asserting gay experience. Steve Abbott wrote, "Gay writers Bruce Boone and Robert Glück (like Acker, Dennis Cooper or the subway graffitists again) up the ante on this factuality by weaving their own names, and those of friends and lovers, into their work. The writer/artist becomes exposed and vulnerable: you risk being foolish, mean-spirited, wrong. But if the writer's life is more open to judgment and speculation, so is the reader's."[9]

Did we believe in the truth and freedom of sex? Certainly we were attracted to scandal and shame, where there is so much information. Shame is a kind of fear, and fears are what organize us from above, so displaying them is political. I wanted to write close to the body—the place language goes reluctantly. We used porn, where information saturates narrative, to expose and manipulate genre's formulas and dramatis personae, to arrive at ecstasy and loss of narration as the self sheds its social identities. We wanted to speak about subject/master and object/slave. Bataille showed us that loss of self and attainment of nothingness is a group activity. He supplied the essential negative, a zero planted in the midst of community.

Now, I'd add that transgressive writing is not necessarily about sex or the body—or about anything one can predict. There's no manual; transgressive writing shocks by articulating the present, the one thing impossible to put into words because a language does not yet exist to describe the present. Bruce translated Bataille's *Guilty* for Lapis Press when I worked as an editor there. We hammered out the manuscript together, absorbing Bataille gesturally.

Five more critics. Walter Benjamin: for lyrical melancholy (which reads as autobiography) and for permission to mix high and low. V. N. Voloshinov: for discovering that meaning resides within its social situation, and that contending powers struggle within language itself. Rolland Barthes: for a style that goes back to autobiography, for the fragment, and for displaying the constructed nature of story—"baring the device." Michel Foucault: for the constructed nature of sexuality, the self as collaboration, and the not-to-be-underestimated example of an out gay critic. (Once at 18th and Castro, Michel pierced Bruce with his eagle gaze and Bruce was overcome!—he says.) Julia Kristeva: for elaborating the meaning of abjection in *Powers of Horror*.

Our interest in Dennis Cooper and Kathy Acker produced allegiances and friendships with those writers. Kathy moved to San Francisco in the fall of 1981; while getting settled she stayed with Denise Kastan, who lived downstairs from me. Denise and I codirected Small Press Traffic. Kathy was at work on *Great Expectations*. In fact, Denise and I appear in it; we are the whores Danella and Barbarella. Kathy's writing gave Bruce, Steve Abbott, and myself a model, evolved far beyond our own efforts, for the interrogation of autobiography as text perpetually subverted by another text. Appropriation puts in question the place of the writer—in fact, it turns the writer into a reader.

Meanwhile, Bruce and I were thinking about the painters who were rediscovering the figure, like Eric Fischl and Julian Schnabel. They found a figuration that had passed through the flame of abstract expressionism and the subsequent isms, operating through them. It made us feel we were part of a cross-cultural impulse rather than a local subset. Bruce wrote,

> With much gay writing and some punk notoriously (Acker the big example), the sexual roots of aggression come into question. There's a scream of connection, the figure that emerges ghostly: life attributed to those who have gone beyond. So in Dennis Cooper's *Safe* there's a feeling-tone like a Schnabel painting: the ground's these fragments of some past, the stag, the Roman column, whatever—on them a figure that doesn't quite exist but would maybe like to. The person/persona/thing the writer's trying to construct from images.[10]

In 1976, I started volunteering at the nonprofit bookstore Small Press Traffic and I became its codirector not long after. From 1977 to 1985, I ran a reading series and held free walk-in writing workshops at the store. The workshops became a kind of New Narrative laboratory attended by Mike Amnasan, Steve Abbott, Sam D'Allesandro, Kevin Killian, Dodie Bellamy, Camille Roy, Francesca Rosa, Gloria Anzaldua, John Norton, Edith Jenkins, Richard Schwarzenberger, Phyllis Taper, and Marsha Campbell; and later Rob Halpern, Robin Tremblay-McGaw, Jocelyn Saidenberg, and others, too many to name, whose works extend my own horizon. Later, guided by Bruce, we started a left reading group at Small Press Traffic, attended by Steve Benson, Ron Silliman, Kathleen Fraser, Denise Kastan, Steve Abbott, Bruce, myself, and others. The personal demolished the political, and after a few months we disbanded. From that era I recall Ron's epithet (which Bruce and I thought delicious), the "Small Press Traffic School of Dissimulation."

More successful was the Left/Write Conference we mounted in 1981 at the Noe Valley Ministry. Bruce Boone and Steve Abbott conceived the idea for a conference in the spring of

1978, and sent letters to thirty writers of various ethnicities and aesthetic positions. Steve was a tireless community builder, and Left/Write was an expression of New Narrative's desire to bring communities together—a desire which informed the reading series at Small Press Traffic, Steve Abbott's *Soup* (where the term New Narrative first appeared), Michael Amnasan's *Ottotole*, Camille Roy and Nayland Blake's *Dear World*, Kevin Killian and Brian Monte's *No Apologies*, and later Kevin and Dodie Bellamy's *Mirage*. We felt urgent about it, perhaps because we each belonged to such disparate groups. To our astonishment, three hundred people attended Left/Write, so we accomplished on a civic stage what we were attempting in our writing, editing, and curating: to mix groups and modes of discourse. Writers famous inside their own groups but hardly known outside, like Judy Grahn and Erica Hunt, spoke and read together for the first time.

Out of that conference the Left Writers Union emerged; soon it was commandeered by its most unreconstructed faction, which prioritized gay and feminist issues out of existence. At one meeting, we were instructed to hold readings in storefronts on ground level so the "masses of San Francisco" could walk in! Bruce and I staged a walkout, which was perhaps less dramatic than we intended, and the Union continued for many years, based at Marcus Books.

During this decade—1975 to 1985—Bruce and I carried on what amounted to one long, gabby phone conversation. We brought gossip and anecdote to our writing because they contain speaker and audience, establish the parameters of community, and trumpet their "unfair" points of view. I hardly ever "made things up"—a plot still seems exotic—but as a collagist I had an infinite field. I could use the lives we endlessly described to each other as "found material" to complicate storytelling, because this material also exists on the same plane as the reader's life. Found materials have a kind of radiance, the truth of the already-known.

In 1981 we published *La Fontaine* as a valentine to our friendship. In one poem, Bruce (and Montaigne!) wrote, "In the friendship whereof I speak . . . our souls mingle and blend in a fusion so complete that the seam that joins them disappears and is found no more. If pressed to say why I loved him I'd reply, because it was him, because it was me."[11]

In using the tag New Narrative, I concede there is such a thing. In the past I was reluctant to promote a literary school that endured even ten minutes, much less a few years. Bruce and I took the notion of a "school" half seriously, and once New Narrative began to resemble a program, we abandoned it, declining to recognize ourselves in the tyrants and functionaries that make a literary school. Or was it just a failure of nerve? Still, I would observe that my writing continues to develop a New Narrative aesthetic—the problems and contradictions outlined above—and I wonder if that is not true of my New Narrative confederates. Now I am glad to see the term being used by a critical community, younger writers in San Francisco and New York, and writers in other cities, like Gail Scott in Montreal, and critics like Earl Jackson, Jr., Anthony Easthope, Carolyn Dinshaw, and Dianne Chisholm. Bruce and I may have been kidding about founding a school, but we were serious about wanting to bring emotion and subject matter into the field of innovative writing. I hope that these thoughts on our project—call it what you will—are useful to others looking for ways to extend the possibilities of poem and story.

Notes:

1. Robert Glück, "Caricature," *Soup: New Critical Perspectives*, no. 4 (1985): 28.

2. Bruce Boone, "A Narrative Like a Punk Picture: Shocking Pinks, Lavenders, Magentas, Sickly Greens," *Poetics Journal*, no. 5 (May 1985): 92.

3. The Black Star Series published *He Cried* by Dennis Cooper and *Lives of the Poets* by Steve Abbott. Black Star still publishes, most recently Camille Roy's *Swarm*, and soon John Norton's *Re:marriage*.

4. Bruce Boone, "Remarks on Narrative," afterword to *Family Poems* by Robert Glück (San Francisco: Black Star Series, 1979), 29.

5. Ibid.

6. See "Robert Duncan & Gay Community," *Ironwood*, no. 22 (1983), and "Spicer's Writing in Context," *Ironwood*, no. 28 (1986). Bruce's studies have led him to Eastern religion—now he's a nondenominational minister specializing in caring for people who are terminally ill.

7. Glück, "Caricature," 19.

8. As glossed by Fredric Jameson, in *The Political Unconscious: Narrative as a Socially Symbolic Act* (Ithaca, NY: Cornell University Press, 1982), 77.

9. Steve Abbott, "Notes on Boundaries, New Narrative," *Soup: New Critical Perspectives*, no. 4 (1985): 81.

10. Bruce Boone, "A Narrative Like a Punk Picture," *Poetics Journal*, no. 5 (1992): 92.

11. Bruce Boone and Robert Glück, *La Fontaine* (San Francisco: Black Star Series, 1981), 63.

"Long Note on New Narrative" was published in *Narrativity*, no. 1, eds. Mary Burger, Robert Glück, Camille Roy, and Gail Scott (2000). It was reprinted in *Biting the Error: Writers Explore Narrative*, eds. Camille Roy, Mary Burger, Gail Scott, and Robert Glück (Toronto: Coach House Press, 2004).

BAUCIS AND PHILEMON

On Passover we filled a wine glass and left the door ajar in case Elijah wanted shelter and food. Maybe he looked like Michael Anthony in *The Millionaire*. Elijah never suddenly appeared, our meaningful repetitions went unchallenged, change was slow for us, the future remote. In a network where all parts communicate, the appearance of a new or revealed term can transform the whole, so I wait for Elijah as though he were the second term in a metaphor, and meanwhile look for secrets to expose. Narration wants to illuminate the inside of a shoe or glove—small surprising darknesses which sometimes deepen into genuine blind spots. That is, narration wants a local where gestures and ideology are conserved and shared over a stretch of time, a sublime to destroy/transform that local, and both the local and sublime to exist at once as they do in a community.

Maybe story (local) and metaphor (sublime) have the same structure experienced at different speeds—a metaphor has two terms, perhaps story's second term is the future. Stepping from our lives to that future, we pause at the metaphor's *is* where time ceases to exist and all forms are available—is that too fanciful? How can we create a local in writing that takes account of the future, the sublime? Levi-Strauss called myth the "imaginary resolution of a real contradiction."[1] That resembles Lukács's exhilarating description of realism, "The more firmly it grasps hold of the living contradictions of life and society, then the greater and more profound the realism will be."[2] I want to chart the contradictions and forces of change, and assert the fiction of resolution. A further exhilaration: Levi-Strauss and Lukács are describing a self as well as a myth or a novel. Movement politics generates autobiography—every person is a compendium of forces. In the lives of the new heroes and heroines the unconscious barrier between (being a historical) object and subject becomes conscious and gives way so easily it's rather dreamy—a secret terrain that was overlooked, then suddenly home. I mean "home": the forces are discrete texts or networks internally speeding against the flat velvet backdrop of no meaning. Many versions of the local are suddenly available, I can take my pick, but they come with quotation marks and so do their stories. The local and sublime become detached from their experiences, not lost but redistributed.

Put quoted sex next to quoted anger next to quoted tenderness—is it a story or a list of items equal to each other? Where in the infinity of equal signs is the referent, the guest who doesn't come? We plump the pillows and wait disconsolate by the phone. But think of all the divine strangers who did bring us their elated appetite—Mary and Joseph, angels, prophets, gods. I like this mix of domesticity and the sublime. Food and shelter, food and shelter, humiliating as a plotline—exactly what we don't want to need. Jove and Hermes disguised as mortals find hospitality with Baucis and Philemon. At the de Young it's a painting in which Hermes sports wings on his jaunty derby with the bland obviousness of a secret in retrospect. Baucis and Philemon are dignified and old in love and poverty; they dish up their best to these gods who just stepped from the flux. How extremely sluggish this couple must appear, clunking around with their rustic human language and crude rituals. Each gesture is a 45 played at 33—which gives Ovid the leisure to make the most of cottage life. The frame these gods provide brings the local to its full realization—the "gods," the "referent," the ultimate generation of difference. Foot bath, shard under the table leg, table cloth. Green and black olives, cornels pickled in wine, salad of endive, radishes and succory, curds and cream, fresh roasted eggs, boiled salt pork, wine, plums, apples, nuts, dry figs, grapes, dates, a honeycomb—a miracle! The bowls brim with superior wine despite being emptied, hospitality sincere as a dream, a measure outside the rational economy of exchange. In this way the sublime is revealed, they fall worshiping. All forms are suddenly available; what does this couple want? To die together, they reply. So when the time comes:

> Old *Baucis* is by *Philemon* seen
> Sprouting with sudden Leaves of spritely Green:
> Old *Baucis* look'd where old *Philemon* stood,
> And saw his lengthen'd Arms a sprouting Wood:
> New Roots their fasten'd Feet begin to bind,
> Their Bodies stiffen in a rising Rind:
> Then, e're the Bark above their Shoulders grew,
> They give and take at once their last Adieu;
> At once, Farewell, O faithful Spouse, they said;
> At once th' incroaching Rinds their closing Lips invade.[3]
>
> [trans. Dryden]

So they become nature; gods supply the mechanics of transformation, of metaphor. It's a quantum leap to a new form fueled by extremity. The essential remains, purged of the human. Baucis and Philemon were inseparable; now they are trees standing forever, a roman numeral II.

Back to aggression: narration wants to seize whatever stands for self and demolish it, kill it along with every model. (Barthes says that narration is the perfect vehicle for the creation of a world—and its destruction, I add.) In story after story we enjoy shivers of agreement as humans become trees, streams, flowers, fish, stars. This is the inhuman version of the sublime. Jove turns two rustics into cellulose and kills all their inhospitable neighbors. Elijah arrives shortly before the Messiah—very last judgment-y, all secrets revealed, end of history.

Jean Baudrillard posits the following version of self: "Each person sees himself at the controls of a hypothetical machine, isolated in a position of perfect and remote sovereignty, at an infinite distance from his universe of origin."[4] I read this with a thrill, acknowledging what pertains to me: the universe of origin, the multinational system that forms me and yet is as impossible to understand as . . . Still, it's hard to be an astronaut for long without laughing, and not only to share Baudrillard's scorn for the ineptness of a self whose story is miniaturized as an astronaut's citrus drink—I'd laugh at (make art from) any version of self, even one that does a better job of providing a local. I write about these forms—that are myself—to acknowledge and then dispense with them, to demonstrate their arbitrariness, how they disintegrate before a secret (the world, the body). The world wants you to become the world—at once a point of origin and death, furious, full of catastrophe and transformation. Let the sublime come, say I, but—ah—first a rehearsal: I hedge, I stage the upheaval inside a story, like Elijah's cup.

Notes:

1. As glossed by Fredric Jameson, in *The Political Unconscious: Narrative as a Socially Symbolic Act* (Ithaca, NY: Cornell University Press, 1982), 77.

2. Georg Lukács, "Realism in the Balance," trans. Rodney Livingstone, in *Aesthetics and Politics: The Key Texts of the Classic Debate within German Marxism*, by Theodor Adorno, Walter Benjamin, Ernst Bloch, Bertolt Brecht, and Georg Lukács (London: Verso, 1980), 39.

3. Ovid, "Baucis and Philemon," trans. John Dryden, in *The Works of John Dryden*, ed. Vinton A. Dearing, vol. 7, *Poems: 1697–1700* (Berkeley: University of California Press, 2000), 243.

4. Jean Baudrillard, "The Ecstasy of Communication," in *The Anti-aesthetic: Essays on Postmodern Culture*, ed. Hal Foster (Port Townsend, WA: Bay Press, 1983), 128.

"Baucis and Philemon" was published in "Non/Narrative," *Poetics Journal*, no. 5, eds. Lyn Hejinian and Barrett Watten (May 1985).

MY COMMUNITY

In 1966, when I was nineteen, in order to compete for acceptance to a student exchange program between UCLA and the
University of Edinburgh, I took a battery of psychological
exams, which included a long written test. Two of the questions
I remember well: describe a male friend and describe a female
friend. This part of the sixties was still connected to the fifties,
even though the Beatles arrived in '64. Most of the things I felt
were literally nameless to me because of my age and the age of
the decade. Impossible, really, to recapture the unnamed after
learning to use words. The child's world is replaced by the language the child acquires.

I wrote that Andrea was short, nice legs, nice body, nice
breasts with small nipples that pointed up, and dark hair she
wore in bangs and pulled back—I avoided the word barrette. I
wrote that she had full lips and dark brown eyes with dark eyebrows and lashes. That her nose was rather big, but she was still
pretty. That she had a good personality *and and and* was fun to
be with and made me feel good and also she was *bright*.

I deprived Larry of a body—he was a brain almost in the
science fiction sense: his hobbies were astrophysics, baroque
music, and calculus. He was given a telescope by Rocketdyne to
track satellites. I described the telescope that, like Larry, was
pointed at the stars.

My test was a lie. I had just finished Benjamin Franklin's
Autobiography. In the tidy little testing room I had a stroke of
inspiration. I realized that if I answered the questions as
Franklin, I might create the impression of a normal man. In

fact, I was incredibly anxious about Andrea's body. We are necking, the boring lights of the boring Valley twinkle below my parents' boring station wagon up on Mulholland Drive. It's like boring exercise. I make goofy jokes to keep alert. I'm confused when the car fills up with smell—I don't recognize it and I don't like it at all but I am impressed when Andrea says that I'm at least partly responsible for it. I'm always mentally averting my eyes from her vagina even though I have never seen it—have only the vaguest notion of what's down there—even though it's my supposed geographical goal. Someone told me they like it if you push down on it, so I push down and she does like it. She sort of guards it, but with a puzzled expression.

I was able, had the writing skill and observation, to delineate most of Andrea's body more accurately and her character too, a mix of starts and stops, bravery and affectation. I had the skill to describe Larry's tapering fingers, cornflower eyes, convulsed laughter. The writerly ability to skew these descriptions was bound up with a homosexual's sickening, unwanted knowledge of the fiction of gender roles, which led to knowledge of the difference between a dishonest fiction and an honest one.

I felt no guilt for distorting my relationship with Andrea and Larry—what did I know about undistorted relationships? Like many of the boys and men I knew in the West Valley, Benjamin Franklin seemed gruesomely soulless, a caricature in his bland unconscious egotism, his endless energy to dominate what may be thought of as fate or at least circumstance; certainly his own body, that proximate example of the world. And for my invented narrator, Benjamin Franklin, myself as a clod, I felt contempt and fear. I had a secret I wanted to keep from him above all. The secret did not allow me to live in my group. I was alone. I had no world, no community—just the despicable pink satellite of my body, and in outer space there is no moral life or camaraderie, just self-preservation.

Franklin was the model of daily exertion. I was sluggish and aroused from lack of meaning. There was no darkness or perversity in him because there was no shame. I felt these thoughts rather than thought them. But I had chosen the right model: personality as a Skinner box.

It's strange to invoke all this antique fear, the terror of track and field, injured pride at the bus stop, the ambient sarcasm that never got an edge on its enemies or even found them. I did feel guilt for not being the oaf I described. Any fiction, any version of the self wants you to become it. That's why a dishonest fiction is immoral. I laughed with vertigo when I was told in confidence by the chatty examiners that I'd received the highest score ever recorded on that test.

I'm describing an inability to make experience with the materials at hand, which is to say that I lacked experience because I lacked a language. That year my selection of poems for the UCLA poetry contest was titled "5 Aspects of Death." I really didn't know what to write about, I was without subject matter. I lived in LA and it would be at least a decade before Dennis Cooper started taming LA by making its emptiness a literary subject—by locating LA's emptiness in the ardent life of the flesh.

Am I exaggerating? Homosexuality was against the law. Was I a crime? I located Homosexuality—the disease—in psychology texts: grim reading. Was I a case history? Could I be cured? (Later, I would read Freud predictively, like a horoscope—*This one's for you, Hysterie*—never sure which gender to apply. Am I a male with a female rising sign?) I stumbled on Petronius's *Satyricon* at the Woodland Hills Public Library, amazing, but too late, too late for life in ancient Rome. Still, in literature I was on the right track, a world was appearing.

It wasn't until 1968 that I discovered Frank O'Hara in Donald Allen's *New American Poetry*. O'Hara's world I recognized as the kind of utopia I could enter. He lived among artists—wasn't I an artist? He was witty and deep—I could be that. He was on the cutting edge, a bit hysterical—I could be hysterical. He seemed to say it was hip to take for granted what I had agonized about. I kept waiting, as a writer, for my "voice." What voice? The self I knew was a novelty act, a timid small-time manipulator who, when perfectly safe in the bosom of his family, became a tyrannosaurus rex. I didn't know who I was, but also, I didn't know where I was supposed to be. The freedom of O'Hara's community was represented in his poems by formal innovation, by language choice—flighty, engaged, romantic. He was excited. Didn't I want to be excited?—to throw off all my loathsome boredom and anxiety? With the zealousness of a convert I became O'Hara. The mess and quick breath of his poems corresponded to my life. His longing and friendships and way of being became mine.

Looking back, there can have been little similarity between O'Hara's elegant, conversant life in savvy New York art circles, and my horny, somber hippy life. I even went back to the land (as if a person raised in Cleveland and LA had ever been to the land in the first place). I took O'Hara with me, mulching the crops and dropping organic mescaline, listening to Led Zeppelin and Wanda Landowska, being isolated in a commune. So again I was a traitor, nameless, a spy working against the common good, alone in the world, but not without a world—one was taking shape.

When I was sixteen, I used to memorize poems by John Keats, my hero, and then write them out just to see what it felt like to be writing incontestably great poetry. Later I read O'Hara with a religious faith that I would become the art I was consuming. After Frank O'Hara came Proust. But I never could become Proust—I spent a year with him—a mountain range as great as Shakespeare and as impossible. One could try for the felicity of phrase, already an antique goal in Proust's time. One could imitate the construction of metaphors so empowered that both terms parade along parallel lines with the equals sign aloft between them. What I took, and in that sense what I became, was the murmuring, the whisper that is a meditation that unfolds on itself, making itself up as it goes—that I could tell a story and also be the one to endlessly speculate on its meanings and the nature of storytelling itself.

Proust willed into literature a society that was passing away. O'Hara told the story of itself to a rarefied community of lovers, friends, writers, and artists. I wanted to identify with a community—to be the community telling itself its own story, to link my fate to the community's rise and fall, to be that crossroads of history and personal life. This was an exotic idea for someone raised in the suburbs of Cleveland and Los Angeles. I thought it could be a solution to the trap of psychology, and a way to gain strength from—instead of being muted by—the contradictions of my period. Eventually I found Burroughs and Genet, Allen Ginsberg, Gide, Djuna Barns, Baldwin, Spicer, H.D., Duncan, Garcia Lorca, and Cavafy, residents of my first real hometown. I look at my neighbors so that I can know who I am. Their writing could be difficult, engaged, learned; they could say anything, pitched at some extreme verge, almost religious in their devotion to the power (and their awareness of the limitation) of words. It was a writing that validated daydream and nightdream, revolution and sudden vast reversal, the severely reduced, the flamboyantly inclusive.

Any art wants to take the place of your reflection in the mirror and call for your recognition. It makes you become it like a magic spell—with words, images, representations. That is why a new self, like a new aesthetic form, like any new approach to art, is something of a scandal. That's why readers experience shock and outrage, or relief and urgency. New form, new content demand a new way of being, a new way of seeing your own life, just as new vocabulary calls forth its meanings in your life. It is at this starting point that an art movement, or a political movement, has moral life. The appearance of a new self in fiction will be tested and taken as a demand as much as a description. A dishonest picture is a traitor, an enemy of the common good.

I am making a big connection here between writing, coming out, and community. But learning to articulate, to be free, created a double movement in me, in that the secret of my sexual identity gave way, not to the cost-effective complacency of a Franklin, but to the larger secrets of the self in its body, the physical thing that we are that can no more enter into the sphere of language as enter into the space created by a mirror.

When I say body I mean the old-fashioned genre-novel orgasm that explodes like lightning, the colonized country whose present can't be articulated, and yet it is the answer to every economic and cultural puzzle, the material state of meaning; I mean a burst of laughter that cancels the social contract, the knowledge of death, unity with matter, the disjunction out of which step gods and monsters. The body is the first secret. Any story hides and then reveals the body—whether in the form of sex or death or a secret. Flesh is what has value. A secret is the most seductive thing. Like the body it is hidden or buried and then comes to light. A story reveals the body in order to verify existence, yet it's an incomplete revelation; we fall into the mystery, then return. Like a daydreamer, the novelist tries as many combinations of sex and death as possible, to bring the body forward.

So it would be sloppy to say I moved away, came out and became free, because one can only measure this brand of freedom, which is the freedom of language to make representations, by contrasting it with the state of captivity (the dishonest fiction) which the present is for everyone.

Still, I want freedom, *especially* in my hometown. Recently I've been masturbating to the image of myself as a woman, passive, tended, and penetrated by two lyrical young men. Sometimes this woman is in a porn movie and one of the men is black. Sometimes I'm a small Asian woman with a rather small cunt and he is seriously endowed, and there's some question about the mechanics of this, but everyone is very patient; they gently brush my nipples and this lovely black man known for his finesse keeps licking the sides of my clit until my sense of my own twin parts dissolves in turmoil—the walls of my vagina become at once yielding and urgent—and in fact his cock does go in, very slowly at first—congratulations all around—and then I experience a pleasure more convulsed than I have ever known.

I write about this fantasy in the context of this essay and the life I lead. Of course I feel queasy portraying a passive Asian woman and an endowed black man. Their sex happens to be taken from life—as though that made a difference? My community has not developed a language to unravel these strands of identification, desire, and racism. I haven't allowed myself to be woman since early teenhood, so now I am in a position to wonder: Have I repressed that image for thirty years out of shame for not resembling the face in the mirror my community holds up, first of a normal man, later of a feminist woman, and finally of a normal homosexual?

"My Community" was published as "Marker" in *Dear World: Queer Art & Lit*, no. 1, eds. Camille Roy and Nayland Blake (1991). It was reprinted as "My Community" in *Discontents: New Queer Writers*, ed. Dennis Cooper (New York: Amethyst Press, 1992).

FAME

Realtors say there are three conditions that determine value: location, location, and location. These realtors must understand that the postmodern question is not *Who Am I?* but *Where Am I?*—*Where is the place of the other?* Could one apply the realtors' observation to a literary practice and assign value according to location?

1. I am going to talk about the use of real names and true stories. The classical writers used names—Sappho did, Catullus and the rest. But it's hard to consider very ancient literature because its motivation is swamped by the universality heaped on it. I may wonder what is universal about this description of a man from Sardis—

> You are no country fellow, neither
> lout nor pigkeeper:
> not Thessalian born; neither
> Erysichaian: not a sheepman... [1]

—but I do wonder for a few seconds in the silence after reading it. Did Alcman want to be universal, to leave something in his work that could be completed only by future generations? Or did he just want to endure, mocking mortality like a stone sculpture?

2. The history of the eternal in the West is a tale of subtraction. The religious landscape of the Middle Ages teems with daily life. By the eighteenth century, that landscape is idealized and depopulated (*Voyage to Cythera*); by Cezanne's time, the idealized

atemporal content becomes eternal forms, forms latent in a land-
scape, modernism's rediscovery of the universal in form itself.
Were these boxes and spheres always nostalgic for a golden age?
Certainly more nostalgic than the eccentric medieval crowd.

3. In the fragment we see a postindustrial ruin—that is, a ruin of
language. Robert Smithson's little essay on art in gardens allowed
me to understand the fragment in writing. It may clean the
windows of perception, or combat the tyranny of unitary meaning,
or express women's experience, or convey spiritual states, or
escape the confines of self, or bring the finished work closer to
the process of writing, or break the fiction of narration, or make
words opaque; but more, the fragment of language evokes the
melancholy pleasure of a ruin, the destruction of a place to live,
the falling away of human scale, the relinquishing of meaning,
the falling away and recontextualizing of human scale to include
the nonhuman, the unshared, mysterious, and unsharable—
which is shared.

4. I am fascinated by the representation and sale of community
by the media. TV turned a corner with Angela Lansbury's
Murder She Wrote, the miniaturized coziness of Cabot Cove
populated by actors who portray not the natives, but the more
recognizable character actors of days gone by. We don't suffer
undue suspense. We guess from the first scenes who the killer is:
he's probably that mean guy who kicked the dog. The Miami of
Miami Vice is the flip side, decorative malaise. Both shows are
quite reassuring, and I would want to avoid the contempt Jean
Baudrillard heaps on such miniaturizations of community life—
his famous description of Disneyland, for example. He doesn't
acknowledge the needs that these shows partially satisfy, or at
least indicate. In not acknowledging our needs, he will never
know if we are generating our own solutions.

Anything we can say about nature, self, or community bears
the lie of the partial truth—because we are speaking from the
inside. But speaking from the inside can become a strategy of
conservation. Bataille uses Freud, but he remains the patient—

that is, sick—instead of being the doctor—that is, Breton. Bataille takes Freud's science, his belief in a cure, and turns it back on itself; Freud's versions of the myths become merely their latest manifestations in a continuity of reworkings, a long meditation on the self in the grip of tragic destiny.

5. We can observe communities predicated on the family either breaking down or regrouping, and newer communities inventing themselves in the context of urban life, like the gay community's use of bars and cafés and other commercial spaces. Most things about community we can't know until they have been lost, like extended families and leaving the front door unlocked, or newly invented, like the culture forged to care for people with AIDS, and using anonymous sex to eroticize urban alienation. So when communities are eroding or inventing themselves, the structures of personal life become visible.

6. *Someone* is always famous for fifteen minutes—an exemplary life with book contracts and movie rights. All this urgency is fueled by a hunger for personal life and human scale, the need to know people in common, the desire to recover the wholeness of life. Since we increasingly can't know each other, let's know Fawn Hall. And then let's all be known.

The characters in Cabot Cove are examples of the already-known, of appropriation. As a literary practice, appropriation is used to give the lie to the sovereignty of the mind and to challenge the distinction between public and private. Revival of the known is behind every kind of appropriation—from Ruskin's *Sesame and Lilies* and revival architecture, to Venturi's *Learning from Las Vegas* and today's retro styles. They are a strategy to reintroduce human scale, to bring the already-known into a dynamic relation with the present, a response to our hunger for community and shared experience. The already-known is a postmodern subject.

7. Appropriation restructures the meaning of an existing construct by changing its location. So, the Old Testament becomes useful

when it demonstrates that the coming of Christ has been fore-seen. Jonah prefigures Jesus, the three days in the fish equals three days in the tomb. When something is known, it is either the relation between social actions in the broadest sense, like Jonah, or it is the knowledge of the body and death, and that knowledge is . . . So the self lives and approaches death in narration. Other ways to say that: continuity and disjunction in narration, social scale and the sublime in narration, community and the body in narration, the representation of time and timelessness. With allegory comes ruin, because allegory is based on splintering meaning. Decay, rust, as Smithson observes, is the monument's first new context.

8. There are contradictory reasons why I use "real" people in my work, and the contradictions comfort me. I suppose any literary practice should derive from contradictory sources and motives. The work that wants to clear away the obstructions of late capitalism will be rightly seen as one of those obstructions. So I name names to evoke the already-known, to make writing coextend with the world, to examine the fiction of personality and the fiction of the word. Foucault, in an example of his own theory, shows how the dynamics of sex have become increasingly visible and susceptible to manipulation—that is, in a double movement, sex becomes the kind of sex that could be manipulated, just as that kind of manipulation is called into being by power. I propose self-community-story as a tonic for the loss of human scale; by naming self-community-story I participate in their disintegration, their progress from invisibility to something to be named and manipulated—to be reintegrated later in a new context that history must provide.

Prolonged scrutiny can become an expenditure of self, a potlatch of self. I've come to experience the unreeling of inte-riority and sexual disclosure as such a loss, and also part of a historical trajectory. It's writing that privileges the aggression of naming—an ongoing colonization of self into one's own lan-guage. Once something is named, you are in relation to it. Name the disease to cure it.

9. We want to see a story as we see other representations: being hiding behind appearance—that is, hiding and revealing the body. But the use of real names reorders connections and disjunctions. I do mean fragmentation. I don't want to make the predictable distinction between story and fragmented writing. In a postmodern switch, naming names creates the open form of modernism by putting quote marks around the entire story, turning the story into a fragment, an example of story. The story floats—as gossip does—between the lives of the people who are its characters, and the lives of its readers. The problem of figure and ground becomes a social one, and some of what is existential in the content is subtracted and reintegrated in the relation between reader and writer. The depth of characters remains partly in the same world as the reader. (By depth, I mean the sense that the story is real—as you are aware in a dream of the different levels of commitment, sometimes caught in the story, other times so aware of dreaming that you can go back and restructure events.)

10. With real names and true stories, what could the reader observe?

a. I could draw different conclusions from those the writer makes. This proposes an openness of meaning, is against omniscience. It establishes a point of view that allows unfairness—lets fairness be an issue. Kathy Acker's letters from Rosa in *Great Expectations* are exemplary in their injustice.

Again, openness of meaning allows for different points of view—not irony with its proliferating points of view that all exist on one plane, but social spaces constructed differently.

b. I could meet these characters, establish relations, stories of my own. For instance, an ad that appeared in the *Coming Up* personals began "Part Fawn, Part Desperado." The man advertising himself said two favorite authors were John Berger and Robert Glück—he turned out to be Jack from *Jack the Modernist*! Why not call him up?

c. The story is partly controlling the narrator, and the narrator is only partly controlling the story—chance exerts its influence.

d. The story is ongoing—even if a character dies there would be more to discover.

e. The characters are produced, ready to go, generated by the world and by their own histories—they are ready-made images, people as readymades.

f. Insofar as personality is an illusion, using real names wants to make the illusion of the book coextend with illusion in the world. For example, I want people to represent themselves in my work. I take conversations from letters, and ask people to rewrite their own dialogue, so the fiction of personality can enter.

g. Since the story actually happened, I am not invited into events transparently—I am excluded as a documentary excludes, or as a photograph, which documents, along with its subject matter, my lack of participation. But I can register how events tally with my own experience. The story excludes like a documentary, but invites another relationship, like earth sculpture, where we measure ourselves against some actual arrangement of space and scale.

h. Using real names promotes a different relation between the writer and myself that carries some risk, a sacrificial relation like some performance art. What I witness is always the same: any story hides and then reveals the body.

(We take it as our due that if our skin breaks, it heals. The pleasure of horror writers, like Jim Thompson and Poe, or writers of pornography, is that they exacerbate an itchy sore. They are like Sade in that their lack of forgiveness is a form of integrity. Are they angry at the characters for being merely human, merely animals, only words? We find in them the novelist's—and the daydreamer's—desire to give their characters every combination of sexual or violent contact in order to reveal the body.)

i. The characters are not "universal," yet there is a second source of awe (the first being the body, hidden and brought forth)—they may "live forever, defeat time," like the man from Sardis in Alcman's fragment (*not marble nor the gilded monuments*). In fact there is something eerie about making representations of people, something uncanny. "Objects that were useful in life did not function in death, objects that simply 'modeled' life on earth became functional in the world of the dead"—Han Tomb catalogue description.

j. As a reader, I have come to think of Bruce Boone's description of me in *My Walk with Bob* as an actual memory—yet I don't remember it. "It's easy enough to imagine Bob asking me, Bruce, how can you get a moral edge on the void . . . When I say the word void I imagine Bob picking out cucumbers at the produce counter of the Noe Valley market, anxiously smiling of course, weighing prices against textures against looks in the shipment of the day."[2] It's like a story told about me when I was a child that I have come to remember and even use to ascertain who I am. So this description can be taken as a demand—the demand, in fact, of any writing—a magic spell turning me into it. There is also something sickening in seeing my name there—me and not me, because it is myself in Bruce's psychic life, the me in relation. A Bob who acts too much like himself, revealing the made-up nature of who he is.

Notes:

1. Alcman, untitled poem, in *Greek Lyrics*, trans. Richmond Lattimore (Chicago: University of Chicago Press, 2013), 36.

2. Bruce Boone, *My Walk with Bob* (San Francisco: Ithuriel's Spear, 2006), 34–35.

"Fame" was published in "Knowledge," *Poetics Journal*, no. 10, eds. Lyn Hejinian and Barrett Watten (June 1998).

TRUTH'S MIRROR IS NO MIRROR

I'm interested in the way we exist for each other in language. My stories take their authority in part from being the kind of stories people tell, stories that create "a fair field full of folk"—that is, a local, enclosed and heated. But TV miniaturizes and sells intimacy, and daily life collapses or bottoms out into commodity; is not the destruction of human scale the major event of the twentieth century? Modernism's sublime replaced the one disappearing in society. Now the assertion of a local also becomes a conscious (rather than naïve) political endeavor—one that characterizes the autonomous movements and rainbow coalitions of postmodern politics. The local is on the front burner of feminist and progressive agendas, architecture, and city planning, and it has generated its own historians: John Boswell, Philippe Aires, and Michel de Certeau.

> Jack sat next to me; he looked worried, said "Gossip is crude."
> I reasoned that the depth he missed in a single story could be found collectively in a hundred. He cocked his head, attentive, so I became interesting. "The people who know your story are as important as the plot. Gossip registers the difference between a story one person knows and everyone knows, between one person's story and everyone's."[1] (*Jack the Modernist*)

I name names and give dates to locate stories in lives and in history. Like any neighborhood gossip, I follow the dictates of my plot but not beyond my reader's credence. Documentary seems to clear away all systems of interpretation—"just the facts" remain. I don't aspire to docudrama: William Carlos Williams's factual cat steps into the flowerpot. I don't know what that reportage means, severed from its context and the appearance of motive. It claims a purity (spirituality even) based on the truth of origins—of perception, of language—salvation myths I mistrust. And if the commodification of daily life demonstrates anything, it "brings home" the local's true ongoing origin as a construct. Like the Romantics pointing to nature, we can articulate the shape of the familiar at the moment when it is no longer occluded by the smokescreen of the natural; that is, just as the local is lost to us.

While I want to write about the self as a transparency, that's not the whole story. The self is a depth *and* a boundary. To show the necessity and impossibility of narration, I want to borrow Lacan's mirror stage, the moment when a child, about six months old, recognizes itself. Lacan based his essay on comparative physiology (kids and chimps). He described "the transformation that takes place in the subject when he assumes an image."[2] Here is my body, the undifferentiated world. My self is projected outside of that into differentiation, a "fiction" linked to socially elaborated situations.

Lacan's model is so literal: I have a mirror, I was a baby. Writers often set image/self against anarchic reality as a dopey ballot measure: "I vote *for* nonrepresentation . . ." But Lacan discovers the physical relation that links these contraries. I nudge Lacan's baby out of the way and substitute myself. I then enjoy a realization that includes the baby's lack of terms one giant second ago (nonrepresentation, his ignorance of space and difference) and also his self's moment of origin, the origin of a fiction, a Genesis story deeper than the modernist estrangement that takes language by surprise, and anterior to inner life and psychological first causes. My image (two dots and a line?) makes a tremendous assertion of inevitability and the box-in-a-box variety of expectation (self anthropomorphizes self). The image contains the world as all images do from that moment on. Isn't it a writer's job to articulate and challenge that proposition? When I write about that image I have a narrative. When I change the scale to include the body, the constructedness of the narrative/self becomes apparent—narrative flattens into a construct. I am describing a nonironic doubling, holding two points of view at once, rather than irony's doubling that operates on (and doubts) the single plane of the author's voice.

An originary moment. Thirty-eight years later I catch sight of myself before I am prepared and the mirror returns a different kind of image. It's akin to my own voice pronouncing a word incorrectly—the world becomes noise, losing meaning as it shifts out of context. Instead of phonemes, I see a dying animal in the mirror. Some source of pleasure surprises me, my expression, gesture—my *self* stands out, glaringly artifacted. The disjunction between matter and self engenders an instant of vertigo and an excitement close to pride: this animal is going to die. "The tension which then arose in what had hitherto been an inanimate substance endeavored to cancel itself out. In this way first instinct came into being: the instinct to return to the inanimate state."[3] This desire—or "instinct," as Freud says—to return to an inanimate state lasts only an instant, *dwelled on*. Then nostalgia and language falsify the experience with an urgency based on "self"-preservation.

I call disjunction that sudden change of scales, the double awareness of self (narration) and anarchic body (the sublime). The sublime: nothing, piercing laughter, a catastrophe, a fire at night, a violent orgasm—anything that expresses a void which our communities have filled with religions and monsters in order to understand the absence of ground. This awareness of disjunction between self and body is an experience that a community, to be a community, provides its members. A self lost in the greater being of a god or lost in the horror of the alien would be lost like that baby's image in the mirror before the moment of identification. We realize the mistake in the system, which is that the system *is* a system. The understanding that meaning resides in systems gives a luster to nonmeaning. The self is not so much lost as "seen through."

If narrative is a self, disjunction is being, an "effect" that can occur between two bits of representation:

to proper to   behindless   weigh in a   rotating
rectilinear   our plated, *embosserie des petits cochons*
    plient feint   insensate, round   bands of immense
release   fell, a crudity   form of the   assignment—
increase   by venture   populace animated by   appeal[4]

We want each of Charles Bernstein's fragments in these first lines of "Islets/Irritations" to participate in a larger context—whether by joining forces with fragments to the right and left, above or below, or through the promise of a sentence and the intimations of a paragraph. In this way we express our desire for a face that contains the world. But thought and being do not have identity if meaning is an institution. When the fragments don't jibe, when thought fails, our being spills into the gaps, tries to fill them. The smaller the fragment, the more being, until the unit becomes so small that there is an equality among fragments; they cease calling to absent contexts, their sameness of scale eliminates disjunction.

By disjunction, I also mean pastiche, the disequilibrium caused by, say, genre narrative's collapse into metaphor—becoming a public self—in Dodie Bellamy's *Letters of Mina Harker*:

Bob is at the front door prolonging his goodbyes: "Mina are you planning to have a baby?" *He laughed as if it were a joke as if I Mina Harker amorphous figment of multiple imaginings would or could ever stoop to quotidian existence* I say "Who? Me? No! NO BABIES!" . . .
    I am eager for his ejaculation as I was for Emma Woodhouse or Elizabeth Bennet to be married.[5]

Is this Bellamy's *life? politics? genre horror? fiction? psychology?* Allegory's meaning doesn't settle. The "unit of representation" becomes several selves, which are themselves systems of interpretation.

> My body is so full of holes it's a fish net flung into this cold
> dark ocean more holes than any demon doll's I stick toilet
> paper in my ears in case it's the devil talking *between a reality
> that possesses no consistency and appetites that are limitless there
> is no hold for a mediating consciousness.*[6]

In fact, a carnival of mediating selves doesn't so much dismantle the "I" as discredit it with laughter and disgust. Each identification risks the catastrophe of disclosure, a stake through the heart. The risk both makes and unmakes a local. "Don't tell anybody are the three most erotic words in the English language, ask anybody at the Café Flore. In the 1985 remake Medea doesn't need a knife, she has the phone."[7] Finally, the letter form blurs private and public categories. The reader—inside, outside, conspirator and voyeur—is invited into the problem of location.

Lydia Davis investigates location by merging parable and case history. In both, story is taken as an example of many such stories—an example of story itself sidestepping the problem of inside/outside, where the hero is a function of his story (as we are of ours). Story becomes deeper (that is, less classical) as the hero becomes less rational. Davis's protagonist loses her location as a man in a parable does, but with the most particular of interiorities, a case history. In "Once a Very Stupid Man," the woman is the "bearded man" because "anyone writing at the next table in a café might be considered to be a bearded man"[8]—or is she located "in" her boyfriend's life? Is her boyfriend located "in" his own life? Disjunction can be seen as the riddle of location that overtakes the simpler problem of identity. "And he looked and looked, but it was a vain search; he could not find himself."[9] Revamping Socrates's injunction, we ask the image in the mirror not *who am I?* but *where am I?*

The degree of belief at any given moment in the existence of a self—as a depth—determines the degree of narrativity. Absolute faith is hardly necessary. With narrative comes mimesis, explanation, destiny, complexity, time; tensions based on manipulation of meaning and/or action; and dynamics of power and sex. Narration is not passive; it is demanding. It is a magic spell. What can be said about this spell can be said about a dream: it hides and then reveals its secret (the sublime/body), or it encloses suffering and the self's powerlessness (revenge, wish fulfillment). Fredric Jameson's definition of ideology could also be applied to self and narration—"the imaginary resolution of a real contradiction."[10]

If I write about the historical constuctedness of this mirror self (history of subjectivity, the personal as political) I am in "metatext"—the story of the world. If I focus on the body, my subject becomes a member of a species, which happens when I describe how it feels to breathe or sweat.

The identification with the image in the mirror strikes me as a model for identification with art, an identification that demands, like any ideology, the suspension of disbelief. The reader's identification is the fuel that gives a new aesthetic its scandal. But even if I take the "permanently partial" self as subject, I'm trapped (entrapping my readers) in a fiction, an ideology. Moreover, the self becomes master. In that sense narration is authoritarian and its destruction—by its slave the body—revolutionary. But if I present the self only as a construct, a nonsubject, I write from the void, a location even more improbable than the self. I'd want to regard these positions—the only ones that exist—as untenable, mutually exclusive, inseparable.

Are there models for this double view? Critical writers like Barthes and Kristeva take modernism (disjunction) as text and history (narration) as context and critique—or they reverse these terms and reveal discontinuities of history, a shifting of scales that allows both for the collapse of the self into trope, on the one hand, and identification with narrative and writer–audience connection, on the other.

The other day I went to see *In The American West*, Richard Avedon's mean-spirited show at the Pace Gallery. Avedon's subjects are doubly lost. First, they are part of larger, unknowable historical matters. Second, the scale of Avedon's biological-glass-slide-white-art-gallery background severs them from their own narrations. The photos are glamorous; that is, they convey a mix of invitation and rejection. But when we identify with these subjects, we feel humiliated; if we remain ourselves, we feel ashamed. The subjects contain the great momentum of their narrations first as potential energy, and finally as a metaphor. "The relative insufficiency of peripheral existences is absolute insufficiency in total existence" (Bataille).[11] By collapsing his subjects into tropes, Avedon breaks their nineteenth-century-novel personas which imply that they will end up in a different place from where they are now. In fact, the point is that their appearance reveals them to be examples of a story that can't change. The disjunction between his subject "matter" and his technique creates a gap that we struggle and fail to fill, spilling into being. Our own failure generates awe and fear. Who is taking the risk?—his subjects, Avedon, or ourselves? His subjects are ourselves in the mirror at the moment of seeing our death, except they remain unconscious, dying animals dressed for distorted lives. They are equivalent to unworkable selves, degraded and exoticized communities, degradation of the local.

Avedon's characters are portrayed as unconscious as fictional characters unaware of the boundaries of the novel they inhabit. Behind Avedon's social critique is the more acute contempt of the artist for subject matter. We are invited to feel contempt for the image, as I did for the self in the mirror, the contempt blocking identification.

I am reminded of Flaubert's anger at his characters—form's exasperation with representation—as though Mme. Bovary or Pécuchet were robots passing themselves off as human. Flaubert's art underscores their artifacted nature, disallowing them depth and continuity as though to punish them. Exasperation with the artifice of representation leads to an exasperated narrative, like Beckett's *Molloy*, a literature that looks for authenticity by asserting the materiality of its medium, so that the writing appears to coextend with language itself. But that strategy dead-ends when language appears to be as artificial as the despised fictional personalities—including the writer's "real" personality—and moreover equal to them, artifice being the common denominator. Isn't that lack of authenticity what postmodernism means?

I wonder if we are at the point of reversing Flaubert's scorn by accepting an artificial self, with its own scale, depth, and continuity. Eastern religions respond to a "made-up" world with compassion—but with fatalism that is the flip side of Flaubert's scorn. To the degree that we "see through" the ideology of the self, both inside writing and in the larger fiction of personality, we suffer from and enjoy a self-contempt that is close to bragging. Or is it a Freudian pleasure based on an instinct to return to the inanimate?

Is the nameless body the key to this mystery and every mystery?

I wonder if it's possible to be aware of the artifacted nature of the self and not be contemptuous of it?—to understand it as a construct and be moved by its depth?

Notes:

1. Robert Glück, *Jack the Modernist* (New York: SeaHorse/Gay Presses of New York, 1985), 10–11.

2. Jacques Lacan, "The Mirror Stage as Formative of the I Function as Revealed in Psychoanalytic Experience," in *Écrits: The First Complete Edition in English*, trans. Bruce Fink (New York: W. W. Norton & Company, 2006), 76.

3. Sigmund Freud, *Beyond the Pleasure Principle*, trans. James Strachey (New York: W. W. Norton & Company, 1961), 32.

4. Charles Bernstein, *Islets/Irritations* (New York: Roof Books, 1983), 1.

5. Dodie Bellamy, *The Letters of Mina Harker* (unpublished manuscript, 1985). The final version of Bellamy's *Mina Harker* was published in 1998 by Hard Press (West Stockbridge, MA).

6. Ibid.

7. Ibid.

8. Lydia Davis, *Break it Down* (New York: Farrar, Straus, and Giroux, 2008), 140.

9. Ibid., 139.

10. Fredric Jameson, *The Political Unconscious: Narrative as a Socially Symbolic Act* (Ithaca, NY: Cornell University Press, 1982), 77.

11. Georges Bataille, "The Labyrinth," in *Visions of Excess: Selected Writings, 1927–1939*, trans. Allan Stoekl (Minneapolis: University of Minnesota Press, 1985), 176–177.

"Truth's Mirror is No Mirror" was published in "Postmodern," *Poetics Journal*, no. 7, eds. Lyn Hejinian and Barrett Watten (1987). It was based on a talk given at the St. Mark's Poetry Project, New York City, December 1985; and rewritten in 1987 for "In Context," a three-day residency at Intersection for the Arts, San Francisco, which included two lectures and a reading by myself, as well as lectures by Kevin Killian and Dodie Bellamy.

WHO SPEAKS FOR US: BEING AN EXPERT

I'm teaching the Writers on Writing class at San Francisco State this spring. Writers come in and talk about their work, and I was struck by a common theme. Many writers talked about a "child" in them. The image: an ideal child, the creative life of the artist, constantly distracted, besieged, and hemmed in. The image interested me because it seemed so particular to here and now. What would it have meant to Dante or Shakespeare, to whom being a child mostly equaled small understanding, undeveloped faculties? And how does it tally with the maladjusted children we writers probably were?

So I thought about it, helped by Philippe Aries's *Centuries of Childhood.* Aries belongs to the Annales School, a group of French historians who chart the history of subjectivity—of attitude and worldview. I learned that in earlier times play was integrated into our lives to a degree we can hardly imagine. I came to the conclusion that when these writers said "child" they meant flexibility and open-ended play, resistance to uniformity, "a promise of bliss," polymorphous utopia. The distinctions we make between child and adult are recent, and only recently has childhood claimed a special province. Like other books on the history of subjectivity, *Centuries of Childhood* maps the dolorous transition from an integrated society to one that specializes. Childhood itself is something of a specialization, and our ability to be flexible—playful—has been reclassified as childlike:

In 1600 the specialization of games and pastimes did not extend beyond infancy: after the age of three or four it decreased and disappeared. *From then on the child played the same games as the adult, either with other children or with adults.*[1]

In the society of old, work did not take up so much time during the day and did not have so much importance in the public mind: it did not have the existential value which we have given it for something like a hundred years. One can scarcely say that it had the same meaning. On the other hand, games and amusements extended far beyond the furtive moments we allow them; they formed one of the principal means employed by a society to draw its collective bonds closer, to feel united.[2]

It is important to note that the old community of games was destroyed at one and the same time between children and adults, between lower and middle class. The coincidence enables us to glimpse already a connection between the idea of childhood and the idea of class.[3]

These separations inform our models for art and writing. Flexibility, resistance to uniformity, are hallmarks of twentieth-century art. Literature doesn't look modern unless its surface is messy or playful, or constructed in some way that resists closure (as a limit: Derrida's "language without discourse").[4] Nineteenth-century realism and its descendants have come to be associated with work. (Think of Balzac's output and Flaubert's endless complaints— "working like a mule.")[5] The charge leveled at modern art by a self-righteous working world has always been "a child could do it." This is rightly threatening, and the accusation underscores the connection between childhood and art.

So most experimental writing has an adversarial relation to professionalism, to work-ethic mentality; a resistance to fetishizing the "expert," or whatever is authoritarian. I'm also thinking of performance art—a kind of art that says "no experts"—where we find flexibility, spectacle, and the "child" emotions of awe and fear.

But when the avant-garde talks about itself, it becomes extremely professional. If the language that addresses experimental writing has any charm, it is often based on difficult syntax and terms that want to be technical, associated with science. Maybe this expertise validates play by making it look like work, and this may be just another separation into parts that characterizes late capitalism. Or is this still Wordsworth's division between the spontaneous and the analytical?

When we say public speech—whether spoken or written—we mean setting or reaffirming or challenging the terms that legitimate discourse, and ultimately legitimate writing. The expert sets terms, an act of will because it's difficult to marshal ideas—they seem to prefer disjunction. A new set of terms brings codes to bear on each other, legitimates new work, and creates the native soil of future writing. We move toward or away from a given set of terms, but we are rarely indifferent. (This is a mixed message regarding the role of the expert—it's born of mixed emotions.)

"The diegetic function of this sequence is thoroughly incommensurate with the hyperbole of its presentation."[6] I lifted this sentence from an article in *October*. To my mind it says, "I am an expert." It's long on terms, short on discourse. If we rewrote this sentence—say, "The diegetic presentation of this hyperbole is hardly commensurate with the fluctuation of its sequences"—would its effect be altered? But these very terms carry urgency—they are a language that constitutes a (campus?) community. Of course the terms will be simpler for a wider community.

For example, gay male discourse usually carries some perfunctory citation to sex. We often see ourselves and are seen by others as purveyors of sex. So any gay journal, whether literary or simply a newspaper, has lots of sex in it. Sex is the terms: if it's not in the text, it's in the visuals. Gay Christmas card? Naked Santa. Naked housecleaning service, naked accountant, naked driving school. In these terms we invest our subjectivity; they invoke group activities that are gay related, and in general they reaffirm our attraction to one another. In this way gay men recognize that a given journal or newspaper pertains, and certainly these terms carry an urgency that has more to do with directing one's subjectivity than emptying the libido. These images invite and exclude much the same as the semiotic critical vocabulary of experimental writing.

An article by Dennis Altman in *Socialist Review* illustrates the cross circuiting of discourses. The article was called "Sex: The Front Line for Gay Politics";[7] it was flanked by a sexy Joe Brainard drawing and an ad for Gay Sunshine Books. One book in the ad was titled *Meat: How Men Look, Act, Talk, Walk, Undress, Taste, & Smell.* Readers subsequently attacked Altman's essay; many tried to delegitimize it based on the drawing and the ad. "We emphasize that we consider the pornographic advertisement that follows Altman's article to be offensive, politically incorrect and damaging to *SR*"—that from part of the *SR* collective itself.[8] And another letter: "However, what bothers me most of all is the concluding frame of the article—the ad for 'Gay Sunshine Books.' To my mind this ad is completely irrelevant to *SR*'s political concerns and purposes, and I find its appearance in *SR* as poor judgment in the extreme."[9] Here two kinds of discourse meet. Naturally there is resistance. One group's terms can be the exact formula that invalidates another group's terms. What would happen if you belong to both? *SR* is not friendly to experimental writing, and would not consider semiotic analysis, so what happens if you belong to three hostile groups? I suppose the answer is that you have a pretty average writer's life, but that does not make public speech any simpler. Unless you are motivated to connect the dots, to make these codes inform each other.

Although earlier models persist—romantic, aristocratic, ivory tower—experimental writers want to be the edge of the new. Newer than new: in fact, critiquing the new. We are self-consciously critical of the various technological vocabularies. The most rewarded expert produces the most insights by de-expertizing the other experts, giving their partializing codes the lie by positing a more extensive unification. He finds common codes or brings one code to bear on another, and shows us to what extent the commodity permeates writing, sex, and other "last bastions." So, the case of the *SR* controversy: I might use the terms of the Left to portray the gay ad as a commodification of sexuality, but then I would turn the tables and say that commodification of sex is part of a community as it exists—and use that notion to critique the Left's blind spot in the terrain of sexuality, community, and the production of desire. In the end I will have played the part of technician with dexterity, producing an insight larger than either set of terms.

Then it's not surprising, historically speaking, that experts create a maximum power imbalance. In horror movies, after all the lyrical supernatural events (transgression, awe, flexibility, spectacle, fear), we meet the expert, the scientist with a stack of books who says, "Yes, these events really happened."

To claim that events happen, you must have confidence in your perception. But there is a second kind of confidence based on physical safety. A speaker feels physically safe in the world, or deals with the fear of physical harm, urgency to speak tipping the scales. And there are different ways to speak. When I was a kid, adult men all seemed to be experts. They talked politics with authority. The basic message was authority; it was tedious and frightening. The women were more tentative, ironic; still, they exchanged information and, as opposed to the men, all the women talked. Both groups reaffirmed their friendship, the terms of their community, but the women were a lot more fun. But now you are getting the idea that I'm introducing the theme of gender. The experts tend to be men, and there are objective reasons why men feel physically safe in the world. (How much better, then, to be without a body completely. The moral of *Donovan's Brain*, for example, is that without a body we would seek limitless power fueled by limitless arrogance.)

When I start to speak, when I think about starting to speak, I am confronted with a cliff, vertigo, to jump or not to jump. Here I am a child again—but in this version of childhood, speech abides by the absolute verdict of a fairy tale, one wrong word and you're out. As I get used to speaking there is a psychic cost, some restructuring. Going from an object to a subject— whether as an individual or as a movement—first I experience the urge to account for myself completely. So now I occur in language. I master techniques to claim the audience, physical techniques and the going vocabulary. What comes with practice eventually becomes part of me. I must know how my presence is felt—in fact it becomes part of my bag of tricks, an expert's bag of tricks. If I send it out into this room—a warm presence, Jewish/gay, with a subtext, not too buried, saying "don't hurt me"—and I master the projection of this presence, then I gain something to manipulate but lose something integral. (That's why we resist being described—it limits us.) As a second option I could junk my personality and opt for scientific objectivity, arrogant, blank as a TV test pattern. What I gain from all this is that I become part of other people's psychic lives. That's power. I set the terms that will govern their imaginations, shape their subjectivity. I also create for myself more elbow room in my own writing. I will no longer be afraid to speak, but the audience will be afraid of me. And rightly. I will be an expert who represents oppressed minorities. After all, when there are power inequalities favoring one side, like racism and sexism, inequalities of other kinds often gather on the other side.

In an ideal community, I would be reciting the terms the community gave to me. The greater the power differential and the more I am fetishized as an expert, the greater will be the distance between my audience and me. That's why movements and communities are wary of experts. The Right prefers "common sense." The Left criticizes "elitism." And the more I turn my audience into a classroom, into children, frightened and bored, the less chance there will be of any real community. One way to open the discourse—if that is a goal—is to arrange for more people to feel a personal stake. In a community of writers, a bottom line will be which kind of writing, *whose* writing, is taken seriously, written about, discussed. Enlarging this canon would expand the terms. Finally, if we want more people to engage in our discussions, then we must pay attention to what is physically threatening—body language, tone of voice, and other expressions of power imbalance.

Notes:

1. Philippe Ariès, *Centuries of Childhood: A Social History of Family Life*, trans. Robert Baldick (New York: Penguin Books, 1979), 71.

2. Ibid., 73.

3. Ibid., 99.

4. Jacques Derrida, *Of Grammatology*, trans. Gayatri Chakravorty Spivak (Baltimore: Johns Hopkins University Press, 1997), 279.

5. Gustave Flaubert to Louise Colet, March 20, 1852, in *The Letters of Gustave Flaubert: 1830–1857*, ed. Francis Steegmuller (Cambridge: Harvard University Press, 1980), 157.

6. Robert Burgoyne, "Narrative and Sexual Excess," in "Rainer Werner Fassbinder," *October*, no. 21 (Summer 1982): 60.

7. Dennis Altman, "Sex: The Front Line for Gay Politics," *Socialist Review* no. 65 (September/October 1982): 74-84.

8. *Socialist Review*, nos. 75–76 (May–August 1984): 124.

9. Ibid., 125.

"Who Speaks for Us: Being an Expert" was published in *Writing/Talks*, ed. Bob Perelman (Carbondale, IL: Southern Illinois University Press, 1984). It was reprinted in the *Poetry Project Newsletter*, no. 113, ed. Tim Dlugos (April 1985). It began as a presentation at Intersection for the Arts, San Francisco.

ALLEGORY

There are too many reasons for allegory's emergence as the post-modern mode, which suggests that it's firmly in place and everyone is merely trying to account for it. Allegory substitutes one text/language for another; it reads itself; it is a collection of forces, of voices, of "levels." What if all levels exist at once and the ladder is suddenly removed, or better, never really existed? Could these shifting, expanding meanings operate as anticipation and take the place of a future? Of course allegory isn't naturalistic; perhaps its rival is symbolism, which wants to regain a world of sympathetic magic where words *are* the things they name. That is, allegory sees itself and history as created events; it dawned as a precapitalistic mode to resolve cultural conflicts. The early church needed a double view and invented allegory when it rewrote Virgil and Ovid by adding commentary and exegesis. It made the Old Testament prefigure the New and shifted reading dynamics to privilege interpretation—a dynamics extending outward from the work. So, Jonah prefigures Jesus by jumping overboard, sacrificing himself, and spending three days inside the fish, the period of Jesus' death. Allegory and other forms of multiple meaning, like puns and anagrams, declined with the class that sponsored them (think of Spencer and the monarchy) and took an adversarial position (Blake, Mary Shelley). To be understood, life must be read.

Allegory's pedagogic uses are obvious. Venus is naked because lust (a crime) can't be hidden. But let's put it another way: the didactic acts as a framing device that creates the local. Using commentary, they made Virgil applicable. The local is a necessary component of any community, and an allegorical poem can be local and at the same time claim or recover that other component of community life: the sublime. By local, I mean intimacy; the circumstance of knowing others and being known; being the subject of one's story; sharing gestures over a period of time; sharing ideology. By sublime, I mean transgression of ego boundaries; merging; transcendence; horror/awe; discontinuities of birth, sex, and death.

I want to discuss some poetry by a brilliant feminist group whose locus is the magazine *How(ever)*. Their imagery is often appropriated—another meaning is added. So Rachel Blau DuPlessis "refabricates" the lyric tradition in her long work, *The History of Poetry*: "not on hills but 'hills'/nor by water, but 'water'/or from desire, but from 'desire.'"[1] Like the early church and the pagan patriarchy that went before, they rewrite the myths: DuPlessis in her "Medusa" and "Eurydice," Beverly Dahlen in *The Egyptian Poems*, Frances Jaffer in her "Great Day for the Virgin." Reclaiming female myths has been a project of the woman's movement—think of Judy Grahn, Susan Griffin, Monique Wittig. For the innovative poets in *How(ever)*, "the myths of a culture are embodied in its language, its lexicon, its very syntactical structure."[2]

Kathleen Fraser's poem "Medusa's hair was snakes. Was thought, split inward" begins, like most allegories, in a state of perplexity.

> I do not wish to report of Medusa directly, this variation of her writhing. After she gave that voice a shape, it was the trajectory itself in which she found her words floundering and pulling apart.[3]

The first line slyly alludes to eyes averted from the fatal Medusa and, more importantly, tells us indirection will be the theme. The "variation"?—words and communication generally. Having been given a shape, language is "writhing." Fraser brings the myth to a local problem, local event.

When he said "red cloud," she imagined *red*
but he thought *cloud* (this dissonance in which she was feeling
trapped, out-of-step, getting from here to there).[4]

Language is gender-identified, thus conflict is staged within the sign. Put another way, postmodernism loves/hates modernism's revolt from representation. It isn't only the sublime/undifferentiated in "Medusa" that's being grasped, but an attempt—via detours and hesitations—to recover a true local with its interruption and plurality: what *can* be known, which may be problematical, even just a set of relationships. As opposed to the confines of a false local:

Historical continuity
accounts for knowing what dead words point to
[. . .]
M. wanted her own.
Kept saying *red dog. Cloud.*[5]

Medusa needs the possibility of interpretation, doubling, "thought split." *Red* can pun for *read* dog, read cloud. *Red*: the emotional adjective set against the factual nouns—"she *imagined* . . . *he thought.*" Fraser's poem works at once as a story and example, the poem itself a site of multiple readings, of the "voices" (current poetry usage for allegory, it seems to me) that influence, surround, inform, and are our lives.

Can she substitute *dog* for *cloud*, if *red* comes first?
Red tomato.
Red strawberry.
As if all this happens on the ocean one afternoon in July,
red sunset soaking into white canvas. The natural world.
And the darkness does eventually come down.
He closes her eye in the palm of his hand.
The sword comes down.
Now her face rides above his sails, her hair her splitting
tongues.[6]

The "distance" between signifier and signified that characterizes much experimental writing is given a local meaning. And there are other dimensions in allegorical writing. Space and time are patterned (the sunset is a painting of a sunset, the story is a metaphor). The glimmer of the distance between commodity and noncommodity is a dimension, too; and desire has its own time, space, and death. Red is a sound or verbal token; a cloud or sunset or blood; subjectivity; allegory.

This writing joins a modernist tradition that sees itself as besieged by or besieging linearity—for feminists, patriarchal linearity. The new elements are the sublime and the local: they establish ties to readers' actual lives both in keeping with the tenets of the women's movement and in the spirit of a postmodernism that wants writing to know its readers. Fraser's Medusa is a sublime multiplicity, a myth apprehended through language, through cultural mediations like the Renaissance iconography of "Now her face rides above his sails." Medusa is born of an actual conflict—she does not want her language to "point," she wants the voluptuousness and risk of all meanings at once. So the poem is an allegory about allegory.

In modernism form grew simpler, the assumptions more complex. Mondrian's *New York City*, with its glimpse of a future society, resembles the Murray of Tullibardine tartan—compare their significance to their respective clans. In modern writing "form" is reflexive. Allegory wants content to be reflexive too. That is, allegory wants to understand the world, self, and narration as constructions—impure ones.

> I have come so far
> I have made this journey
> in the dark
> through the rocks and dry sand
> of the Other World
> I walk on my own feet
> my legs are intact
> my backbone upright
> I see with the Eye of Horus

My shadow joins me
my double
my soul[7]

Beverly Dahlen's "Opening the Tomb to the Soul and Shadow" begins with allegory's pilgrim motif and a narration. Its purity of construction doesn't evade but amplifies the question: What is this poem *about*? Its relationship to us isn't structured as a hierarchy. Fraser's allegory reads itself. A mournful silence surrounds Dahlen's *The Egyptian Poems*; silence, empty, for us to fill. Dahlen calls her ongoing long poem *A Reading*, but here the riddle is ours. The local is ourselves, offstage.

Who is this?

This is the god who was not a child
the first one before you
the last one behind you
the god of no face and no flesh
who nevertheless
faces you

Explain this.

This is the god who
came to himself and knew his own name.
In that name
naming. And the great train of gods
was called out of the darkness
of his mouth.[8]

This poem's title, "Of the Origin of the Gods: a Catechism," suggests pedagogy. Like *A Reading*, it describes that place where words and life impinge: "In that name / naming." Is Dahlen "rescuing" the Egyptian Book of the Dead? Craig Owens says, "Allegorical imagery is appropriated imagery; the allegorist does not invent images but confiscates them. He lays claim to the culturally significant, poses as its interpreter. He does not restore an original meaning . . . Rather, he adds another meaning to the image."[9] Is Dahlen's code Jungian archetype, Freudian unconscious, framing an exotic souvenir, literal, mystical philosophic, ornamental—or all of these? Are they "untranslated" hieroglyphs, the model of emblematic writing? Let's use a Lacanian grid, because in these poems naming = identity = objecthood = death. Speech is already a dead language, a "gate" to a dead/named world: "That their eyes look back at me in the instant I pronounce / these words, that I thus draw them out of the darkness / and enter into their company" ("The Gates").[10] I think Lacan's Name of the Father applies, parental authority considered as a linguistic function, and the notion of the mirrored self as other ("the god of no face and no flesh / who nevertheless / faces you")—a structural irony (doubleness) that always refers to that first sharpest cruelty of names and categories, the creation of the self with its double abdication from the world and from the body ("My shadow joins me / my double / my soul"). So the "darkness of the mouth," where language is, is death and the underworld. Walter Benjamin: "To be named—even if the name-giver is god-like and saintly—perhaps always brings with it a presentment of mourning."[11] Well, *that* could be the subject of these poems.

Behind Dahlen's Egypt is H.D.'s, a "site" like Fraser's Medusa that rejects names and categories: timeless, genitive, dead, bodily—sublime. I am not suggesting one "true" reading of Fraser or Dahlen. We should see their meanings as a secondary multiplicity, with the understanding that the primary may no longer exist if it ever did; or else if once a primary existed as a utopia, now it exists as a break—beyond language, just beyond, a *via negativa*.

I want to apply some of my notions about the *How(ever)* group to a writer with a different agenda. Here are a few paragraphs from *Safe*, a book-length "prose piece" by poet Dennis Cooper.

The man grapples forward and locates a skull in Mark's haircut. He picks out the rim of caves for his eyeballs and ears. The lantern jaw fastens below them, studded with teeth. He comes to the long shapely bones of Mark's shoulders, toying with them until two blades resembling manta rays swim to the surface. He clutches his way to both elbows. Ribs ride short breaths to the touch. He grasps Mark's hips and their structure floats up to him. He strokes through a reef of wild femurs which keep up the ass [. . .]

Mark hears the man cum. Okay, so that's over. He raises up and glances over his shoulder. The skeleton turns to stare at its lover. Whatever it's thinking, it's always looking like it's laughing at the expense of a boy who's in sparkling focus. The man's eyes are spooked when they look at him.[12]

Tricking is a local occurrence to many gay men and, more importantly, *reading* about a trick is a local event to most. Copper retains his distance by going too close—he reveals an intimacy that contains its own opposite, so he's critical. But not of the function sex has here and in his community. He jumps some (social?) hurdle and *knowing* becomes a place of danger, dissolution of ego boundaries, death. At the same time, Cooper is so close he's abstract, his scene becomes a tableau: Death and the Maiden, *In Voluptas Mors*. Think of a Flemish vanitas—literally, *emptiness*—the overturned cup or pitcher; memento mori. On the apple the caterpillar means death but also resurrection. Is meaning only decorative, like Justice Triumphant? An allegorical frame of mind can read crumbling medieval walls as the crumbling monarchy. If personality in late capitalism is also a ruin, how would we allegorize it? Benjamin said:

> Everything about history that, from the very beginning, had been untimely, sorrowful, unsuccessful, is expressed in a face— or rather in a death's head. And although such a thing lacks all 'symbolic' freedom of expression, all classical proportion, all humanity—nevertheless, this is the form in which man's subjection to nature is most obvious and it significantly gives rise not only to the enigmatic question of the nature of human existence as such, but also of the biographical historicity of the individual. This is the heart of the allegorical way of seeing.[13]

That is, the subject must contain its own "nonhuman" or sublime. Think of Dahlen's "underworld," her language-death axis, or Fraser's Medusa's severed head—or better, her "floundering and coming apart" of language itself. People who build a community or merely "inherit" the community they write about share this double impulse to claim their world in words and stake a claim in the "beyond."

Cooper's passage owes something to pornography and to horror, the religious genres. (Consider H.D.'s Egypt, with its sexuality and the body—rising from the dead?) Allegory welcomes the blunt conventions of genre (and mythology), but as trope. Cooper turns genre into pastiche with pastiche's assertiveness, so what was originally intended to engage now distances in order to accommodate new meaning. He rewrites Venus's nakedness by giving his hero a second death—an economic one.

> Mark combs his hair in a mirror. The man comes out dripping, puts on a robe and starts straightening up. Mark asks for money. The man shakes his head. The boy's face blurs as he does. Then it clears, but he still sees the skeleton there. It's a premonition. Its glee is the truth behind Mark's bored expression. Mark puts his hands in his pockets. A light through the open door silhouettes him in his last few seconds. He lowers his eyes. "Bye."[14]

Cooper's "porn" yields its commodity relations: Mark is worthless, he becomes a silhouette, a shadow for his "last few seconds," and by the time he slips away he is a ghost. Cooper writes about sex the way the Romantics wrote about Nature. That is, they each react to commodification of sex or nature, tamed and abstracted, for sale—yet they describe the loss of ego boundaries in that loss, that ruin, that *naming*.

"Any person, any object, any relationship can mean absolutely anything else," says Benjamin about allegory.[15] He also describes a late capitalism where meaning has come loose from its moorings. Or rather, abstraction generated by the commodity gives us a double view, the precondition for allegory that the church once promoted. Put too simply, if we see an apple both as itself and as its price, equal to similarly priced apples and oranges, how do we see our time, our bodies?

Perhaps allegory accommodates "rewritings" of ideology and self as externals that name us—as Robert Duncan says of his poet self, "a made up thing and at the same time a depth in which my being is."[16] Perhaps this signals a new relation to audience—not vanguardist or utopian, but inviting, shared.

Notes:

1. Rachel Blau DuPlessis, "Crowbar," *Sulfur*, no. 8 (1983): tk.

2. Francis Jaffer,"Why However?," *How(ever)* 1, no. 1 (May 1983): 1. *How(ever)* now exists as an archives: http://www.asu.edu/pipercwcenter/how2journal/archive/print_archive/index.htm.

3. Kathleen Fraser, *Something (even human voices) in the foreground, a lake* (Berkeley: Kelsey St. Press, 1984), 20.

4. Ibid.

5. Ibid.

6. Ibid., 21.

7. Beverly Dahlen, *The Egyptian Poems* (Berkeley: Hipparchia Press, 1983), n.p.

8. Ibid.

9. Craig Dworkin, "The Allegorical Impulse: Toward a Theory of Postmodernism," *October*, no. 12 (Spring 1980): 69.

10. Dahlen, *Egyptian Poems*, n.p.

11. Walter Benjamin, *The Origin of German Tragic Drama*, trans. John Osborne (London: Verso, 2003), 224–225.

12. Dennis Cooper, *Safe* (New York City: Sea Horse Press, 1984), 48–49.

13. Benjamin, *German Tragic Drama*, 166.

14. Cooper, *Safe*, 49.

15. Benjamin, *German Tragic Drama*, 175.

16. Robert Duncan, introduction to *The Year as Catches: First Poems (1939–1946)*, in *The Collected Early Poems and Plays*, ed. Peter Quartermain (Berkeley: University of California Press, 2012), 11.

"Allegory" was published in *Ironwood*, no. 23, ed. Michael Cuddihy (1984).

THE CHARM OF DIFFICULTY

One afternoon in the fall of 1965, at UCLA, I noticed a small sign that advertised an on-campus poetry reading by Robert Creeley. The reading was starting right away. A poetry reading, I said to myself with wonder. Aren't I a poet? Shouldn't I go to this reading?

I had no idea who Creeley was, and I doubted that the administration would deliver the real poetry goods to us students. I sat in the back of the huge auditorium. The reading was sparsely attended. Creeley was already at the podium. He was wearing a tan corduroy jacket and sandals—rather informal, I thought, even inappropriate. On the other hand, two professors in black suits were sitting on the stage emitting a gruelingly clerical sense of occasion. Someone had stationed a potted palm by the podium, signifying the presence of culture.

If you've ever heard Creeley read, you will know exactly what I heard. His voice is choppy and averted; he seems to trip at the end of each short line. He read poems that I found later in *For Love*, his first big collection, poems that would become famous. He laughed at something in a poem—what was funny? Another poem was about buying condoms—weird. I couldn't make out what he was doing. Here was a "living author," a rare bird on campus. In classes, our exemplary modern was T. S. Eliot. Dylan Thomas, safely dead for twelve years, took us to the brink of the new.

Listening to Creeley, I became nauseated. Shouldn't I, a poet, be able to understand any poet writing in the present time? Yet here was an aesthetic that did not admit me. Creeley seemed to be making up his poems from the inside as he went along. After the reading, a flock of black-suited vultures surrounded Creeley and carried him off to dismember at some reception. Creeley looked so totally pained that I thought, maybe he *is* the real thing. One of the poems Creeley read that afternoon is called "I Know a Man":

> As I sd to my
> friend, because I am
> always talking,—John, I
>
> sd, which was not his
> name, the darkness sur-
> rounds us, what
>
> can we do against
> it, or else, shall we &
> why not, buy a goddamn big car,
>
> drive, he sd, for
> christ's sake, look
> out where yr going.[1]

In retrospect, Creeley's poem is not hard to understand. It has a narrative and can be taken as a little allegory. What was my problem? Why does new form create a scandal? Why did some blurry haystacks and oranges outrage the first audiences of the Impressionists? That audience could not see their own experience (organization of meaning, sense of space) reflected back to them, so the paintings seemed to reject their experience. Creeley's poem said to me, "You think the world has a unified meaning, but that's false. The world makes itself up as you make it up, piece by piece, arbitrarily, out of your own perceptions. If you don't know how you perceive the world, then you don't know who you are." As Creeley wrote in an essay from 1966, "The road, as it were, is creating itself momently in one's attention to it, there, visibly, in front of the car. There is no reason it should go on forever, and if one does so assume it, it very often disappears all too actually."[2]

Two things strike me. First, DIFFICULT might really mean that a pre-planned meaning does not exist. A very disjunct experimental poem may be easy to understand, because I am supposed to "cowrite" it—that is, experience it through my own set of associations, rather than "decode" the work and "unpack" its symbols. The degrees of coherence and disjunction we recognize in the world (and turn into literature) represent our deepest engagement with language, and so with reality. Second, innovative writing wants to keep me in the present, which can be experienced as a kind of DIFFICULTY. Most writing invites me into a guided daydream with its telescoped sense of time. In much innovative writing, I am thrown back into my own present, the present of the reading instead of the present of a story. Until that becomes normal, it's hard work, like learning to meditate.

To an astounding degree our culture does not know itself, and by that I mean you and I don't know ourselves, perhaps starting with—and caused by—the effect we have on the world. We can't seem to unite feeling and event. Our culture seems reluctant to communicate with its own realities: our labor takes place in conditions of raw capitalism a world away, death and old age are locked up in institutions, our wars don't make it to the news—yet we are titillated by sex and violence in the form of distractions and false crises of every sort that keep the whole culture slightly crazed. The horror and splendor of our lives exceed this threadbare vision. If there is a reason for difficult writing, it is to break this shallow "fictional" plane where most of our life is spent.

My nausea during Creeley's reading was caused by the lack of recognition. I could not see my own experience (organization of meaning, sense of time) reflected back to me in his poems, so his poems seemed to cancel my experience. No wonder I felt sick. In a way, it was the nausea of plenty—too many possible meanings, too much awareness of time. My own discomfort led me to poetry magazines that printed Robert

Creeley's work, and from there I began to piece together the literature of the present that would become important to me.

Now, when my students complain that they hate innovative writing, I warn them: strong feeling—even hatred—suggests a first acquaintance with something you may come to love.

Notes:

1. Robert Creeley, *For Love: Poems 1950–1960* (New York: Scribner, 1962), 38.

2. Robert Creeley, "Notes Apropos Free Verse," in *Collected Essays of Robert Creeley* (Berkeley: University of California Press, 1989), 493–494.

"The Charm of Difficulty" was published in the *Stranger* (Seattle), Spring Literary Supplement, April 20, 2000.

ON CRITICAL WRITING

Critical writing makes obvious claims to science and objectivity, but I also read for new formal models, new language, and prose that is lush, precise, and self-conscious. Look how this sentence, by Fredric Jameson, becomes the tracking shot it is describing:

> Beauty and boredom: this is then the immediate sense of the monotonous and intolerable opening sequence of *The Shining*, and of the great aerial tracking shot across quintessentially breathtaking and picture-postcard "unspoiled" American natural landscape; as well as of the great hotel, whose old-time turn-of-the-century splendor is undermined by the more meretricious conception of "luxury" entertained by consumer society, and in particular by the manager's modern office space and the inevitable plastic coffee he has his secretary serve.[1]

Suspense in critical writing arises from manipulation of meaning. When time slows down, subject matter's share of the page is based on importance rather than story's demand for a discovery. Like Egyptian murals, the king is huge and slaves are tiny. Or the Last Judgment, where final values are assigned. So Baudrillard may fan out a metaphor, develop both terms at once, travel a leisurely circle around an image to release its meanings, indulge in melodrama:

> The whole of science and technology were recently mobilised to save the mummy of Rameses II, after it had been left to deteriorate in the basement of a museum. The West was panic-

stricken at the thought of not being able to save what the symbolic order had been able to preserve for 40 centuries, but away from the light and gaze of onlookers . . . Whence that historic scene of the mummy's reception at Orly airport.[2]

I read critical writing for its detective novel adventure and risk, to find out the identity of the murderer (I already know the victim). But the dead may have risen (or not) in the "text" that the book addresses, like Kristeva's study of Celine, an exegesis enhanced and undercut by difficult prose and fragmentation. The writer can either mime a global disunity or offer the whole of meaning as a fragment (like Barthes's *S/Z*). Stylistic complexity conveys total complexity; one moves through it, coming upon perceptions and realizations based on, and about, limits set by perception and understanding. Jacques Lacan: "In the subject to subject recourse we preserve, psychoanalysis can accompany the patient to the ecstatic limit of the '*Thou are that*,' where the cipher of his mortal destiny is revealed to him, but it is not in our sole power as practitioners to bring him to the point where the true journey begins."[3]

Exegesis takes apart, casts in doubt, some example of the self—but it remembers in the mechanism of its activity (that is, explanation) that other self, the reader. So it delivers a "non-subject" inside an "argument of the book." Exegesis provides us with an allegorical model—the world is a book, says Mallarmé, says Jabès, says Blanchot, says Barthes, says Derrida. It's an attractive proposition for a writer.

I borrowed much of the lyrical melancholy of my first prose from the Frankfurt School—especially Adorno's *Minima Moralia* and Benjamin's *Illuminations*. Their writing gave me access to my own experience and also ways to express it. I took from them the miniature meditation, the energy produced by applying high style to low subjects, and the energy generated when two codes are brought to bear on each other.

In a sense I was borrowing a classical education. The resounding periods of most European writers (like Milton and Barthes) are born of a curriculum that includes, if not amounts to, immersing in classical literature, and composing Latin imitations of Cicero, Seneca, and others, as well as imitations of those who imitated the Romans. These students felt (were taught) that the tradition they were gesturally assimilating was theirs by virtue of a lineage that led directly to them. So Barthes, with complete confidence, begins his little essay on Garbo's face (as I conclude my little essay on critical writing) with this confection: "Garbo still belongs to that moment in cinema when capturing the human face still plunged audiences into the deepest ecstasy, when one literally lost oneself in a human image as one would in a philter, when the face represented a kind of absolute state of the flesh, which could be neither reached nor renounced."[4]

Notes:

1. Fredric Jameson, "Historicism in The Shining," in *Signatures of the Visible* (New York: Routledge, 2007), 86.

2. Jean Baudrillard, *Simulations*, trans. Paul Foss, Paul Patton, and Philip Beitchman (New York: Semiotext(e), 1983), 18–20.

3. Jacques Lacan, "The Mirror Stage as Formative of the *I* Function as Revealed in Psychoanalytic Experience," in *Écrits: The First Complete Edition in English*, trans. Bruce Fink (New York: W. W. Norton & Company, 2006), 81.

4. Roland Barthes, "The Face of Garbo," in *Mythologies*, trans. Annette Lavers (New York: The Noonday Press, 1991), 56.

"On Critical Writing" was published in *Ottotole*, no. 2, ed. Mike Amnasan (Winter 1986–87).

MY MARGERY, MARGERY'S BOB

Margery Kempe is a novel of obsession, grief and farce, loss of self and excess of self. The unrequitedness of life in general is conveyed through the specifics of a love story. A woman who lived in the first part of the fifteenth century tries and fails to become a saint. Her steamy romance with Jesus is framed by Bob's obsessive love for a young man, L., until the two stories merge to become one: "Bob" becomes Margery, L. becomes Jesus. Bob's ability to enter the fifteenth century is "underwritten" by Margery's own travel through time to the events of Jesus' life.

I did not want *Margery* to be an historical novel, a genre that hardly interests me (unless executed by Flaubert and a few others). What *is* an historical novel? A time machine that seems to restore another era and give us access to its citizens. That is, we get to know Alexander the Great. There's a lie involved, but is that lie different from the lie fiction generally tells? An historical novel describes people and events we are already loyal to because they occur in the world we inhabit, yet they are unapproachable for that very reason. Alexander the Great will always be unknowable, his story beyond my control.

I wanted to use Margery's story, but also to let it alone, to retain the Margery who coextends—however distantly—with the world the reader inhabits. What drew me to Margery's life could only be known by us in the present: the difference between her high aspiration and her failure. In a way, my book is about what Margery could not know about herself—the mix of periods her story embodies (medieval, modern). I feel this describes my own condition—a mix of periods in which scales of judgment, of interpretation, do not jibe. Will the future understand this disparity?

How to use historical matter and be true? True to what? Over the course of five years I grappled with this question. I had to import a version of integrity into the genre. How do you not lie in fiction? Some modernist (and premodern!) answers: to "bare the device"; to assert the reader's present time (the time of the reading, art as object); to challenge linear time; to expose the writer's point of view; to meld figure and ground. Then how use historical matter? I pressured the genre by bringing my relation to this slice of history into the book. History is endlessly porous; so instead of creating a middle distance, I used extreme close-ups, historical long shots, and autobiography.

My books usually contain an element of collaboration; in this case I asked about forty friends for observations and memories about their bodies. Those intimate details are applied to—that is, stitched into—remote fifteenth-century characters. Interior life is clearly attributed—in the acknowledgements! Some of these observations have been published by their authors. They are not descriptions of fictional characters in the usual sense, but random pleasures and fears that couldn't possibly be known from the middle distance. They atomize interior life, pressure the idea of historical recreation (locating Ed's fear of death inside the Vicar of St. Stephen) and at the same time they summon a community (of friends, of physical anarchy) in which to stage my obsession. Physical life, obsession: history as disjunction, a gap.

I created an aesthetic relationship with history by setting limits. I refrained from reading a book about Margery till I was done with the novel, confining myself to her self-description. I limited descriptions to certain aspects of fifteenth-century life, especially clothes, food, and physical gestures. I did not read conventional histories to "fill in." Instead, I married my prose to Margery's, confecting a sentence halfway between us, feeling Margery and the period through the rhythm of her language (another kind of collaboration). Most of the texts I used were books of hours, saints' lives and such from the fourteenth and fifteenth centuries, following the model of Tzvetan Todorov's beautiful *Conquest of America*, a reading of many texts from the period.

I am interested in the puzzle of using real people in fiction; my fictions have been autobiographies. I suppose I have staged Margery's story in the theater of autobiography, building aesthetics out of the interpenetration of fact and fiction. For me, the world of fact is made up of fiction, from "ideological state apparatuses," to the sale of lifestyle, to the all-and-nothing of language itself. And, of course, the world of fiction is a fact.

Is autobiography a subset of history? I'm an autobiographer, and Kempe, the failed saint, wrote the first autobiography in English (in about 1430). This is only one of the parallels I make to give the historical matter a vector. I draw together the emergence of the modern self and the end of the modern self, the decaying society in which Kempe lived, the decaying society in which I live, and our respective plagues. L.'s ruling-class status equals the divinity of Jesus. (In the fifteenth century, gods were closer to mortals—about as close as a Rockefeller.) The two stories are like transparencies; each can be read only in terms of the other.

The present extends in all directions; it orders the future and reorders the past. Margery's story can be taken as one huge metaphor to describe Bob's state of mind. That is, as the second term of a metaphor that describes the present.

But writing about a historical subject does not mean writing from the other side of history. That's what makes me uneasy about the fashion for movies and books that seem to "restore" a period as one would restore a house—a distasteful tourism masquerading as good taste. Antique restoration is a postmodern mode, from *Masterpiece Theater* to the many fundamentalisms in this country and abroad. It is a postmodern desire to want a city or even a parlor to be an exact duplication of an earlier period. These fundamentalisms all speak to the yearning to be authentic, to be part of a recognizable order.

Instead, I feel I am a contributor to Margery's life, an event in her posthumous life, and she has certainly contributed to my own sense of myself. Our lives are intertwined. Her posthumous life's twists and turns allow me to adopt that line of thought. Margery did me the favor of disappearing for four centuries. She was all but forgotten except for a few lovely prayers. She is a twentieth-century phenomenon. Her book was discovered in the library of Col. Butler-Bowdon's sixteenth-century manor house and published in 1934. Margery wakes up in this century as though she experienced a wonderfully prolonged coming out in which the necessity to tell her story prevailed. But Butler-Bowdon, her Prince Charming, referred to her in his preface as "poor Margery." She was disappointing—her vulgarity, self-aggrandizement, and the faults in her piety. The distinct phases of her reputation duplicate other coming outs: first the establishment was ashamed of her because she was a noisy woman and inadequate saint; then feminism glorified her strength; and now the great maw of cultural studies absorbs her life, which becomes one more example in the history of subjectivity and daily life.

"Queering" the past (as the MLA puts it) is hardly a issue for me: what else can I do? Margery prostrated herself "with inordinate lust" before the "members" of world religions—I can do no less. I am more attracted to dubious moments of explosion and disjunction than, say, to the life of Michelangelo, the world-historical genius who defines his period. *Margery* is a queer version of disintegration that includes (takes with it) a central myth of our culture. Perhaps I am as angry as Cousin Bette, and perhaps anger is a defining position. I don't mind a reaction of shock—there's plenty of aggression in the book. Shock, confusion, sexual arousal—all acceptable.

The actual forms we take are a kind of extremity we are driven to in a quest for love. We exist to desire and be desired. Or, more roundly, we make ourselves "different" and "same" in order to be loved (if only by the world). And behind this is the mystery of form, how weird and even unendurable it is to be one thing (race, sexuality, gender) rather than another.

When I become Margery, I can no more "control" the import of my literary drag than I could if I dressed as a woman, pursuing an inner necessity whose explanations and effects would be contradictory at best. But maybe that impurity, which is an expression of a problem rather than a way of containing or explaining it, is the way I handle the ever-crossing circuits of narration.

To make an object of the book, to suppress figure and ground, I developed a kind of minimalism amid the excess. I piled up declarative sentences. I used birds and bird calls every few pages. I researched where a certain bird would visit during a given season, say, "the whickering trill of a grebe" in Margery's vision of the Holy Land during December, 0000, the year of Jesus' birth. And I hung the novel on four words—*exalt, exasperate, abandon, amaze*—that appear again and again, a reduced version of the whole book.

Margery is a tale of middle-aged breakdown (those other middle ages) for Margery and Bob equally. By the end of the book, both accept the partial truth of life in the moment—including an acceptance of death, which in the logic of the book means the reduction of the fear of death, and so the end of obsession. Still, Bob and Margery persist in wanting to be lifted out of history and see their books as another stab at rewriting the end.

"My Margery, Margery's Bob" was published in *Shark*, no. 3, eds. Lytle Shaw and Emilie Clark (Fall 2000).

1982

PREFACE TO *ELEMENTS OF A COFFEE SERVICE*

Don Allen asked me to write a preface for these stories. At first I was reluctant—I think I already had my say, at least for this round. Still, I can show you what I had in mind when I wrote them.

In 1975, Ed and I visited Guatemala. We stayed a few weeks in Santa Caterina, a terraced Mayan village that descended to a lake made from the valleys of three volcanoes. One day we dropped acid. Was it Window Pane? White Lightning? (That reminds me: When I was fine-tuning "When Bruce was 36 (Gossip and Scandal)," I called a pharmaceutical company in Palo Alto to find the correct spelling of the name of a prominent counterculture scientist. Joan, the woman who answered, became very excited. "Owsley? A *great* man! *Hey*, remember blotter acid? Yellow Stingers? Orange Sunshine?" In those days Joan's name was Kismet and she lived in a macrobiotic commune. "Stay cool, Bob, and *hey*, let's you and me take another walk together down Memory Lane.")

Anyway, for once I didn't become aggressively lonely and Ed didn't withdraw into geometric patterns suffused with light. Instead, we went for a swim and then returned to our orange nylon tent where we made love. When we closed the flap, the nylon dyed our bodies a pure orange. In the adjoining yard, a girl wove a red cotton belt on a small backstrap loom. She was seven or eight. All afternoon she sang one wistful song: the song had no words and its end seamlessly met its beginning.

A nice experience—but not enough for a story. Did Ed and Bob love each other? Maybe—be more specific. I'd want to know how they usually got along. They didn't. Different styles? Not good enough—what's behind style? Different psychologies? Not good enough—what forces created those psychologies? Different backgrounds? Ethnicities? That's getting there. Different class backgrounds? That's interesting.

Why were they intruding on the fragile life of an Indian village? Did they believe hippie openheartedness gave them a ticket to go anywhere? Well, yes—but don't be too hard on them. They were well-meaning, selfish, and dumb. Besides, the USA also felt it had the right to go anywhere. It taught them that. At what point does this attitude become sinister? Discuss. Finally, was the sex good? It was great. In fact I'd want to share it with you, relishing it. How could anything diminish by one caress that orange lovemaking?

The physical details should be so intimate they bring the story past the show-and-tell stage of psychological nuance into a shared sensory region; the politics should touch as close as t-shirts or socks. Speaking through the story, I'd want to hear voices that sustain me: from my friends; from the gay, feminist, and left communities; and from the community of writers, living and dead. I think these voices would locate our afternoon—and afternoons in your life too—in the history of our times.

"Preface to *Elements of a Coffee Service*" was written in 1982; it wasn't used.

CARICATURE

The lack of adequate social forms breeds satire and caricature, and historically they have taken a cautionary role. Communities—especially those that are disintegrating—are also conservative. "Community" tends to be conservative; it prefers "self"-preservation, and sees change as a threat. The Golden Age is past, not ahead. Generally humor has not challenged institutions, but reprimanded them. Aristophanes chastens philosophy; Rabelais ridicules Church failings without touching basic tenets; Molière exhorts the court to be less petty. Even a fabliau, a life affirming form, demonstrates the system is a grid for life to work around.

While acknowledging the conservative viewpoint, I'd like to discuss satire and caricature as forms that avoid the split between the hero and society, and show how types and narratives are drawn from the communities in which they derive their meaning.

Satire uses types and character systems that have been set up already; they enjoy an a priori relation to life, which they retain "posthumously" (after the demise of their communities). In the medieval tableau *Death and the Miser*, the characters command immediate belief even at this distance. It's a satisfying comedy about death. The stylized elements do not mean the writer abandons "real life." Rather, he aligns himself with the history of a community, and focuses its types on a real issue.

An example: Jonathan Swift's slightly dense concerned citizen is the forerunner of the modern sociologist or economic planner determined to correct social evil with a scientific plan. (Types have a genealogy, as do speech inflections and body language.) This time the humanitarian's civic goodwill tackles the problem of Ireland: his

"Modest Proposal"—to eat Irish babies. This type was built out of contradictions in the same way as the figures in mythology. It is an embodiment that takes energy from—and returns it to—the community. That is the crux of this essay: if the community is a given, so are its types. That's why satire and caricature are often used more effectively by conservatives who believe in their communities than by those of us who want to change society structurally and who were not located in an expressive community until very recently.

Using type and caricature is antipsychological. "The roundness of the value system which determines the epic cosmos creates a whole which is too organic for any of it to become so enclosed within itself, so dependent upon itself, as to find itself as an interiority—i.e., to become a personality."[1] George Lukács sees the epic hero as a person who *is* a community, a totality in the one person. (Poets who want to create a totality seem to mark off an area that will substitute for community, like the idea of Gloucester for Olson, or the idea of Paterson for Williams.) The problem with a psychological model is that it tends to lift people off the map, setting them down in isolation where they have only themselves (and their interiorized parents) to account for their suffering. Even the pronoun "I" has changed meaning, leading to the twentieth-century's psychological burden. In Chaucer's gallery, the "I" is relatively straightforward and naïve. For example, characters have only first names, as people did by and large in medieval society.

New forms cannibalize the contents of earlier forms, so that in Balzac's cast of characters we find the ambitious clerk, the great lady whose long suit is patience, the witch in the form of a poor relation. They look backward to fairy tale and romance. According to Lukács, Balzac energizes them in a new form, the novel, whose power—lacking a real community—was its ability to convey the whole picture, the totality, by dint of sheer enumeration. By the time we come to Rimbaud's "Je est un autre," the "I" has become nostalgic and reflexive; it looks at itself from the other side of the window. The desire to be free of that "I" has become the refrain of our century, expressed on the one hand by fetishizing scientific objectivity, and on the other hand by turning to conservative religious ideals.

As the world grows less believable, the writer's struggle to convince becomes all the greater. STYLE (Lukács would say lyricism) can suggest meaning; if you breathe hard and long enough on your page, it will appear to breathe also. The world appears and disappears depending on how you phrase things: unique phrase, unique writer, unique world. Free-floating intensities replaces tensions from connections, storytelling. Mallarmé's brilliance lies in his ability to make a sentence, along with the world, do the disappearing rope trick: he pipes the rope up straight, climbs it, pulls the rope up after him, and vanishes. DOCUMENTATION borrows its authority from science; it's psychology, the science of interiority. Time spends its energies numbering the days (not seasons) of the hero's life. William Carlos Williams will "catch" a piece of life, in content and form. The writers gets life "into" writing as though life were a case history, a chunk of language, or a fact under a microscope. A tableau: you are standing here and life is standing over there. "Please get into my writing, Life." "I'll come closer and flirt but I'm not going all the way."

The cowboy, the detective, the traveling salesman, the wacky housewife, the ivory-tower intellectual bring a story with them. This surely changes the focus of pleasure derived from the writing. Since types originate in the community, the point of view will at least overlap with the community's, although not necessarily be it, as, according to Lukács, it is in the epic. Narration counters the modernist proposition that anything can be put next to anything, that everything diverges and agrees to the same extent. Narrative pleasure derives from the accuracy and imaginative use of given material, like the medieval concept of *matière*. Only in this case, the *matière* will be the lives of members of the community, the life of the community itself. As for ideas, the pleasure stems from their "rhyming" with the reader's own.

In this light we can see the personal histories and journals of movement writers as extensions of this idea of type, where the writer offers him or herself as an example. From my point of view, this is the happiest solution to the psychological "I."

In the following section of three short essays, I will make some observations about specific caricatures.

Lucy

Ozzie and Harriet and *I Love Lucy* are two sides of a coin. The coin's name is hysteria. In *Ozzie and Harriet,* the characters move woodenly through their lives, feel nothing. No problem is so large it can't be settled by a polite exchange. Arms dangle uselessly, it's "uncool" to use them expressively—or the face, or the voice. Feeling is repressed and devalued, and displaced—to where? Ricky's great adenoidal music. The joyous music of the fifties and sixties, knocking on the libido's door. Behind the crowd in the school gym, even Ozzie will snap his fingers genially, although Harriet apparently can never unfold her arms. The Nelsons don't appear to suffer. They don't feel trapped in their wooden bodies and lives, unlike their TV audience. If the Nelsons became human the comedy would end. Harriet sits in the living room reading brownie recipes from the *Ladies' Home Journal.* Brownies from previous recipes wait in the kitchen (gee thanks mom). Life is effortless, everything is "normal."

Teenagers aimed their fierce love at this neutrality. Their aspirations took shape in the space between the impossible image and their actual world. Ricky and his family dealt with the anxieties of the Cold War by embracing neutrality. In loving him, we embraced neutrality. The question is, what are you allowed to express when you aren't allowed to express anything? In the larger culture, indifference became a Cold War aesthetic. Jasper Johns turned Old Glory into a neutral object; Rauschenberg produced all-white paintings. In 1953, Cage, responding to the white paintings, wrote, "To whom / no subject / no image / no taste / no object / no beauty / no message / no talent / no technique (no why) / no idea / no intention / no art / no feeling . . ."[2] In the same year, we had book burnings.

Ozzie and Harriet's strength is its male caricatures. In *I Love Lucy* the terms change with the changed sexes. No event is so tiny it can't explode into arm-flailing acrobatics. A typical plot has Lucy trying to mark out a place for herself in opposition to Desi's wishes. So she must sneak. She costumes herself as a dancer, gets a job, and her wig attacks her. She goes into the bread-baking business and the dough rises and rises, emerges from the oven, and keeps emerging. It grapples with her. Lucy is the archetypal wacky housewife—a child, or better, a pet. There are plenty of variations, Rosalind Russell's Auntie Mame and Phyllis Diller's characters. To Lucy's credit she can also become angry, depressed, but the dominant mood is cheerful—a cheerfulness that masks the defeat of instinct, a repression immense and secure. It's almost beyond our power to see past it.

Lucy's high spirits, like Ozzie and Harriet's neutrality, is a machine that works regardless of circumstance. In the cultural sphere her counterpart would be the New York School—especially Kenneth Koch and Frank O'Hara. If their enthusiasm seems factitious, or even—as it seems to me—the flip side of a large-scale depression, at least it signaled a desire to feel something.

Porn

Pornography enjoys a clear relationship between the types of its community (defined only in part by sexuality) and a manufactured product—a movie, book, or magazine. The rostrum of sexual characters—the masochist, the sadist, the stud, the leather man, and the character defined by a particular fetish—can readily be found outside a theater or novel. All in all, there's no going back to the types from village life, or ethnic family life, but even if you live in a society in which communities are eroding, you can still be a member of the S/M community.

Are there two pornographies, straight and gay? But they overlap. Take the character who is fantastically desirable and also exploitable. (From pop culture—Marilyn Monroe and Joe Dallesandro.) In *Behind the Green Door* Marilyn Chambers is taken by force. The movie is a giant fantasy rape. The plot goes from struggle against the rape to "going over" to pleasure. Finally, she enthusiastically gives up her will, even to the selection of partners, positions. In straight porn, the exploitable heroine eroticizes her situation.

Gay porn's exploitable heroes are also dumb, but many plots center on the hero's education, and in the end power relations are more flexible, ambiguous. In Billy Farout's *Fresh From the Farm*,

Rags McClusky is defined in terms of his cock—metonymy. He starts out from an isolated dirt farm and, under various male auspices, he ascends to the highest social stratum—private jets, New York penthouses—his ticket being looks, an open manner, and his cock, which is referred to by name as "Dong." Like porno star John Holmes—the man with twelve inches—Rags's cock characterizes him. In the first chapter, "the unconscious lump of his fat prick almost doubled back on itself like a puppy sleeping under the denim."[3] In the final chapter, after learning what he learns, Rags gives up wealth and fame, falls in love with a naïve young man, and nurtures him. That is, Rags's cock nurtures him like a mother: "Joey was being driven to the limits of passion, milking the big stud's cock . . . milking it up and down and trying to drag out the cream." Then Joey, "felt his own cock banging off like church bells"—a marriage made in heaven.[4]

Pornography shows character systems in a pure form. The characters have little or no psychology, they act as a function of the plot; they carry a plot with them, the plot and the characters are interchangeable. The cat-burglar, the housewife, the traveling salesman, the milkman, the nun, the repairman—pornography builds these characters in order to tear them down. Often the types are borrowed from an earlier period, or from the edges of society (like Rags with his farm background), or from prisons, the army, the church, the macho occupations, because types have slipped away (with community) to the fringe.

So character systems must be established all the more clearly for pornography to be effective. By effective, I mean that it must destroy these systems and types, and social typology in general; it must break up social reality. Pornography is successful to the degree that the characters shed their social relations and become only their animal bodies. Can this be called anarchistic?

Writers sometimes borrow porn character systems. The classic example is the Marquis de Sade; his vile seducers and transgressed heroines bring issues of power and domination to a point. Pauline Réage's *Story of O* uses this same system as a vehicle for her existential bonbon. In Kathy Acker's writing, Sade's eighteenth-century libertinism translates to an anything-goes anarchism:

"All I ever do is play with myself. I don't care about politics."

"When the cop arrested Clement, Clement hit him over the head with the end of a bottle. What d'you think of that? At his trail Clement said: 'The policeman arrested me in the name of the law; I hit him in the name of liberty.'"

"Berthe, do you think it's better to fuck a man for money, or just to fuck for free?"

"Then Clement said: 'When society refuses you the right to existence, you must take it.'"

"I'll fuck any way I can get it. I love to fuck so much."[5]

The brilliance of this writing lies in its juggling of systems— porn, detective, high art, sexual, and political. This kind of pastiche generates great energy, but these genres have quotation marks around them embracing and disclaiming at the same time.

Roseanne Roseannadanna

As an exercise in description I asked my second-grade class in Berkeley to describe their teachers. One teacher had a withered leg. The children tensely described her from head to toe without mentioning the obvious, until finally it was blurted out—though phrased tactfully—by the "bad" boy.

Gilda Radner created a character for *Saturday Night Live* called Roseanne Roseannadanna, and Roseanne's humor is based on the fear and silence that surround good taste. Challenges to good taste reveal class antagonisms because the ruling class owns good taste. It goes with the territory. Laws of deportment are violated as we descend economic rungs, until we come to the bottom of the bottom, to Roseanne Roseannadanna, who can't help calling things by their right names. She has no "class."

Roseanne is a newscaster. On one show her assigned topic is the escalation of the prime-lending rate. She immediately alters the class perspective by complaining about soaring rents, which leads into a brief discussion of rent prices at East Hampton, and from there to her personal attack on the ruling class. In good proletarian fashion, Roseanne moves from abstract to concrete. She's at an East Hampton social gathering where the rich and famous are "sweating like pigs." Just a minute ago she said that poor people can't pay their rent, now she has the fashionable rich eating poorly. Adelle Davis food, roughage and crudities; "pig food," she calls it, "that rots and stinks up your insides," that moves through your "pipes" like "Liquid Plumber." She focuses on Yves St. Laurent going in and out of the toilet: when he comes out with a wet spot on his pants she yells, "Hey Frenchy, did it rain on your zipper?"

Jane Curtin breaks in. Jane is the anchorperson, upper class, preppy, a perfect foil for Roseanne. While Roseanne talks, Jane's polite smile grows increasingly frozen, her expression shot with dismay, until she realizes there is no way to recover the situation by ignoring it; that is, by not naming it. She says, "You're making us all sick. You were supposed to talk about a man who wants to buy a house!"

Roseanne deflects this with one of her homilies: "Well it just goes to show you, if it's not one thing it's something else, if it's not that, it's another . . ." She concludes with a prayer that her grandmother, Nanna Roseannadanna, taught her:

> Now I lay me down to sleep
> After a lot of roughage I did eat
> I hope I die before I wake
> Cause another washing the sheets can't take.

Roseanne characteristically zeros in on that cornucopia of bad taste, the crotch. She demystifies people who have become abstract images. On another show, she has Gloria Vanderbilt go through a lot of acrobatics in her tight jeans because of a genital itch.

The anger in this humor stems from Roseanne's working-class, ethnic background. I asked people about Roseanne's accent; to my delight no one could place it. Latin American? Italian? It's just ethnic. True to ethnic form, she was raised by an extended family, with a grandmother, Nanna Roseannadanna, a black aunt, Savannah Roseannadanna, and a religious aunt, Hosanna Roseannadanna. She uses homilies and sayings, she makes her point with stories rather than documentation. The Roseanne character draws on the energy of a working-class/ethnic community—she expresses that community's anger and contempt for the ruling class by challenging codes of behavior. Even in repeating these stories of Roseanne, the intensity of that anger can be felt. These jokes are insulting—they are meant to insult. But what, in all this, leads to structural change?

These are distorted images of distorted lives. They are based on types in the world, but their relation to a community is tenuous at best, because an audience of isolated individuals consumes them. In fact, they are models of isolation. Yet to the degree that they look backward, they also have the possibility of looking forward.

But how? How can we use these images, and others like them, in a dynamic relation to the future? As it is, the community is repressive, the images are negative. Lacking a program, Roseanne Roseannadanna and Lucy are pressure valves to release tensions. But we can turn this proposition around if we see them in this light: they defend a community.

Types, caricatures, narrations, satires, which depict social rather than psychological relations—what if these become literary strategies of a progressive community? For example, the lesbian-feminist community. Here are a few paragraphs from Judy Grahn's "The Psychoanalysis of Edward the Dyke." In this extract, Edward confronts scientific objectivity:

> "Dr. Knox," Edward began, "my problem this week is chiefly concerning restrooms."
>
> "Ahhh," the good doctor sighed. Gravely he drew a quick sketch of a restroom in his notebook.
>
> "Naturally I can't go into men's restrooms without feeling like an interloper, but on the other hand every time I try to use the ladies room I get into trouble."
>
> "Umm," said Dr. Knox, drawing a quick sketch of a door marked 'Ladies'.
>
> "Four days ago I went into the powder room of a department store and three middle-aged housewives came into it and

thought I was a man. As soon as I explained to them that I was really only a harmless dyke, the trouble began . . ."

"You compulsively attacked them."

"Oh heavens no, indeed not. One of them turned on the water faucet and tried to drown me with wet paper towels, but the other two began screaming something about how well did I know Gertrude Stein and what sort of underwear did I have on, and they took my new cuff links and socks for souvenirs. They had my head in the trashcan and were cutting off my shirttails when luckily a policeman heard my calls for help and rushed in. He was able to divert their attention by shooting at me, thus giving me a chance to escape through the window."

Carefully, Dr. Knox noted in his notebook: 'Apparent suicide attempt after accosting girls in restroom.'[6]

So here is the killer cop, the repressive matron, the callous doctor—and a newcomer, the healthy lesbian. The reader must say the word "dyke," perhaps for the first time. The laughter is based on the solidarity of a community. The community confronts a danger—the world according to textbook psycho-logy—which taken individually causes pain and hurt. Our laughter is an acceptance of Grahn's accuracy. More than that, our laughter implicates us; it signals an agreement, a complicity with Grahn's point of view. So in the end we have agreed to challenge that danger, to fight against it in our lives. For all its stylization, I could call this writing realism, in that realism demonstrates a writer's "access to the forces of change in a given moment of history."[7]

Political songs are examples of type and satire that defend working-class communities. In 1940 Woody Guthrie wrote "The Union Maid," drawn from events at a meeting he attended, and picket lines are still singing it. In fact Local 2 sang it in the Hotel Strike in San Francisco in 1981:

This union maid was wise
To the tricks of the company spies;
She couldn't be fooled by a company stool,
She'd always organize the guys.

I'd also like to mention a thirties song called "Picket Line Priscilla":

> She could make the vigilantes
> Run like ants were in their panties.

And:

> Said the judge with smile seraphic
> Thirty days for blocking traffic.

These types embody the courage, humor, and optimism of the group. Like "Edward the Dyke," they stem from a community and at the same time help to create that community.

At movement readings I was interested to see members of the audience come up afterward and say where the writer had got it right (*yes, that's my life*) and where the writer had got it wrong. Can we produce writing that enjoys as much integration as a Kijoku storm chant? Well, no. Does that leave our writing as formal (its meaning as nostalgic) as the Kijoku chant behind glass in *Technicians of the Sacred*? Modernist aesthetics at once welcomes and resists commodification, but writing can be integrated only to the degree that it identifies with a community, a shared ideology, a place and time.

I read a story at a gay reading about being queer-baited. The audience responded throughout with shouts of encouragement and acknowledgement. Afterward people told me I got it right. I read the same story to an appreciative university audience, and afterward people said they liked my transitions. I hope they *were* innovative transitions, and, who knows, this audience might become a community of writers. But the first audience showed a spirit of collectivity in the authorship, where both audience and writers are responsible to their community. This responsibility is not moral blackmail. It releases the writer from the burden of psychology and gives the writer access to history. The writer is a member of a community and will rise or fall with it. Here begins a truly collective writing.

How can we use caricature and type without merely substituting one character system for another—that is, how can we bind these systems to lived experience, to praxis? Bruce Boone and I have thought about one tactic, the use of "text-metatext," where the text is the narrative (with its time span, characters, and action), and the metatext is a running analysis, its point of view based on the future, or a real community. It embodies the critical spirit of the audience that measures the effectiveness of literature—and other manifestations of its community—according to its own experience and ideas. The metatext can be in the form if an essay, or meditation; it can have its own characters and stories. A simple narration can put the reader on the far side of the proscenium arch. The metatext cuts naturalistic illusion. It includes the reader, it asks questions, asks for critical response, makes claims on the reader, elicits commitments. In any case, text-metatext takes its form from the dialectical cleft between real life and life as it wants to be.

Notes:

1. Georg Lukács, *The Theory of the Novel: A Historico-philosophical Essay on the Forms of Great Epic Literature*, trans. Anna Bostock (Cambridge: MIT Press, 1971), 66.

2. John Cage, quoted in *Difference/Indifference: Musings on Postmodernism, Marcel Duchamp and John Cage* by Moira Roth (Amsterdam: G+B Arts International, 1998), 66.

3. Billy Farout, *Fresh from the Farm* (San Francisco: Parisian Press, 1972), 10.

4. Ibid., 143, 145.

5. Kathy Acker, *Essential Acker: The Selected Writings of Kathy Acker*, eds. Amy Scholder and Dennis Cooper (New York: Grove Press, 2002), 65.

6. Judy Grahn, "The Psychoanalysis of Edward the Dyke," in *The Judy Grahn Reader*, ed. Lisa Maria Hogeland (San Francisco: Aunt Lute Books, 2009), 16.

7. Fredric Jameson, *Marxism and Form: Twentieth-Century Dialectical Theories of Literature* (Princeton: Princeton University Press, 1974), 204. Jameson develops this insight from the works of Georg Lukács.

"Caricature" was published in *Soup: New Critical Perspectives*, no. 3, ed. Steve Abbott (1985). It was first presented at 80 Langton St., San Francisco, 1983.

MY 2 CENTS

> Circumstantially, I am posturing as a woman of inchoate origin
> [problematically, I can hear you saying].
>
> —Gail Scott, *The Obituary*

Every aesthetics is an aesthetics of class.

In thinking about a poetics of class that knows itself, it's instructive to look at the history of feminist poetics. In the first place (if you could call the sixties and early seventies the first place), an innovative feminist poetics seemed to be disallowed. If you were going to make a feminist poem recognizable to feminists or to the avant-garde, feminism was content. Formally innovative poems founded on radical politics took their cues from Marxist and socialist critiques which did not include sexuality, gender, or, somehow, class.

At the same time, as Joan Retallack points out in her essay ":RE:THINKING:LITERARY:FEMINISM," "Textual traditions that have enacted and explored modes culturally labeled Feminine have oddly—or, as we shall note, not so oddly—been practiced until recently more by men than by women . . . Perhaps one of the most remarkable things about our present time is that women are finally socially and politically powerful enough to undertake the risks of this 'feminine' challenge in their own texts."[1]

I think Retallack answers Kathy Lou Schultz's question, "What's a working class poetic, and where would I find one?"[2] Women did not will a brand-new poetics into being, but claimed existing forms, recognized the feminist possibilities in them, and then elaborated them. I'm describing a kind of territory war where the victor wins the ability to recognize herself as well as achieving recognition from the larger writing scene (and with it a portion of psychic life on which to stage her writing).

When feminist publications like *HOW(ever)* started gathering innovative poetry already being written by women, I heard complaints that the women were not doing anything new. But they certainly were, because they brought feminism over the great divide from content to form. Once a critical mass of writing (and assuming) had been achieved, people no longer said that women were not making something new, and "suddenly" disjunct form could be feminist poetics. "Suddenly" there was a tradition of feminist experimentation that included Gertrude Stein, Lorine Niedecker, and many others. "Suddenly" there were writing models from French feminism, like Monique Wittig and Helene Cixous.

I don't think I could look at a page of words and say, "Oh, here's a working-class form." A working-class aesthetics must claim part of what is already there, apply it to the disjunctions and silences of class, and build a writing that brings new meanings and new applications to innovative form. Can we look at avant-garde form in the twentieth century and recognize class as one of its sources? One day (perhaps today!) the answer will be, of course!

It is an interesting moment to be thinking about class. Class inequities are more brutal than ever and yet until ten minutes ago (I am thinking of the Occupy movement) all discussion seemed to be silenced by a "mainstream" which was ready to give away zillions of dollars to the super rich rather than depress itself by addressing homelessness and health care. Was that moment of silence also a moment of power? I doubt it. If there was an aesthetics of class, it may have been founded on the abjection and dissonance that inform genre-bending writing by, say, Lawrence Braithwaite, Camille Roy, Dodie Bellamy, Gail Scott, and Eileen Myles. Can Occupy—this surge of negativity—change the discourse? Following the logic of this essay, Occupy would redefine the meaning of unity: unity is dissonant.

It seems to me that Scott's superb novel *The Obituary* is a model for what can be accomplished. It tells a story from all fronts at once and locates itself between English and French. It's a no-holds-barred book, in that it conveys a huge and even brutal sadness, a daring sadness, along with other valences. Scott has put so much pressure on language that she has made her own kind of poetry—it's an amazing book, really. The city itself—and the disjunctions of place, language, and race—are lived in the most detailed ways, without prudery, and they create schisms in identity that are so present they are hard to endure. That is, the alienations that occur inside the self (class, race) are realized on a formal level, and so here is an example of a splendid leap from content to form.

Notes:

Epigraph: Gail Scott, *The Obituary* (Toronto: Coach House Books, 2010), 12.

1. Joan Retallack, ":RE:THINKING:LITERARY:FEMINISM: (three essays onto shaky grounds)," in *The Poethical Wager* (Berkeley: University of California Press, 2003), 112–113.

2. See Kathy Lou Schultz, "Talking Trash, Talking Class: What's a Working Class Poetic, and Where Would I Find One?," *How2* 1, no. 2 (September 1999). https://www.asu.edu/pipercwcenter/how2journal/archive/online_archive/v1_2_19 99/current/alerts/schultz.html.

"My 2 Cents" was published in the Forum section of *How2*, Vol. 1, no.2, on "Class & Innovative Writing," eds. Kathy Lou Schultz and Robin Tremblay-McGaw (September 1999). It was reprinted in *Lipstick Eleven*, no. 2, eds. Robin Temblay-McGaw and Jim Brashier (2001); and revised and reprinted in *Open Letter* 14, no. 9, guest ed. Lianne Moyes (Summer 2012).

HIS HEART IS A LUTE HELD UP

POE AND BATAILLE

> During the whole of a dull, dark, and soundless day in the
> autumn of the year, when the clouds hung oppressively low in
> the heavens, I had been passing alone, on horseback, through
> a singularly dreary tract of country; and at length found
> myself, as the shades of the evening drew on, within view of
> the melancholy House of Usher.[1]

The first sentence of Edgar Allan Poe's story ends *basso profundo*
"House of Usher." The House is a symbol, so complexity, mystery,
and resonance devolve on it; meaning moves toward it like metal
shavings to a magnet. In a recent schlock made-for-TV *House of
Usher*, the narrator (and his wife!) urge unwilling peasants to drive
them at dusk through the wasteland to the House. This theft from
the vampire myth is apropos—the undead (Roderick, Madeline;
Dracula) are cultivated, barren, old blood . . . really old. Perhaps
Roderick and Madeline are Jews. They are from "an ancient
race."[2] Usher can be a Jewish name—the Tribe of Asher. And
there's Roderick's arabesque (Eastern) expression and aquiline
nose, "of a delicate Hebrew model."[3]

In both "House of Usher" and Georges Bataille's *Story of
the Eye*, there is an overriding sexualization of death and a
corresponding reordering of the senses.

To the degree that they use genre, Poe and Bataille have an
understanding with us—we consent to receive pleasure, nonproductive, nonimproving. Then it's Poe's show, he trundles out the
Gothic furniture with the proviso that his lute be *our* sensibility.
Like gossip, this pleasure is based on a manipulation/transgression

of shared codes and a continuum of experience. That's why Truth in fantasy usually defaults to common dualities—Good and Evil, God and Devil, etc.—just as porn likes "types," the cat burglar, the sailor.

Like much nineteenth-century American prose (Hawthorne, some Melville) Poe's is warmed over, awkward and arty. It's distant from the center of the power; you have to work at detail if you are far from the informing idea. "It was the misfortune of Mr. Pinkney to have been born too far south. . . . We pardon his hyperboles for the evident earnestness with which they are uttered" ("The Poetic Principle").[4] Poe's overproduced rhetoric lets us know we're in for a full-blown experience—it's all worked out: the elegiac bell of "dull, dark and soundless," the memorial "autumn of the year" and "shades of evening."

> I know not how it was—but, with the first glimpse of the building, a sense of insufferable gloom pervaded my spirit.[5]

The eye of the story enters the impressionable realm—the spirit is invaded with a glance, that is, through the eye.

> I say insufferable; for the feeling was unrelieved by any of that half-pleasurable, because poetic, sentiment with which the mind usually receives even the sternest natural images of the desolate or terrible.[6]

We rely on the narrator to organize time and space for us, and to render the intangibles—"I say insufferable." What traits create high perception? Poe had a formula: in the "Purloined Letter," a detective story, visual acuteness is based on an impulse toward order—"ratiocination"—combined with an equally high ability to sustain ambiguity. Our narrator in "House of Usher" is cut from the same cloth but we understand past him.

For example, the narrator says the House is not poetic, not pleasurable. This is a strategy, because we *are* poetic, receptive to pleasure. This tease helps to pin down the reality of subsequent marvels, and it prepares us for one of horror's delicious moments: the opaque doubter, our most atheistic self, joins us and is converted. The conversion and the pleasure are religious: terror, a secular awe.

Horror asks for our faith in order to attain a more inclusive humanity—the uncanny. Pornography is also religious—"I am a beast!" It says that our portrait must include this assertion. Because they diffuse boundaries, this awe and sexuality are guilty pleasures; formerly they may have been part of a ceremony, but now they are sold to us.

> I looked upon the scene before me—upon the mere house, and the simple landscape features of the domain—upon the bleak walls—upon the vacant eye-like windows—upon a few rank sedges—and upon a few white trunks of decayed trees—with an utter depression of soul which I can compare to no earthly sensation more properly than to the after-dream of the reveller upon opium—the bitter lapse into every-day life—the hideous dropping of the veil.[7]

Poe writes thirty or forty years after the first Gothic rush; his story is an auteur version, less vulgar, less energetic, but more penetrating. He adds symbolism, analysis, and psychology. Psychology, like our narrator, will try to undermine fantasy by positing Science as the larger myth. Poe is one stop on the train from Gothic fairy tale to case history of the criminally insane. Symbolism (meaning becomes problematical) and analysis (the resistance of the materials) will become pastiche in Bataille—he will complete the modernist quote marks around genre.

The narrator invokes that criminal of the senses, the addict. (Roderick's "morbid acuteness of the senses"—enclaves of body knowledge.)[8]

> There was an iciness, a sinking, a sickening of the heart—an unredeemed dreariness of thought which no goading of the imagination could torture into aught of the sublime.[9]

For the third time the narrator asks us not to consider the sublime, and to see the House as pro-death (vacant eyes, etc.).

Roderick and Madeline are barren; their embrace concludes in death. The "atmosphere" manifests itself in Roderick's senses—hearing, taste, touch become more important. Wordsworth says Analysis goes with Death. In this Backwards Land the narrator is life, analysis, sight; and the House is death and sensation. Our narrator is good at seeing. Seeing interested Poe—it's the basis of the detective story and it corresponds to analysis. We unite death and sensation despite and because of our narrator's objections.

Reordering the senses challenges accepted boundaries as do Evil and Death, those other challengers. Later, there's Rimbaud's *dérèglement de tous les sens* and a whole Axel's Castle full of sensual experimentation in out-of-the-way locales. The sublime moment in our time, the late sixties, chose play over work and elevated sensation.

> What was it—I paused to think—what was it that so unnerved me in the contemplation of the House of Usher?[10]

I paused to think: This gives Poe's horror its auteur status. Poe inters character after character, but what activity does justice to the mental atmosphere of suffocation and horror? There is a gap between meaning and action; the symbolic takes up the slack.

> It was a mystery all insoluble; nor could I grapple with the shadowy fancies that crowded upon me as I pondered.[11]

From now on the realistic and the supernatural will keep bracketing each other, making the story impossible to "understand" though sponsoring an "elasticity of mind," which is useful at the conclusion of "The Mad Trist" when Roderick and Madeline embrace in a blaze of overloaded fuses. The House divides and recombines (like the sister and brother?) in the tarn: the narrator is expelled and death, sex, Madeline, Roderick, and the House *become one* in that collapse.

> I was forced to fall back on the unsatisfactory conclusion that while, beyond doubt, there *are* combinations of very simple actual

objects which have the power of thus affecting us, still the analysis of this power lies among considerations beyond our depth.[12]

The problem of fantasy: what can a true map of the world look like
if this landscape is an example? Still, his atomic theory (combinations) doesn't tell the whole story because he can't see why it works.

> It was possible, I reflected, that a mere different arrangement
> of the particulars of the scene, of the details of the picture,
> would be sufficient to modify, or perhaps to annihilate, its
> capacity for sorrowful impression; and, acting upon this idea,
> I reined my horse to the precipitous brink of a bleak and lurid
> tarn that lay in unruffled lustre by the dwelling, and gazed
> down—but with a shudder even more thrilling than before—
> upon the remodeled and inverted images of the grey sedge, and
> the ghastly tree-stems, and the vacant and eye-like windows.[13]

It's odd that someone riding all day—fatigued—at the urgent
request of his friend—hurried—would conduct an experiment
with sensibility and perspective—the Picturesque. He looks at the
image of the House mirrored in the lake—no, still ghastly. Its
image isolates the terror. The House will end up in the lake, one
with its image. The business of the two views carries an analytical
meaning but the horror subverts the analytical. The narrator uses
his eyes, the House is blind; he tries a different view, still blind. He
fails to see *imaginatively*, so the House will be beyond his scope.

> I grew up very much alone, and as far back as I recall I was
> frightened of anything sexual.[14]

The first paragraph of Georges Bataille's *Story of the Eye* breaks into
three distinct beginnings. The first sentence presents an "I"
abstracted from its surroundings, a sense of psychological data. We
recognize a writer, a personality. We don't realize at once that he is
merely an urge toward transgressive sexuality, toward Evil.

First person presupposes the encompassing context. Evil creates
human potential in Bataille; he sets equals signs between sex, death,

Evil, and (replacing Poe's nature) the unconscious. Since this counters the models of our "crass machine age," the Evil becomes avant-gardist, an enclave *against*. But isn't personhood on the way out?—on its way to becoming a text, merely one more element in a story? Bataille dismantles the individual with disjunction and banality, with a cold treatment of genre and a free-for-all of literary codes. Romantics saw nature as separate, as subject matter; the moderns see the self in the same way (name it and it's lost, owned).

"I have always been afraid." (Actually *angoissé*: anguish or anxiety, more ambivalent.) We who write about sex internalized society's dictums—we never recovered from the shock of sex itself; we communicate our amazement. The writing is aggressive, something of a revenge. Everything is visual. Information from the other senses tends to normalize and diffuse the surprise of sex.

This story, like much of porn—like most of Sade, in fact—is about education; it's a Bildungsroman. The first sentence sets up the anxious hero who will learn. The book concludes with his participation in the defilement of a priest. After Sade, who could take the defilement of a priest with complete seriousness? Bataille's heroes *are* reduced: instead of Juliette's Sherman's March through Europe, we have the narrator's and Simone's tireless legs pumping always pumping on their bicycles, and later their modest trip to Spain. When the priest succumbs, or better, converts—Yes! Yes! I *want* and *need* and *crave*!—we feel he's come over to our side.

> I was nearly sixteen when I met Simone, a girl my own age, at the beach in X. Our families being distantly related, we quickly grew intimate.[15]

This second beginning—the furniture of nineteenth-century narration. The inspired X invokes the nineteenth-century's "effect of the real." (Poe also used initials to give his stories an air of docudrama.) Bataille imports this stilted prose to advance the plot, as it puts quotation marks around plot itself. We relish its patina as one more refinement. It's Poe's decor. That is, it's a museum. The strangeness of subject matter now extends to narrative style. The quotation marks around storytelling, the multiple beginnings, give us notice: to the degree this story is about being a story, it's not a story. The first paragraph is not an example of "reframing," which develops an idea while placing it between the audience and writer; the paragraph simply heads out three times, parallel, evoking three traditions—hence its startling energy.

The narrative itself disappoints in the same way that pornography and Poe's horror do, because it's not equal to the meaning:

> But on a sensual level, she so bluntly craved any upheaval that the faintest call from the senses gave her a look directly suggestive of all things linked to deep sexuality, such as blood, suffocation, sudden terror, crime; things indefinitely destroying human bliss and honesty.[16]

It's the task of horror and porn to constantly replace image with image, each more intense than its predecessor, but what image could equal the intensity of this sentence?

In 1839 the trappings of Evil were a stage company devoted to its diva, Sensibility. For Bataille, sensibility is just another actor in the troupe, and subjectivity has retreated to tone. One imagines a tonal coherence, the high-chanted monotone of Corneille.

> Three days after our first meeting, Simone and I were alone in her villa. She was wearing a black pinafore with a starched white collar. I began realizing that she shared my anxiety at seeing her, and I felt even more anxious that day because I hoped she would be stark naked under the pinafore.[17]

The third beginning is porn: Simone's black pinafore and starched white collar suggest a nun's habit, but more likely it's a schoolgirl's uniform. In any case it invokes the rather formal tradition of nasty pictures: "I hoped she would be *stark* naked." Porn wants structures and roles in order to overwhelm them. The effect will be complete when the characters are animals, abandoning life's starched collars.

If Poe's story is about Death and Bataille's is about Sex, this particular sex and death are twins who live in a single breath. The sex in Bataille is about obsession and power, disconnected from the body. In *Story of the Eye*, the ultimate image is an eye (distance, analysis) inserted in a cunt—sexual seeing, reordering the senses. It's at the far pole of the erotics of self, the manipulation of image, distanced and objectifying. Death in Poe is the result of heightened sensation—death presents a body that is frantically activated. Language (narration, analysis) fails when it approaches what directly pertains to us, the working of our senses. It's none of its business. The old ballad supplies the voice that Roderick lacks.

Notes:

1. Edgar Allan Poe, *The Fall of the House of Usher and Other Tales* (New York: Signet Classics, 2006), 109.

2. Ibid., 115.

3. Ibid., 113.

4. Edgar Allan Poe, "The Poetic Principle," in *Essays and Reviews*, ed. G. R. Thompson (New York: Library of America, 1984), 83–84.

5. Poe, *House of Usher*, 109.

6. Ibid.

7. Ibid.

8. Ibid., 114.

9. Ibid., 109.

10. Ibid., 109–110.

11. Ibid., 110.

12. Ibid.

13. Ibid.

14. Georges Bataille, *Story of the Eye*, trans. Joachim Neugroschel (New York: Urizen, 1977), 3.

15. Ibid.

16. Ibid., 6.

17. Ibid., 4.

"His Heart is a Lute Held Up: Poe and Bataille" was published in "Close Reading," *Poetics Journal*, no. 2, eds. Lyn Hejinian and Barrett Watten (1982).

WRITING SEX BODY

I was moved by Taylor Brady's description of a body that is "buffeted, fragmented by the very forces it stands in for . . ."[1]

Sexuality: I'm not only homosexual—but I'm always homosexual. In some circumstances, I am Homosexuality. When I enter a room, it's a homosexual room; when I leave, it renounces homosexuality. My homosexual breath spins the atoms Socrates breathed. I put my sexuality on the world as Española puts gender on words. Glück lives in a Glück world, to paraphrase Wittgenstein. Compelling sexuality, alarmingly threadbare. It furiously weaves a world on top that frays off in mismatched threads at the bottom.

Gender: What a strange page the body is, covered at once by so many stories. The awareness of this arbitrary and total saturation is founded on my experience as a gay child, which made me a kind of prepubescent Tiresias—though in my case it wasn't the knowledge of pleasure I gained, but the toxic awareness of gender as artifact, and all I could predict was my shame. I remember that time very well, buffeted and fragmented by the barren effects of gender. I tried to stiffen. Gender seemed fantastically arbitrary since I seemed to be encased in the wrong one. Maybe in one's twenties the human shape seems inevitable, but ask a queer boy who is six, or any fifty-year-old. That the body is matter only makes the body more fantastical—at this point, who would take matter seriously?

About twenty-five years later I was working on a story called "Night Flight." It was about an infatuation that lacked a narrative—"a feeling with no outlet, followed by a question mark."[2] Pursuing the logic of the story—to unite feeling with event—I borrowed a plot that seemed to be the same size as my emotion. I chose one of Sade's *Crimes of Love*—wonderful valentines that are nothing but plot. In it, the unfortunate heroine is seduced by her brother, bears a child, then murders her grown-up son while defending her honor against him, then marries her father, then testifies against her mother, which sends that lady to the scaffold. She doesn't realize till the last page that they all are her relatives and related to each other. I turned her into a man named Felix, the object of my obsession, and I was writing along till I got to my hero's pregnancy and motherhood. For a few days I was stumped. Perhaps I was curtailed by the assumptions that belonged to the audience in my imagination?

In an elated trans moment I realized that I would simply make Felix pregnant and then a mother. A mother with a masculine pronoun. Even now I wonder what gap was crossed.

I'd had dreams in which I become pregnant—not a problem. So why did the ability of men to bear children temporarily vanish? And my feeling of pleasure when I passed through that resistance resembled the gratified desire in dreams, when it's understood that I'm pregnant and I am roundly congratulated. Why was gender so porous in one region of my imagination, yet so opaque in the realm of writing?—a realm entirely public and entirely private. I wish for freedom in writing and in the dimension of flesh and blood. I'm tired of the two old sexes. In *Margery* I wrote, "Gender is the extent we go to in order to be loved."[3] I meant gender is a weird extremity. I don't want to be a real woman, though perhaps I did when I was Tiresias. Certainly I don't want to date a real man, I like them a little femmy.

I wish we were more like orchids which, in order to please their pollinators, take the form "of little birds, lizards, insects, man, woman, of sinister fighters in a death embrace, of lazy tortoises basking upside-down in the sun, of agile and ever chattering monkeys screened by fronds," as Kenward Elmslie says in *The Orchid Stories*.[4]

One of my heroes is Pierre Molinier. He was a wonderfully awful painter and a fellow traveler of the surrealists. His thrilling photomontages—which he made late in life, from the 1950s through the early '70s—mix autobiography and fantasy in ways that New Narrative aspires to. His palette was meager: his body, a room, a patterned screen, and a few fetish objects—a plaster hand, a whip, a mannequin leg, a female mannequin head, a shoe with a dildo attached to the heel, like the wing on Mercury's sandal. With these materials he staged an ongoing performance of imploding categories. "The contradiction between shame and performance is played out in these secret spectacles memorialized in Molinier's photos," writes Earl Jackson, Jr.[5]

The shame of these transformations makes a performance of such art. Don't tell me I'm promiscuous, even though the Bob of *Jack the Modernist* is fucked in public. Perhaps I'm "dishing up" the shame I felt in the first place, as a first place. Why write about body and sex unless they are problems? Dodie Bellamy writes, "no way can I stand in front of an audience reading this stuff and maintain the abstraction the 'author' . . . To regain some of that privacy I have desexualized myself in public, have stiffened, as if to say, 'This is not a body.'"[6] I love that *stiffened*—to ward off judgment, as though turning into a corpse, or a man. I know that shame: "As I age I clench over my spasms rather than arching backwards from them," I wrote in *Margery Kempe*.[7] At a reading, I know that line is coming. A story told this way reveals the life of nakedness. After I put my orgasm in words, I can't look people in the eye. Nakedness becomes a goal, as though absolute nakedness can be *achieved* (with the understanding that one image simply replaces another, endlessly).

Not endlessly: Kathy Acker's sex-drenched books did a curious thing without the presence of Kathy's body to support them. In

"The Madness of Day," Maurice Blanchot says, "I must admit I have read many books. When I disappear, all those volumes will change imperceptibly."[8] I thought Blanchot had lapsed into a sentimentality that marred his terrific story. But when Kathy died, I felt her words *rustle* into another position. They "stiffened." Her words moved outward as they adjusted to her death, there was more white space between them. Kathy's life no longer gave them scale, or bound them with a current of tension and changeability.

A hip magazine called *Cups* interviewed me in 1995, and the sympathetic editor asked, "You are against safe sex, right?" I was mildly dumbfounded till I realized he was looking for the transgressive formula, as though I was going to whip out my *Junior Woodchuck Guide to Transgression*. Everywhere pieties proliferate. What is *appropriate* transgressive writing? The present becomes a theme along with the resistance of the present to being described. The impulse to shock becomes an interesting social event when it bridges the disjunction between what experience looks like and what the culture thinks it is *possible* to say. One has to add that some part of the culture will be asking for that kind of transgression.

Where does the "falsehood" of fiction become a dream that leads to a psychological truth, as though a piece of writing fares past a certain point of extremity to be analyzed as a case history? Writing about sex invites such unwanted extraliterary assumptions to be made. The writer's pride or shame (of being a body feeling pleasure, a compendium of unruly urges) leads the reader beyond the page. Was the *Cups* editor wrong to assume that I promote barebacking? I recognize in myself a certain urgency, mated with a certain reluctance, to answer these questions.

My audience makes assumptions. I am not surprised. That confusion of fact and fiction, of actual bodies and words, gives power to sex writing; a writing that can't be contained by explanation. Put another way, it demands to exist in the same world as the reader's body. Where is the autonomy of the text? The reader is led in directions as divergent as spiritual abjection, solitary pleasure, and communal joy. Sex writing brings a dissonance or even helplessness into the activity of interpretation.

I felt the same way about Stanley Kubrick's *Eyes Wide Shut*. I revere Kubrick, but I don't know how to understand this film. Tom Cruise listens to Nicole Kidman's confession of desire for another man. She's naked, and the rich lust she describes is like the opposite of her sliver of a body. Fueled by his wife's story, Tom goes on a night journey that takes him to an orgy. The sexuality in this movie is as smutty as a sixties sexploitation film, where the women are naked—breasts breasts breasts—and the men rarely take off their Nehru's. The orgy illustrates the challenge of presenting sexual enormity visually. Sex is a comedy, the mechanical optimism of many pistons. (To describe sex is one thing. To *arouse*, writing mimes the rhythm of sex, the tension and release, conforming to a dramatic structure in a kind of decency.) The most exciting moment of the orgy is when the master of ceremonies orders Cruise to get undressed. Even through his mask you can see him thinking, "Is this in my contract?"

He doesn't get undressed. The banal sexuality of the movie may belong to Cruise's character, Dr. Harford, rather than to Kubrick, and the movie itself may portray the disgust of marriage, the terror and contempt Harford feels after living for years in close proximity to his mate's libido, at once a compelling force and a threadbare fantasy.

That is a goal: to unframe writing about sex and the body, to derail the mechanisms that make a unified position. I'd like to recommend Juan Goytisolo's *Makbara* for its stew of point of view, class, desire, and filth.

Sometimes late at night I watch the Playboy Channel while I floss. I would never pay for such dumb entertainment, but I discovered that the actors have been degraded into splashy bands of color for the nonsubscriber that pump pump pump, folding into each other like taffy on the verge of representation, resolving in an instant of clear image—more reward than tease—before resuming existence as a kaleidoscopic lava lamp on speed endlessly squishing into itself. Completely legible is the background music—thump thump thump, porn porn porn—as well as the cries and grunts of the dear actors. What a faithful representation! As though through eyes wide shut, then opened for an instant: oh that's an ass, a leg, a tongue. Here's overflow, here's a paradise of sensation, here's the modernist present, here's no-mind, here's living in eternity 24/7—find it on the Playboy Channel!

Notes:

1. Taylor Brady, "Part-Writing, a Response in Part to Dodie Bellamy's 'Sex/Body/Writing,'" to the Poetics List, September 30, 2000. https://listserv.buffalo.edu/cgi-bin/wa?A2=POETICS;1bc56d94.0009.

2. Robert Glück, *Elements of a Coffee Service* (San Francisco: Four Seasons Foundation, 1982), 58.

3. Robert Glück, *Margery Kempe* (New York: High Risk Books, 1994), 57.

4. Kenward Elmslie, *The Orchid Stories* (New York: Doubleday, 1973), 7.

5. Earl Jackson, Jr., "Pictures at an Atrocity Exhibition" (unpublished manuscript).

6. Dodie Bellamy, "Sex/Body/Writing," in *Pink Steam* (San Francisco: Suspect Thoughts Press, 2004), 144.

7. Glück, *Margery Kempe*, 12.

8. Maurice Blanchot, *The Madness of the Day*, trans. Lydia Davis (Barrytown, NY: Station Hill Press, 1981), 9.

"Writing Sex Body" appeared on the Poetics List (SUNY-Buffalo) for "Poetics List Colloquium," Group 1 Number 3, September 2000. My essay responds to Dodie Bellamy's "Sex/Body/Writing" and the conversation it generated.

BATAILLE AND NEW NARRATIVE

In the late seventies, Steve Abbott, who always knew what to read, discovered Bataille. He told Bruce Boone about Bataille and Bruce told me. We were reading *L'Érotisme*, which appeared in France in 1957, so it is one of Bataille's last books. We read Mary Dalwood's translation, published by Walker and Company in 1962 as *Death and Sensuality: A Study of Eroticism and the Taboo* and republished by the Arno Press in 1977. (In 1986 City Lights republished this as *Erotism: Death and Sensuality*.) Reading *Death and Sensuality* was essential to the beginning of New Narrative. I am describing a kind of cultural intervention that gave us access to our own experience. Reading it again after thirty years, I am amazed by how much of my writing is derived from it.

During the seventies, representation of the gay community was a vexed subject. This community was inventing itself during those years and loyalty to it meant that we present a healthy gay identity. Sex was supposed to be good for us. Pornography, for example, often took the form of a Bildungsroman, and sex was often staged in natural settings to frame its naturalness. Negativity was understood as internalized homophobia, and we did not have a language to think about loss of self except as a result of social injustice. By negativity, I mean concepts of sacrifice, loss, and the "experience of nonknowledge": "we achieve the power to look death in the face and to perceive in death the pathway into unknowable and incomprehensible continuity—that path is the secret of eroticism and eroticism alone can reveal it."[1] (Parenthetically, we also lacked a language to deal with our own sexism, racism, and class antagonism.) Yet how could a serious literary work, a character, community, or even narrative exist without negativity? Bataille writes, "Only negative experience is worthy of our attention, to my thinking . . ."[2]

Most writers who addressed gay (not yet queer) subject matter wrote coming-out stories that occurred in the family, where loss, waste, and insufficiency could be found in exactly the preferred terms, them against us. These years produced an onslaught of such coming-out novels and, by comparison, few novels about the communities in which gay people—including the writers of these novels—were living.

I suppose every group or community or friendship or nation has a stage where it enacts the story of itself. The largest forum in our national culture is the family, so an American story must reach that stage to become recognizable. I think that's why the traditional family structure is hotly conserved in our country, at least in the imagination. (Italy legalized same-sex marriage, as did Spain, South Africa, and Norway, so they must not be guarding the family in the same way. Perhaps their politicians do not have to drag their children onstage?)

The coming-out novel did the work of locating homosexuality inside the family. Perhaps the best of these novels, because it is the exception, is Edmund White's A *Boy's Own Story*, in which the ability to betray marks the entrance to adulthood, and the hero does not actually come out to his family or to anyone except perhaps to his victims. What is conveyed is that power is erotic, and that a person who makes a secret of his sexuality undermines the group and, in general, the common good. Like Bataille's fictions, White's novel undermines rather than supports the idea of the family. More true to the form is Robert Ferro's *The Family of Max Desir*, in which Max seeks to integrate his homosexuality and his lover Nick into his Italian American family.

The family was a strangely remote institution in the lives of most gay men. It was like the old country: a way of life, a set of gestures, and even a language that had been left behind. Certainly the ever-radical hippie credo that helped shape the beginning of the gay movement—that play is more important than work—could not be affirmed in the family context. In a sense, our writers were faced with the problem of finding a public stage on which our actual lives could be portrayed.

To like ourselves was an important if exotic undertaking that countered the infinite hatred that had been leveled at us. It was important not to appear to be sick, since we had been pathologized. This led to strange configurations. These were the glory days of a community-based S/M that often described itself as a spiritual path leading to self-fulfillment, balance, therapeutic good, and fundamental equality. These terms come from Geoff Mains's *Urban Aboriginals*, published in 1984. You might assume that if anything were sick, if done correctly, it would be S/M. Leather men and women wearing Nazi paraphernalia were exploring power in arenas of safe play. Bruce and I had a catch-phrase—*he must not like himself very much*. After all, that was the greatest crime. We would say it, for example, when someone had gone way too far down the road of erotic asphyxiation.

In *Death and Sensuality*, Bataille demonstrated that the common good could equal the annihilation of the self. Bataille investigated communities in two contexts—anthropology and the avant-garde. What is a community? According to Bataille, it is "an undefined throng of possible existences."[3] Bataille's Acéphale was a secret society whose rituals were supposed to reignite a lost spiritual brotherhood in Europe and send that revelation outward. It was a community that wanted freedom rather than power, a release of energies that could not be controlled. What is the meaning of freedom? *To live at the limit where all systems break down.* When Bataille investigated a particular society, like the Native Americans of the coastal Northwest or the people of the Middle Paleolithic, he looked at rituals that were instances of a counter-economy: that is, an economy of loss, of sacrifice and expenditure, rather than of conservation. In this sense, transgression meant that the rule of order, expressed by a taboo, was violently broken to give expression to this counter-economy. The goal, or at least the result, was to go past the bounds of self to become a continuous rather than a discontinuous being—not continuous with the local community, but continuous with heterogeneous matter. There was an erotic element to these rituals, but they were not generally organized around sexual expression. In Bataille's novels, on the other hand, transgression is certainly wedded to sex. "Flesh is the extravagance within us set up against the law of decency," he says in *Death and Sensuality*.[4]

Here in one stroke is a self at once grander and more porous than the pallid, ironized being who inhabited stories in the *New Yorker*, or the character of the wronged innocent in my own community. Here is a series of chance ruptures rather than a coherent system or an autonomous being. We must do violence to our inner selves in order to call our existence into question and to "bear a negation that carries us to the farthest bounds of possibility."[5] Here is an attack on the self—or better, an expansion that lifts it outside the box of psychology and the confines of the family, where it had languished for so long.

Our situation was less avant-garde and more postmodern than Bataille's, if postmodernity can be characterized as a politics of groups. These kinds of questions were being asked: Should we gay people think of ourselves as a separate social class? Should we be a separatist movement? Is there any value in electoral politics? Should we focus our energies on revolution? What part does feminism play? What part does Marxism play? What part does the commodity play? Are male and female homosexuality the same thing, or should their adherents be understood as two groups? Here was a community in the throes of self-description, not an example from prehistory, anthropology, or utopian aspiration.

So for us there was a double movement: sex was a central stage that affirmed communal life—that is, as a site of loss and release from the bounds of self—and it was also the stage of our new-found identity. Identity politics called forth its own kind of obedience, including protests and self-censorship. For example, my lover reported to me that in one of the first Gay Freedom Day parades in San Francisco—1972?—men gave each other blowjobs on the back of a flatbed truck. Later, there were furious debates about what and whom this annual parade would include. NAMBLA (the North American Man/Boy Love Association) was a problem— did the group make the community look bad to other people and to itself? The parade committee wanted to get rid of the wrong kind of homosexual in favor of the right kind of homosexual. In 1991, Dennis Cooper was attacked for depicting young men as disposable objects. A man in the audience at Different Light Bookstore stood up and denounced him, and this man's group, Hookers Undivided Liberation Army, published a sort of *SCUM Manifesto*—*Dennis Cooper Must Die! Must Die! Must Die!*

Insufficiency, instability, uncertain readings, impossibility. How to locate and articulate the annihilation of the self within this community when the community itself was in the process of rejecting annihilation from above and sanitizing itself from within? Sex was already at the center of my community—as it well might have been, since the inner necessity to join the ranks of perverts had to be strong enough to break the actual law as well as the sundry prohibitions we had internalized. Since courtship had been forbidden to gay men, it was the sexual act itself that claimed our attention. As Michel Foucault observed, gay courtship—even learning your lover's name—often occurred after sex rather than before, and this is still the case.

The loss of self that was intrinsic to sex, the transgression of laws against homosexuality, the building of a self founded on sex (whether as a gay man or as a member of some other sexual underground) complicated a sex act that was, on the other hand, easy to find. If I characterize our sex from that era as a public orgy, it may be that a public bond connected even private sex acts, which were preformed in spite of social and legal injunctions and in defiance of what was understood as good health. All sex acts have a public aspect, but perhaps in different ways. An orgy may have been the public forum in which my community described itself to itself. According to Bataille, any sex breaks a law, if the law is meant to keep us proper, our bodies clothed and unpenetrated.

Bataille enabled me to recognize the negativity in the heart of my community's erotic life. A community takes part in what Bataille called "inner experience." Inner experience contests the limits of language and opens us in endless and incomplete relation. The subject is an impediment to communication, and communication opens us outwards and overflows. About discontinuity, Bataille says: "But I cannot refer to this gulf which separates us without feeling that this is not the whole truth of the matter. It is a deep gulf, and I do not see how it can be done away with. None the less, we can experience its dizziness together. It can hypnotise us. This gulf is death in one sense, and death is vertiginous, death is hypnotising."[6] One does not have to go further in Bataille's thought to see that sex makes an equivalence, that it is a kind of death—a notion he supports biologically, anthropologically, and from his own experience.

We in the New Narrative group—Bruce Boone, Kevin Killian, Dodie Bellamy, Camille Roy, and others—imported Bataille's concept of negativity into our work, which gave us access to the world we were living in. Of course we were also thinking about the possibilities of the New Narrative group as a community. Bruce was writing about what he called the "gay band" led by Jack Spicer, Robert Duncan, and Robin Blaser. He was referring to the Godard film *Band of Outsiders* (*Bande à part*), meaning a criminal group, and that was Bruce's sense in his work on Spicer. Bruce says, "I got the 'ruins' vision of community from Spicer and ran with it in only a slightly different sense. The gay *band a part* has submachine guns, yes, but it is filled with co-conspirators from the other side and some of its loyalties are to the other side (family, straight friends, et al.)— a still underground or hostile and aggressive community. Later they would say in France, the 'non-working' (and hence non-workable) community. There are too many holes in this aggressive community for it to work."[7]

I have told you about some of the things we took from Bataille— here are some of the things I could not use. The female as sacrifice dispatched by the male, both losing themselves in the consummation: "The woman in the hands of her assailant is despoiled of her being."[8] The male image of community, a secret fraternal brotherhood. Transgression, especially in Bataille's fictions, weds a moment of freedom to a sense of sin. While shame and a spiritual or metaphysical anguish accompany this shattering of the bonds of self, reason, sense, and world, the Catholic component was lost on me. A secular spirituality had already seemed to enter the commodity without contradiction. On the other hand, Bruce located in Bataille's collapse of dualities a path to Buddhism and the Gnostics.

In order to make Bataille our own, we had to translate from heterosexuality. For Bataille, homosexuality itself did not seem to constitute a taboo, nor did anal penetration "on its own" constitute an act of transgression. About the achievement in sex of continuity with animals of the same species, Bataille writes, "Curiously enough, this does not happen under exactly similar conditions between individuals of the same sex."[9] How disappointing! Heterosexuals bond with all homo sapiens when they have sex, but we do not.

I want to take a moment to look at Bataille the writer. In the first place, I want to note the strains of autobiography that knock the props out of his philosophical writing. In my favorite sentence in *Death and Sensuality*, Bataille purposefully makes his book unprofessional, "A study that sets out to be scientific minimises the part played by subjective experience, while I on the other hand am methodically minimising that played by objective knowledge."[10] Instead, he gives us lyrical way stations on a *via negativa*: the summit, the opening, sovereignty, the labyrinth, inner experience, heterogeneity, the accursed share, transgression.

Bataille's violently erotic fictions are based on his life, but not explicitly. The performance of his imagination amounts to self-revelation and makes the reader complicit in autobiography on that level. The reader wonders how far Bataille will go. At the same time, the impossibility of willing nakedness and irreversibility onto the page becomes a kind of unapproachable limit, but not more impossible than turning language completely into an object or banishing narrative from words. Shame itself is part of the chain of regulation and we break that chain, along with the rule against hurting ourselves, when we become naked. In any case, Bataille declines to separate writing from life, and he gives us a model of autobiography refracted through genre writing (pornography).

Bataille thought we experience death through the spectacle of sacrifice. My bathhouse scene in *Jack the Modernist* is based on Bataille's conflation of religious sacrifice and the erotic. The reader becomes part of the witnessing audience, experiencing shame and an enlarging loneliness. Extremity is in a sense reenacted to include the reader. "The victim dies, and the spectators share in what his death reveals. This is what religious historians call the element of sacredness. This sacredness is the revelation of continuity through the death of a discontinuous being to those who watch it as a solemn rite . . . What remains, what the tense onlookers experience in the succeeding silence, is the continuity of all existence with which the victim is now one."[11]

I want to close with this quotation to show that writing, inner experience, and community were united in Bataille: "It is from a feeling of community binding me to Nietzsche that the desire to communicate arises in me, not from an isolated originality."[12]

Notes:

1. Georges Bataille, *Erotism: Death and Sensuality*, trans. Mary Dalwood (San Francisco: City Lights, 1986), 24.

2. Ibid., 23.

3. Georges Bataille, *Inner Experience*, trans. Leslie Anne Boldt (Albany, NY: State University of New York Press, 1988), 61.

4. Bataille, *Erotism*, 92.

5. Ibid., 24.

6. Ibid., 12–13.

7. Bruce Boone, e-mail correspondence.

8. Bataille, *Erotism*, 90.

9. Ibid., 99.

10. Ibid.

11. Ibid., 22.

12. Bataille, *Inner Experience*, 26–27.

"Bataille and New Narrative" was presented at the MLA Convention, San Francisco, 2008.

2006

THE GREATNESS OF KATHY ACKER

> Jesus saw some little ones nursing. He said to his disciples,
> "What these little ones who are nursing resemble is those who
> enter the kingdom." They said to him, "So shall we enter the
> kingdom by being little ones?" Jesus said to them, "When you
> make the two one and make the inside like the outside and
> the outside like the inside and the above like the below, and
> that you might make the male and the female be one and the
> same, so that the male might not be male nor the female be
> female, when you make eyes in the place of an eye and a hand
> in place of a hand and a foot in place of a foot, an image in
> place of an image—then you will enter [the kingdom].
>
> —The Gospel of Thomas

I read *I Dreamt I Was a Nymphomaniac: Imagining*, I think,
before I met Kathy or even heard of her. I was snacking on the
stock of the poetry bookstore that I codirected. I could see the
book was provocative and experimental, and the sex kept me
alert. The second chapter contains a passage that begins "Last
night I dreamt I was standing on a low rise of grassy ground,"
and continues to describe a dream that involves family, the art
world and sex. Then the next paragraph begins "Last night I
dreamt I was standing on a low rise of grassy ground . . ."[1] I
began the second passage with a sense of having been there
before, like a dream. Then a dawning sense of wrongness, then
certainly of wrongness and a search for an explanation. A printer's
error seemed the probable cause. Lord knows, the small-press
books in my store contained zillions of mistakes.

I read the second passage more carefully than the first, because if there were any differences between them, I would have the relief of seeing the author making variations, but there were no differences. That made me suffer. Since the second passage duplicated the first, my arousal and emotions were taken from me, and I wanted to hold onto them. "If I don't fuck someone soon know someone wants me, I'll have to ride my horse for three days again: do something wilder. I can't stop myself. I get another drink. My sister who's also drunk asks me to dance . . . she kisses me . . . I ask her and she says she'd like to fuck me."[2] The dream contains many of Acker's themes, always close at hand in any case: suicide, sex, incest, family money, romance, loneliness, the inhumanity of "this society."

Why were my feelings taken from me by this repetition? Because I no longer knew Acker's reason for telling me the dream. Like any reader, I depend on knowing the author's intention to stabilize my reading, because I use her belief to underwrite the intensities that are generated and modulated inside me. Instead, Kathy dispatched these emotions while I was more or less stuck with them. It is a strange loneliness to be abandoned, emotions disowned, choking on the equipment of narrative projection. Kathy destabilized my reading by a strange doubling in which I saw how artificial the emotions were—or were made to be—even as I fell into them. They became an example of emotion, quoted emotion, and the effect of her quote marks was to slide me back and forth between embrace and distance. I am describing an aesthetic effect: I was left stranded with story as the writer leaped into the cold heaven of formal abstraction.

Many of Acker's strategies keep the reader off-balance. That's why it's rather difficult to write about her work, because the best reading is an uncertain reading. I want to offer my confusion as an ideal. Rather than drawing conclusions, developing identifications or thematic connections—that is, making judgments that lead to knowledge—Acker creates a reader who is lost in strangeness. She pitches the reader into a welter of contradictions that do not resolve themselves, but replace each other continuously: a text that hates itself but wants me to love it, sex that dissolves and amalgamates, a disempowered self that tops its heated bottom-act with cold manipulation, a confession that is therapeutic without the possibility of health. Her aesthetic is founded on double binds whose brilliance captivates me as I struggle against them.

The dream passage was repeated a third and a fourth time, and I understood how coldly and elegantly the second passage turned the dream into collaged text. By the fourth repeat I was skimming—I had been turned out of the story and saw it as a block of text. Acker's location had gone from the "I" of the dreamer to the manipulator of text. My own location as reader also changed: I was deprived of one kind of identification in favor of another. When Acker applies pressure to modes of narrating, she compels me to stand with her as the writer of her book, perhaps just living with her through a chunk of time. The theme jumps from, say, incest, to the materiality of print and the notion that texts themselves can be "represented." I feel a kind of joy as I attain that grander perspective. But that position is continually undermined by the story being told.

Acker said in 1989, in the useful interview that Sylvère Lotringer conducted, "The I became a dead issue because I realized that you make the I and what makes the I are texts."[3] When I lost my purchase as a reader, I felt anguish. I gained my footing on a form of identification that was perhaps more seductive, a second narrative about Acker manipulating text and disrupting identity. To treat a hot subject in a cold way is the kind of revenge that Flaubert took. Acker's second narrative acts as a critical frame, where I discover how to read the work: the particular ways in which a marauding narrative continually shifts the ground of authority, subverting faith in the "suspension of disbelief," the guided daydream that describes most fiction. Acker blasts that arrangement wide open by locating the writing in her own life and in the life of the reader and then calling for the reader's disbelief. I read these and other narratives all at once and I am a tag team running from one to another. If identity equals a florescence of narratives, or the materiality of language, then I must give up the sense of myself as a coherent narrative, and no matter how sophisticated my reading becomes, that is always a struggle. Hence my suffering.

If we see the self as the ongoing formation of a subject through the subject's ongoing negotiation with power, in Acker's work that negotiation is profoundly lost, because the self itself is a tyranny from above that descends *like a wolf on the fold,* as debased as the society that gives and withholds value. The self/text is at heart a political system, as nasty as the society it is part of. Self and subjectivity are prisons, the most intimate expressions of a domination that is almost total. "I feel I feel I feel I have no language, any emotion to me is a prison."[4] Struggle equals gestures that fuck with identity.

The heroines of Acker's novels want sex. Arousal may be a drug—"I've gotten hooked on sex"—but it is also a blissful jailbreak from the confines of the self. It is pleasure happening, not the self.[5] I may wish for a world in which I found my identity on the moment of orgasm—we could be squiggles of joy in which meaning proliferates delightfully. Still, to address the distorting need for sex (or a job, or love) a person must appear to be something recognizable—say, a gendered being with "appropriate" emotions. It is a double bind that Acker rejects with a grievance enacted by her narrators and characters. Acker declines to accept the terms of our confinement. She even rejects gender, the form the body takes to "get needs met," and she declines to commit to one or any. "I would rather be a baby than have sex. I would rather go GOOGOO."[6] That is, I want the freedom to have no ego boundaries. If texts and selves are prisons, would it be too fanciful to find a kind of freedom in the nonspace between texts, in the silence and emptiness between juxtapositions? Some of us experience this kind of freedom as anguish, but we prisoners might also experience other kinds of freedom as anguish.

Acker takes revenge on power in "this society" by displaying what it does: it expels people from the human club, rather than include them even at the bottom rung. The assertion of feelings, especially feelings of shame, makes our fear apparent, and even takes a kind of revenge by throwing these feelings back in society's face. She speaks truth to power by going where the power differential is greatest, to a community of whores, adolescent girls, artists, and bums; the outcast and disregarded. The power imbalance itself causes a reversal that confers authority, not to identity—these characters are merely quick sketches—but to the realities of oppression, loss, and degradation. If hegemony defines itself by what it tries to exclude, then the excluded merely need to describe themselves in order to describe hegemony.

In the program where I teach, a student wrote plays that were unrelentingly about sex with toddlers and violence with guns. The students had to perform each other's work. Extraliterary questions swarmed his writing. He worked the nightshift at the sheriff's office. He brought his gun to class for show-and-tell, and he started killing his characters off, characters modeled on the students in the workshop. He was in his sixties, so no youthful high jinx there. Had he acted—was he going to act—on his imaginings? Was I supposed to regard his writing as abnormal psychology rather than fiction? If so, even a fake confession would be part of a true case history.

One unwanted play was about some people waiting for a bus to pull out. The mother of a three-year-old fondles her child's vagina and the baby loves it. The other passengers also love it, and demonstrate other ways to pleasure the child. "Little pink tickle buttons sticking out of the baby's soft cunnie lips. So precious. I spider-tickled them and gave them all little baby orgasms." This goes on and on. The bus driver sighs, "How cute! I guess I'll now call this the 'love bus.'"

One of the characters describes Hopi mothers taking great pride in masturbating their children. I have no idea if they do, but different cultures handle childhood and sex in different ways. The nurses of Louis XIV fondled the toddler king's "drawbridge," as they called it. His little erections put them in a festive mood. Manchu mothers fellated their male infants but never kissed them on the face. Through this kind of "unwanted" information, our author cleverly adds scale to his play, and disallows a judgment based on "community standards." In fact, his play destabilizes our tenet against child sexuality. All the characters on this bus share a vision of acceptable sex and violence (killing adults is okay)—an unimaginable coincidence, yet one that makes our own unexamined agreements seem just as unimaginable.

Finally the students rebelled and the class closed down, so this troublesome student was sent to work with me (wise in the ways of transgression). He was a skillful and even funny writer. I found myself laughing—was that complicity? Was the humor intentional? The ugliness? I could picture the front page of the *Chronicle*: "Teacher Gives A+ to Killer Rapist." Intention itself was blown wide open, so his text was in a sense illegible.

I feel again that I was in the position of Acker's ideal reader, just as I had been in the bookstore encountering Acker's work for the first time. By best reader, I mean that I was implicating myself in ways I couldn't foresee. The power I enjoy—that of a professor judging a student's work—was turned upside down because it was myself I had to judge, along with the power that kept me safe from the text, and safe generally. If I had read my student's work in a book published by Grove Press, or published by anyone, the scandal might have been contained by the form of its publication, and I would have neutralized the danger rightly or wrongly by placing it in a tradition of transgressive literature. In order to make scandal felt continually, Acker finds ways to overflow the bounds of the literary by combining the knowledge she gives us of her life with aggression, humor, unfairness, and shifts in diction and context. "I asked him if he had gotten a letter from Mother . . . 'Were you expecting the dead to tell you what it's like so you can have a new place to spread your cunt lips?'"[7] Cultural tenets are demolished because I can't contain this damage in the box of literature.

Kathy blabs, but not necessarily the truth. Early on, she mixed real and fake autobiography according to set formulas, as she explains in the interview with Lotringer.[8] She manipulates my urge to build a reality behind an I. I want to believe that her story occurs in the world I inhabit: I'm hooked into her out-rageous desires—they must be *real*. But Acker denies me the means to draw a conclusion, a conclusion she is not committed to herself. If this is a performance in writing, what is at stake? Belief in the fact or fiction of events is no longer a pressing issue, because the risk of performing takes its place—if I am not sure of how naked she has made herself, I can still react to the spec-tacle of "how far will she go?" And my risk as a spectator becomes the risk of complicity, that the confessional machinery will somehow get backloaded onto me, that it is my confession in the end. It is my confession because I stage it in my psyche, because it calls a community into being that I am part of, because I already know the story so it is already mine, and because Acker has thoroughly confused belief, doubt, and emptiness.

Acker makes a nether region because she structures extra-literary relationships into her writing, an act which complicates the kind of judgments most readers never need to make. Finally, judgment itself is worn down and falls away in favor of a kind of astonishment. In this sense, you could say Acker creates extra-literary conflict that does not build character either on the page or in the world, as most fictions do, but instead destroys character.

Acker expanded the range of what can be said about the body, and all who write about sex owe her a debt of gratitude. There's no precedent for her patient records of pleasure, coldly observed. "If I concentrate on the air my lungs draw into them-selves, I can feel the nerves around my breasts move and shift in complex patterns."[9] She records consciousness as it moves through the phantasmagoria of daydream and the reality of the body as a first place: "This lasts forever: time intercedes, I can feel his cock expand."[10]

How true the confession and how proximate the complicity that create arousal! Following the lead of Georges Bataille, Acker says that sex destroys limits: "I matter when someone touches me, when I touch someone; the touch matters; so in this way I no longer exist, nor do the men."[11] But there is a contradiction here, because sex is often the place in Acker's writing where recognizable time and space begin. Sometimes Acker borrows from porn—high-class porn by Alexander Trocchi, for example—which has its own time frame of tension and release, and its own characters. But often she is simply looking at sex for a long time. So sex stabilizes as much as destabilizes the self/text. Arousal occurs on a register in which continuity is reinstated. Sex operates as a kind of weather, or middle distance—it takes the place of representation's bric-a-brac. It puts the world in place: here's the "effect of the real":

> The hair curling above the cunt, between the thighs, around the outer lips, in the red crack of the ass touches the thick pink outer lips touches the tiny red inner lips inside the outer lips touches the red berry at one end of the inner lips whose inside grows if it's grazed lightly enough touches the muscles and nerves spiraling as a canal away from the red inner lips.[12]

Acker draws in the reins of all her other preoccupations in favor of close observation.

To present myself as a reader of Acker's sex writing, I include my own extraliterary commitments: both to the body in the form of my arousal, and to the community of sexual experimentation that is supported by such writing. Acker's voice describing sex is most often her "real voice"—as she described it—a voice that becomes more present in her later books.

I want to take this sex-equals-stability another step. That we have bodies, and a relation to these bodies, and a lack of relation to these bodies, is politics for Acker. Flesh is what has value. Kathy and I used to trade nuggets of physical experience. Talking on the phone, one of us would say something like, "She can't have an orgasm unless a third person is watching," and the other would pounce on it. We were on the lookout for an irreducible language, an irreducible chunk of experience to put together with other irreducible chunks to make a language where feeling, event, and words come together. "'I need to fuck guys who fuck really slowly, for a long time, so it just comes over me. I tremble and tremble and tremble.'"[13] A language that can't exist, in which the most ephemeral is the most enduring. A magical language whose words fasten onto their readers' bodies in a kind of onomatopoeic fury. Sex is like a spell, like sympathetic magic: an erection on the page can cause an erection "in the world." Using these nuggets has the same pleasure as correcting the error of generalization, since each one stands for a whole sexuality, a species of one.

Acker's ambition for literature was to site it in a queasy place where autobiography and fiction, politics and myth, become indistinguishable. She brings language to its limits, to the body and emotions—where risk of nakedness derives from and supports a community. "Culture's the way by which a community attempts to bring its past up out of senselessness and to find in dream and imagination possibilities for action."[14]

Certainly she stands with Juan Goytisolo and Thomas Bernhard in the pitch of her hatred for her country, for "this society." Against the loneliness of her experience, Acker posits the ongoing conversation of a group of whores that defines community, a gathering of outcasts that evolves into a band of pirates in her final book. They're already present in her first work, "Politics," about her life as a dancer in a strip joint. These gatherings are composed of women, artists, and freaks who review their relationships with men and power on the eternal stage of night and empire, whether it's a New York City jail or Imperial Rome. This community draws an equals sign between freeing our ability to love and the destruction of the state. Included in that community is Acker's reader; as she says, "When I use language, I am given meaning and I give meaning back to the community."[15]

In 1975 Acker wrote about "A possibility of living in a world to which she's not always alien. San Francisco!"[16] Acker's move from city to city—New York, San Francisco, London—was the story of hope and disappointment. The demand she placed on local communities to support her in an unalienated fashion was more interesting for being unreasonable and unfair. Kathy was always on the lookout for forms of collectivity—art scenes, music scenes, the tattoo or biker "communities"—that tie the fate of the individual to the fate of the group. In her essay, "Critical Languages," she says: "May we write, not in order to judge, but for and in (I quote Georges Bataille), 'The community of those who do not have a community.'"[17] That is, generating text means generating identity. I would like to add, generating identity means generating community. If the idea of community were to begin so heterogeneously, I wonder if the reductionist pitfalls could be avoided.

Acker included her communities in her writing by using real names, by speaking to them directly, and by speaking for them. "Friendship is always a political act, for it unites citizens into a polis, a (political) community."[18] She loved gossip—the glue of any community—and there was never a greater sob-sister. She does not dress up romantic suffering with pretty language. Love, when it's done right, only makes things worse: "It's sick to love someone beyond rationality, beyond a return (I love you you love me). Real love is sick. I could love death."[19] And, "I knew I belonged to the community of artists or freaks not because the anger in me was unbearable but because my overpowering wish to give myself away wasn't socially acceptable."[20]

Kathy was the best girlfriend, because with her you could really complain. "I am lonely out of my mind. I am miserable out of my mind . . . I've got to fuck. Don't you understand don't you have needs as much as I have needs DON'T YOU HAVE TO GET LAID?"[21] Romantic distress was a default position for human communication, and if the truest language is the unique particulars of desire spoken by the community of cock and cunt, then the lack of such communication (which means no agency, rejection, emotional harm, and poverty) makes a communal language of failure. When I was *badly loved*, no romantic bruise was too tiny to examine, no repeat of that examination was too obsessive. Kathy and I gave each other plenty of advice, the blind leading the blind. Bits of these endless conversations worked their way into each other's writing—here are two tiny passages.

This is from *Great Expectations*, 1982: Three whores are talking in ancient Rome. Kathy is the whore Cynthia, I am the whore Barbarella, and Denise Kastan is Danielle.

> Barbarella: I'm both the wife and husband. Even though none of us is getting anything right now, except Danielle who's getting everything, our desires are totally volatile.
>
> Danielle: I can't be a wife. I can be a hostess. If I've got lots of money.
>
> Barbarella: One-night stands don't amuse me anymore.
>
> Cynthia: I think if you really worship sex, you don't fuck around. Danielle fucks around more than any of us, and she's the one who doesn't care about sex.
>
> Barbarella: Most men don't like sex. They like being powerful and when you have good sex you lose all power.
>
> Cynthia: I need sex to stay alive.[22]

This is from my book *Margery Kempe*, 1994:

> It's two a.m. his time; I'm in bed in San Francisco. My life occurs on the heavy satin of his skin yet he won't let me be the cause of stimulation. I give him an ultimatum: Let's live together or break up. He thinks it over a few months: he has the self-confidence to reject me. I write a blistering letter and show it to my friend Kathy. She says, "Bob, you must delete the anger and beg."[23]

"One text subverts another" is the consecrated phrase. Appropriation can express a cynicism where nothing obtains—"my writing is all shit," Kathy once affirmed in P.J.'s, a seafood restaurant in San Francisco—and the process itself can be pitched like a bomb at the custodians of identity. In her hands it's a malleable practice—in her later work Acker uses appropriation to conduct us into a state of wonder. "I'm basically a New Age writer," Kathy said some years later at the same table.

Great Expectations begins with episodes of family life alternating with chunks of Acker's translations of Pierre Guyotat's

Eden Eden Eden, a novel-length sentence fragment on sex and atrocity. Soon the sections infect each other and we see the link between need and violence—that family life and war (in 1982 Guyotat's Algeria looked like our Vietnam) have their common denominator. "*Reality* is just the underlying fantasy, a fantasy that reveals need."[24] Need means need for love on every register. Reality is need in a simpler way than we might be comfortable acknowledging. Acker may be subverting text with text, but need has a different economy: one need equals all needs. One need is not an allegory of all needs; it is all needs.

Another way to describe this economy of need is to say that appropriation is a way to look at the distance between feeling and event. One of Acker's basic tenets is that the world is against feeling. She projects her life into stories that are already known, like porn or the detective genre or canonical works like *Don Quixote* and *Great Expectation*. The already-known is a public stage on which to reclaim emotion. It's a theme in *Don Quixote*—how to love while ferociously transvaluing emotion and continuously redefining world and self. In works like *Don Quixote* and *Pussy, King of the Pirates,* appropriation grants Acker's own story a second fate with its own inevitabilities, its own organization of experience. You could say this fate is a fate in words with its own freedoms and resistances. Once begun, the appropriated text acts as the unforeseen, since Kathy's life must somehow fit into the story.

The rereading that *is* appropriation turns Acker into a reader as well as a writer. "The more I write my own novels, the more it seems to me that to write is to read."[25] Acker jumps the barrier and becomes a reader—displaying that projection of self into the text that shapes, however briefly, a reader's being. That projection of herself is presented as a kind of spectacle to myself the reader, part of my own act of self-projecting. In reading, I am pitched between the true version of the appropriated work, its theft, the facts of Acker's life, and the truth of her psychic life (the "case history" of extremity that writers since De Quincey have been reporting).

I have come to think of the trajectory of Acker writing as going from daydream to nightdream. In the first place Acker took her cue from early-seventies conceptual art, banishing creativity and asserting procedural elements by setting up arbitrary guidelines to set fiction outside intention: so in *Kathy Goes to Haiti*, she used predetermined amounts of real and fake autobiography. She wrote so many pages per day, brute production, which she called "task work." At one point she said she wrote with the TV on, and bits of histrionic soap-opera dialogue filtered through boredom-induced daydreams. Her early work, taken as a whole, can be characterized by daydream—that is, dream riffs of clear motive, immediate longings, revenge fantasies, and wish fulfillment.

Acker used dreams in many ways—the dream maps in *Blood and Guts*, for example. There is a therapeutic aspect to the repetition of the family drama, the litany of obsessions, the report of endless suffering and desire. Writing may provide the same occasion for self-revelation that therapy does—we take for granted that it's good for people to speak candidly in these "confidential" situations. But it is a therapy in which good health is impossible because the dream is turned outward—deprived of interiority, stripped of coherent subjectivity—and it is our culture itself that is sick. The endless recycling of societal messages and oppressions enlarges the sense of impossibility, except perhaps faith in the power of storytelling itself. A therapy minus interior life, antiexpressive, and so turned outward.

In *My Death My Life by Pier Paolo Pasolini*, Acker wrote, "I can wonder whatever I want. I simply see. Each detail is a mystery a wonder."[26] Acker was searching for a way to escape from duality and rational thought. In *Empire of the Senseless*, she dreamt the plot forward. Acker would make a move in writing, like dreaming a plot forward, then see that she was doing it and make a commitment to the strategy, as Carla Harryman observed. After *Empire of the Senseless* was finished, Acker said she was glad to sleep through a night again, since she had been waking herself up for months to write down her dreams. The dreams are recognizable—Kathy moving through a dreamspace where actions seem ringingly emphatic to her and to the reader, though motive is located beyond the grasp of both. Dualities are canceled in favor of an immediate consciousness of the inter-relation and interdependence of things. Acker was using her unconscious like a public commons, the location of image-making that belongs to a community.

I'd like to place Acker's later work with Baudelaire's "Corre-spondences" and Rimbaud's *Illuminations*, works intended to change the world directly through the reality of the imagination. "If writing cannot and writing must change things, I thought to myself, logically of course, writing *will* change things magi-cally."[27] Acker's interest in magic can be seen as the grandest attempt to integrate the extraliterary into writing. Magic, in the largest sense, allows me to link my own experience, desires, and biological self to a grand order. It connects the ephemeral to the largest realty. Acker uses the obscure and emphatic motives of dreams to indicate this unknown organization of the world. Maybe she is rejecting the idea that anything is secret. Her dreams belong to the reader as well as the writer, so the goal of self-knowledge is turned outward as well. My interior life may be cultural glue organizing me from the outside, something to live up to, like the idea of fidelity in the Middle Ages.

Acker founds her aesthetics on distant poles. A sentence like "I'm sick of this society" can seem at once post-punk self-mockery, ugly writing shedding the trappings of literature, an "example of language," a *cri de coeur*, and the "stupid" voice of an adolescent girl who can't be controlled.[28] That girl is a recognizable citizen of the Downtown Scene in New York, while Acker seems to have acquired appropriation and other such maneuvers on the West Coast—in David Antin's classes, for example, and in dialogue with the Language poets.

Acker champions feeling itself, and she is a cold writer working from formulas that generate text. Her continual shifts in scale stretch meaning out of shape, as she packs together extreme statements of far-flung lyricism. Belief is "bent out of shape," an exciting disorganization that isolates each sentence. I must continually renew my trust in the process of reading while my assumptions are demolished. I attain a place of innocence, my affirmation and trust must take place in the present—past affirmations don't matter, past betrayals of that trust must be surmounted. The writing itself gains majesty as the truth of the world seems to be balanced against each sentence.

Kathy Acker had the highest ambition: to reorient literature in a true relation to the present and to crack that moment wide open. In the end, my reading goes from unreadable to unbearable, because Acker intends that I bear the knowledge of chance, which is the acceptance of constant change. That acceptance is also the knowledge of death, the knowledge of my body, which exists (whether I know it or not) in the pure intensity of arousal and dread.

Notes:

Epigraph: Quoted in *Sex from Plato to Paglia: A Philosophical Encyclopedia*, ed. Alan Soble, vol. 1, *A–L* (Westport, CT: Greenwood Press, 2006), 405.

1. Kathy Acker, *Portrait of an Eye: Three Novels* (New York: Grove Press, 1992), 101.

2. Ibid., 106–107.

3. Kathy Acker, "Devoured by Myths," interview by Sylvère Lotringer, in *Hannibal Lecter, My Father* (New York: Semiotext(e), 1991), 11.

4. Kathy Acker, *Great Expectations* (San Francisco: Re/Search, 1982), 24.

5. Kathy Acker, *Hello, I'm Erica Jong* (New York: Contact II Publications, 1982), 11.

6. Ibid., 7.

7. Kathy Acker, *In Memoriam to Identity* (New York: Grove Weidenfeld, 1990), 165.

8. See Acker, "Devoured by Myths," 7.

9. Kathy Acker, *Essential Acker: The Selected Writings of Kathy Acker*, eds. Amy Scholder and Dennis Cooper (New York: Grove Press, 2002), 39.

10. Ibid., 15.

11. Ibid., 33.

12. Kathy Acker, *The Adult Life of Toulouse Lautrec* (New York: TVRT Press, 1978), 26–27.

13. Ibid., 17.

14. Kathy Acker, *Bodies of Work: Essays* (New York: Serpent's Tail, 1997), 4.

15. Ibid.

16. Acker, *Adult Life*, 37.

17. Acker, *Bodies of Work*, 92.

18. Ibid., 104.

19. Kathy Acker, *My Mother: Demonology* (New York: Pantheon Books, 1993), 315.

20. Ibid.

21. Acker, *Essential Acker*, 139.

22. Acker, *Great Expectations*, 110.

23. Robert Glück, *Margery Kempe* (New York/London: Serpent's Tail, 1994), 134.

24. Acker, *Essential Acker*, 115.

25. Acker, *Bodies of Work*, 66.

26. Acker, *Essential Acker*, 195.

27. Acker, *Bodies of Work*, 8.

28. Acker, *Essential Acker*, 37.

"The Greatness of Kathy Acker" was published in *Lust for Life: On the Writings of Kathy Acker*, eds. Amy Scholder, Carla Harryman, and Avital Ronell (New York: Verso, 2006).

TWO

BETWEEN LIFE AND DEATH

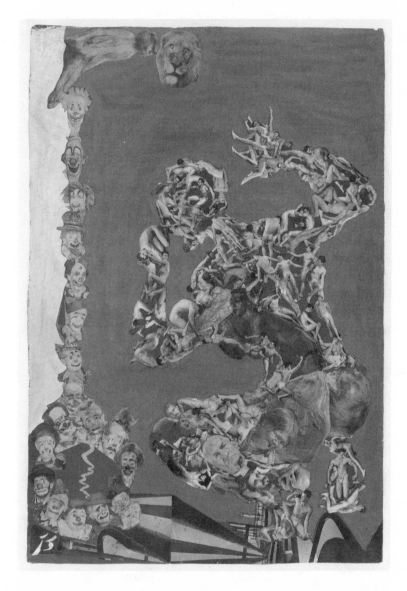

Jess, *The Mouse's Tale*, 1951–54. Collage (gelatin silver prints, magazine reproductions, and gouache on paper), 47.6 × 32 in. San Francisco Museum of Modern Art.

THE MOUSE'S TALE

In 1951 Jess made *The Mouse's Tale*, the first of his large collages—or "paste-ups," as he calls them. Only a few years before, he had been a radio-chemist working on the production of plutonium for the US government. He abandoned science and rational method when he dreamed the world would come to an end in 1974. The nude in *The Mouse's Tale* crouches on contradictory perspectives of a chemical refinery.

Jess's marriage to the poet Robert Duncan also began in 1951, and it lasted until Duncan's death in 1988. Their household made a world, and Jess dispensed with large parts of the world outside. Art was a kind of exalted play that demanded unalloyed sincerity and concentration. Unwilling to be distracted, he discarded his family along with his last name, declined to attend his own openings, and spent years—even decades—on a single work.

The San Francisco Museum of Modern Art acquired *The Mouse's Tale* in 1976, so I've been looking at it for twenty-four years. It always arouses me with its dual dramas legible from different reading distances. First I see the large nude silhouette with its skeletal head and ample butt, fingers splayed in terror. Then I see the abundant nakedness, more suggestive because the eye discovers and coaxes each body out of a shrubbery of more nakedness. The composite nude (like an Arcimboldo or a Surrealist mannequin) confuses life and death, an uncanny effect that Jess complicates by using photographs of living people. They are both fiction and flesh, "characters" who, away from the camera, age and die with us, or before us. Jess puts a strange pressure on the images to be, at once, scraps of paper and actual depths to fall into.

How long can I track little naked men in an artwork in a museum before I seem subnormal to the guards and to myself? I'm amazed that Jess at midcentury could accept at face value the innocence and delight of those *Physique Pictorial*–style photos, the childlike wonder hitched to adult sexuality. He dropped two snapshots of himself—the young beat with a goatee—in his animal-cracker soup of "homoeros," along with a Navajo woman, a minister, a panther.

I was grateful for this startled naked figure whose third dimension always risks being canceled by the myriad perspectives of the men who make him up. Caught in his confrontation with some greater power, he turns away from the viewer, perhaps in self-horror, perhaps unaware that his body is a swarm of Lilliputian exhibitionists, tireless multipliers of sexual urge. It was 1976; I had a ticket to the orgy, but that freedom did not eliminate the pervasive fear.

Beside the nude stands a monkey gallows. Surveying the world, a cat/lion, symbol of empire, is the knot of the rope as well as judge and jury. If the man is found guilty, he'll be hanged by a rope of clowns. Do these soft old spirits say, "Your death is a joke?" The gray universe is already condemned, already hanging in the gaudy noose. If the man is a mouse, then his tail restates the proposition of that universe, Lewis Carroll's calligram, the squiggle-shaped "Mouse's Tale" in *Alice's Adventures in Wonderland*:

> Fury said to
> a mouse, That
> he met in the
> house, "Let
> us both go
> to law; *I*
> will prose-
> cute *you*.—

Come, I'll
take no de-
nial: We
must have
the trial;
For really
this morn-
ing I've
nothing
to do:"
Said the
mouse to
the cur,
"Such a
trial, dear
sir, With
no jury
or judge,
would
be wast-
ing our
breath."
"I'll be
judge,
I'll be
jury,"
said
cun-
ning
old
Fury;
"I'll
try
the
whole
cause,
and
con-
demn
you to
death."

In 1951, Jess was still assimilating the influences of his teachers Clyfford Still and David Park. He discovered fantasies in his own "nonobjective" paintings (and in Still's work). He would enter these scenes for a while, then perhaps paint them out. That is, abstract paintings are romantic environments: vistas of aspiration that generate story along with profound mood. Does that seem obvious in retrospect?

I'm a writer who learned from visual art, and Jess is an artist who learned from literature. In the fifties, he solved the exact puzzle I was working on in the late seventies: how to tell a story that also knows itself as writing—"a made up thing and at the same time a depth in which my being is," as Duncan said of his poet self. Jess declined to recognize a dichotomy between abstraction and representation, or to take sides in a debate that fueled Bay Area art and writing for decades. His solution was pastiche and appropriation—a material-based aesthetics that narrates through the mystery and authenticity of salvaged images.

It would be a mistake to take the two gouache background fields for granted. They are the matrix for the colorless world of the nude: images are drawn out of them with the addition of white or gray. The universe our naked figure dreads is the universe that makes him, a crucible of image-making. If that contradicts without altering the playful Eros of the work, then we are exactly in Jess's terrain.

Maybe some of the nude's anxiety derives from Jess's own horror vacui. Henceforth the paste-ups will be so densely layered with images they'll convey the kind of wonder found in Victorian fairy paintings like Richard Dadd's—a wonder based on abundance and meticulousness, as though the artist performs a slow task in a fairy tale, say, counting grains of sand:

Once there was a mouse vulnerable yet something that—

The chopped-off tail crawls in sweeping motions.

Once there was a mouse that turns you into a homosexual.

Ocular criminal in a gray universe, Fury the cat trapped our citizens in a quaking body.

An incy-wincy mousy called LIBIDO made of nothing—gray and white scraps.

"The Mouse's Tail" was published in *Artforum* 38, no. 7 (March 2000). It was reprinted on *Open Space* (the blog of the San Francisco Museum of Modern Art), September 12, 2012.

YOKO

Sometime in the early seventies my mom said, "Look how lucky John Lennon is—and he has a beautiful Japanese wife!" My mother conveyed to me that she knew I was gay; *any* wife would be a good idea, even if she wasn't Jewish. *Was* Yoko a trophy wife?

Pop culture and high culture got married. Pop culture reigned and Fluxus was not a word in the news. Would high culture *spoil* John?—was a question we could ask then. Yoko had sung with Ornette Coleman. She'd made *Grapefruit: A Book of Instructions*. But it was the Bed-In that I loved her for. Perhaps Fluxus was encountering Situationism, but who knew? It was just vaguely-appealing-but-unsexy John and his squat wife turning the media into a revolt against the commodity for an instant before all reverted back to the John-and-Yoko show. What if these bodies were worth looking at? What if these childish drawings were worth doing? What if this whiny song was a great one? What if we were supposed to *think* a split second before mindlessly identifying?

I have always felt grateful for public nudity. Even in the degraded vocabulary of performance art, nakedness is a strike against the all-encompassing strip *tease* that our culture is. As Yoko remarked, "Those who make revolution *half way* only dig their own graves."

"Yoko" was published in the exhibition catalog *Piece: Nine Artists Consider Yoko Ono* (San Francisco: Kiki Gallery, 1995). It was reprinted in *KIKI RICK YOKO CACA* (San Francisco: Allone Co., 2008), a zine produced to accompany *Kiki: The Proof Is in the Pudding*, an exhibition honoring the Kiki Gallery at Ratio 3, San Francisco, 2008. (Actually it was Saint-Just, not Yoko, who supplied the concluding observation.)

IN GOD WE TRUST / AMERICA'S MOST WANTED

José A. Toirac, Meira Marrero, and Loring McAlpin explore the American rule of law, especially as it is practiced at Guantanamo Bay. As the title may suggest, there are two rooms in their installation, but they are so entirely related that I could say they are two versions of a single room, a room we still inhabit—the American psyche post 9/11. The title has a patina. *In God We Trust* is the motto on the dollar bill, and *America's Most Wanted* conjures images of Chicago gangsters as well as a long-running TV series.

In God We Trust / America's Most Wanted (installation photograph), 2004.

In the first room, three neon signs hang on adjoining walls: Deus, Yahweh, and Allah, the deities of monotheism. Are these the "neon gods" of Simon and Garfunkel's *Sounds of Silence*? The artists stenciled a grid of dollar signs on the walls and then covered them with used motor oil that pools onto the floor. The dollar signs become legible as the smell of the oil becomes apparent, and the fragrance of the oil carries these symbols of a holy war into the body. These are different kinds of abstractions—the neon words, the symbol of the almighty dollar, and the commodity itself—but they are all naked.

In God We Trust / America's Most Wanted (installation photograph), 2004.

In the second room a drama is enacted. The artists covered the walls with enlarged camouflage patterns, painstakingly painted, whose colors morph from the greens and tans of military gear to the orange of prisoner uniforms at Guantanamo Bay. On facing walls, two images confront each other. A silk-screened grid of the twenty-one most-wanted international terrorists from FBI files is flanked by fiery orange. They are Arabs, some apprehended and some still at large. On the facing wall, Coalition troops shower in the desert. In this blown-up news photo, the young men are joshing and looking over their shoulders at the camera. They seem to be looking at their terrorist audience. A boardwalk over sand crosses the floor, connecting and separating the army and the prey (which army? which prey?). In the play of abstract and concrete, this sand resists allegory, just as the oil does in the first room. Above the sand, the conflict occurs; below, the treasure/oil is hidden.

If the terrorists are guilty, are the soldiers innocent? The police procedural–style presentation of the Arabs' photos automatically applies the deadening pressure of guilt to their faces, while the candor of the soldiers' photo automatically confers innocence, even innocent arousal. These naked, young men could also be America's most wanted. I depend on their innocence and glamour because I decline to identity with the terrorists, but then I realize that the power behind the abstractions in the next room also relies on their innocence, both to follow orders without question and to act on their own initiative when orders are left purposely vague (for example, to wrest information from prisoners).

In God We Trust / America's Most Wanted (installation photograph), 2004.

It does not take much time to realize that only a short while after this work was first shown, nakedness itself was used as a punishment by soldiers at Guantanamo Bay, Abu Ghraib, and Bagram. The artists have turned the tables on these soldiers. The terrorists become a kind of male gaze multiplied by twenty-one. In fact, there are only males here, including the gods in the next room. The soldiers' vulnerability and lack of protection from the eyes of the terrorists—some of whom may indeed have been their victims— creates a kind of vertigo of guilt and innocence, nakedness and camouflage, ping-ponging between these walls. Here are heroes and villains, but which is which? Are the gods also enemies, naked as they are and shining forth as they do from different walls?

In God We Trust / America's Most Wanted is refracted through images by Andy Warhol; it was first assembled in Pittsburg in October 2004, partly as a tribute to Warhol in his hometown. The dollar signs and camouflage come from his paintings, and the images of the terrorists refer to his project for the 1964 World's Fair, *The 13 Most Wanted Men*. Warhol silk-screened the FBI's most wanted on large panels and arranged them in a grid on the exterior of the New York State Pavilion. It was up for only two or three days before Warhol, forced by officials to obscure the offending images, covered the faces with silver paint. The guilt/innocence of the FBI's list *and* of Warhol's project thus became a mirror for the attending public.

As for the dollar sign and camouflage, Warhol amazed us by demonstrating how welcoming they were, like all images and symbols, to the spiritual improvement of art. Toirac, Marrero, and McAlpin do not so much appropriate the appropriated (the art world dilating on itself), as return these images to the conflicts that generated them, to their blunt, original contexts—power, guilt, and the shifting parameters of ideology and the rule of law.

"In God We Trust / America's Most Wanted" was published in the exhibition catalog *In God We Trust / America's Most Wanted* (Havana: La Casona Galeria de Arte, 2009). The artists' installation was first shown at the Mattress Factory, Pittsburg, 2004.

ED'S TOMB

Ed Aulerich-Sugai has had AIDS for about six years. He's thinking about buying a niche at the San Francisco Columbarium to house his ashes. I drive him out so we can look the place over. We see its dome floating behind Pier 1 Imports on Geary Street. A little suburb surrounds the Columbarium, and it's not surprising to learn the building was part of the extensive Odd Fellows Cemetery, which became a residential tract in the forties.

British architect Bernard J. S. Cahill designed the Columbarium. It's an ornate, steel-framed, neoclassical building that housed the ashes of 6,700 San Franciscans through this century's portion of eternity, including two big earthquakes. It was always secular, giving rest to an array of race and ethnicity. Perhaps it served the religion of business, as evidenced by the many Masonic emblems and august family names on the oldest niches. The building decayed into a magnificent ruin until 1980, when the Neptune Society of Northern California bought it and began restoration. The niches have increased in value like real estate; a modern annex was installed in the old building to meet the demand. The current wave of customers is attracted by the opportunity to control at least one aspect of death by making an intimate statement in a public space.

This lovely wedding cake of a building houses the private gestures of the recently departed and the lilies and doves of the long gone. When Ed and I enter the honeycomb of circular tiers, Ed's final resting place starts spinning around him. He folds up, but catches himself when he feels my hand on the

Photograph by Kristie Wells.

back of his neck. As he sinks onto a folding chair, I brush his clammy temple with my lips.

In Japan, in the seventeenth century, it was fashionable for a cultivated person to write his death poem, intended to be the last syllables the author spoke. Basho's goes, "On a journey, ill, / and over withered fields dreams / go wandering still." Last words interest me because death gives them such a grand setting. Moreover, language always has a reversible quality. Taking words into death undermines its finality, turning death into a comedy.

Ed and I explore the building. Many of the newer niches at the Columbarium have that brand of comedy—the hilarity of last words. Each niche is a tiny room "where dreams go wandering," covered by a glass pane, a stage with theatrical potential on which to assert, "this is who I am." The private and the public converge. Some people seek the shelter of infancy, teddy bears, and toys. Others display their obsessions—various collections, baseball, Elvis and his twin, gambling, the perfect Martini—in the face of the very death that fueled those obsessions, the very obsessions they used to hide from death.

Ed buys a niche and begins to make his tomb. Later he invites me over to see the tomb before it's installed. It sits on a small drafting table—looking at it makes me weak in the knees. I don't think I have the forward momentum to plan my own tomb: why not just get dumped in the Bay . . . or *whatever*?

Ed's tomb is a diorama, a ground of polished viridian-green marble surrounded by a robin's egg–blue sky across which white clouds with lavender-gray shadows drift. His ashes go in a ceramic vase but he doesn't know how to seal it. I suggest a copper cap that would oxidize into blue-green. The fabricator Michael Brown could do it, I offer.

Ed tells me about the thought that went into the materials— long-lasting pigment, for example, and glue that fixes the canvas to a Plexiglas liner so the cloth will not contact the moist cement. I'm dubious. After you are dead, is there a difference between two hundred and seven hundred years? I think it shows a lack of imagination; Ed still doesn't realize that nothing matters after you are dead, that you are no longer included.

Ed has painted clouds for two decades; still, I think, what does this blue sky say about Ed and his world? I recognize his iso-lation, a kind of inorganic purity. The vase, the stone, the sky. The violence of dying flesh has vanished, what's left is the incor-ruptible skeleton of the world. Long ago, when we were hippie lovers on acid, I hallucinated that the universe was fucking itself, while Ed sat cross-legged, watching crystals endlessly unfold on a white wall. Ed's niche says that now nothing stands between him and the sky. Maybe it's a wish. Perhaps Ed's tomb is the ideal landscape that his ashes, if scattered, might become part of.

The restraint of Ed's installation interests me, a heaven characterized by lack of detail. My heaven would contain even less—as though there is nothing to pass on, nothing to propose, and no forum to say it in. Experience itself is so threadbare that sky effects are the only assertion we can make with confidence. Memorial art supposedly looks backward—old gardens and weathered cenotaphs—but it actually looks ahead and believes in continuity with the future and the value of the world to come. Ed has an idea, however sketchy, of the whole.

The idea that a future exists startles me and reorients me to the present. The recognition of a future is the beginning of a kind of sanity. It is a powerful optimism, an enormous idea. The waste and greed of the Regan–Bush years have created a futureless mood, diminishing our ability to link our lives to experience beyond ourselves. The profiteer who says there is no tomorrow turns that cliché into the daily reality of his victims. Our lack of belief in a future is a symptom of a massive and pervasive marginality.

Acknowledgment of a future seems like the first order of business. But whose future? And whose heaven? Suddenly politics enters. I don't mean that museums should collect worlds and "sublimes" like the *Star Trek* crew, to exhibit otherness for the benefit of an undifferentiated audience. It's true that alien religion is treated with respect on the Starship *Enterprise*. We are allowed to witness belief; what is more fun than Vulcan mysticism with its Noguchi modernism? But the human crew has no faith of its own beyond the sanity of their vessel, and that contrast reduces the aliens to folkways. The curatorial crew should express its faith in the global world of an individual artist and the microcosm of a community or an art practice.

Still, that may not be enough. An exhibition site that is a graveyard or a columbarium might open a "beyond" for an arts institution in more than one sense. What is the answer here? The Center for the Arts could begin as an expression of a given community; a Center event could be smaller and more incisive, abandoning the idea of an ideal stage and a unified audience; it could halt the expansion toward ever-larger events and atten-dances that has become a disease of art organizations, a kind of obesity created by funders who ironically ignore the realities of current private and public funding.

Along with Ed Aulerich-Sugai, I want to mention two other artists whose works convey an inside out–ness, a grasp of time that makes me want to write my stories posthumously. Gran Fury member Loring McAlpin made Hollywood-style Walk of Fame sidewalk blocks to remember porn stars who have died of AIDS. These blocks can become part of the sidewalk outside a porn shop, a sex club, or a museum; they mourn particular deaths, a particular moment in the gay community, and the passing of beauty.

Artist Charles Sexton gave Jerome Caja his ashes to be used as an art material; in a collaboration that is also a memorial, Caja filled an ashtray with Sexton's ashes, and in the cigarette slot he placed a butt with Sexton's face drawn on it. Both Caja and McAlpin frame intensity of loss in a banality that doesn't allow the emotion a dignified (i.e., contained) expression, but sends it spiraling outward.

Ed takes up residence in his tomb—I go out to have a look. I see that Daniel, Ed's lover, has added a photo of Ed to the niche, supplying a human scale that Ed had ruled out. Ed had not planned to face outward, but to display his isolation. His isolation is not antisocial. In fact, Ed asked me to join him in his niche after I die. Now my assessment of his tomb becomes more acute and my conclusions become irreversible—and that is just what I am trying to say in this essay about the opening of an alternative museum. I wish that Center for the Arts and you, the reader of this essay, could accompany Ed and me in his small exhibition space, in his work about death and the future.

"Ed's Tomb" was published as "For the Opening of Center for the Arts" in the first exhibition catalog of the Yerba Buena Center for the Arts, *In Out of the Cold* (San Francisco: Yerba Buena Center for the Arts, 1993). It was revised and reprinted as "Final Nest," an essay on the San Francisco Columbarium, in *Nest: A Quarterly of Interiors*, no. 4, ed. Joseph Holtzman (Spring 1999); and appeared on *Open Space* (the blog of the San Francisco Museum of Modern Art), October 1, 2013, to celebrate the work of Josh Fraught installed at the San Francisco Columbarium. This version, with some matter added, will appear in my novel, *About Ed*.

BOTTOMS UP!

With Chris Komater

Lately, we have been thinking about our national preoccupation with memoir. It's the happening literary form. A memoir is true but literary—a two-for-one deal. Literature rescues truth from the talk shows. So Frank McCourt starved when he was a child. So Michael Ryan is a sex addict. So Greg Louganis is abused, closeted, and has HIV. So Katherine Harrison slept with her dad. There is an element of performance art here. The actions described between the covers of these books occur irreversibly in the world where we live. Not fantasy. It happened, so it can't not happen, unless the writers are lying.

This avalanche of memoirs is not being written by Nobel laureates who discover new elements or new planets, unless these geniuses are also addicted to erotic strangulation. The blurb on McCourt's *Angela's Ashes* states, "Boyhood pain and family suffering become as real as a stab in the heart." That must be how we want to feel at century's end, and this wounded heart has spirituality and politics, and bleeds a thrilling torrent of self. Abjection hits the mainstream.

When Chris hears the word *bottom*, he thinks, "Hairy older men to subdue and glorify with camera and tongue." When Bob hears the word *abjection*, even when spoken by himself, his ears perk up: "Isn't that me? Why does the display of shame, loss, grief, and orgasms appeal to me?—to Bob the writer, Bob the homosexual, Bob the citizen?" In art practices of all kinds, abjection undoes modernist heroics like those of the abstract expressionists (action painters/action heroes) and especially the grandiose art gestures of the 80s. Most of the work in our show is small, miniaturizing, mock-heroic. To tell you the truth, it's a scramble downward. If you want to be recognizable, be a bottom. Even the highest office in the land is occupied by an out-of-control bottom who wants to please everyone. We've heard that the definition of a top is the last person to get to the bottom. Who will be left standing?

With these thoughts, we assembled a show in which eleven favorite artists describe eleven views from the bottom: from a sex-positive position that welcomes new beauty ideals onto the stage of history, to one that takes revenge on the dominant culture, to one that asserts the integrity of pathology. If it's not pitiful and a testament to loss, it's not good art. Bottomness can be seen as a position of political and cultural estrangement, an attitude to materials (threadbare, ephemeral, and ugly), or as a kind of vertigo that informs the creative process. We want to demonstrate· the glories of shame, abjection, and awkwardness, as well as honor heroes and heroines of the bottom.

DiDi Dunphy's "samplers" exact a gruelingly hilarious revenge. DiDi makes tiny cross-stitched embroideries in the style of Mondrian and the post–World War II masters. Rather than asserting the glory of woman's work, she makes a record of female exasperation with little stitches and doll-house minimalist forms upholstered in wipe-'n-wash Naugahyde. Her *California Suite* was inspired by Barnett Newman, who observed that sculpture is something you back into when you are looking at a painting.

Scott Hewicker's science-fair aesthetics illustrate a distance from the centers of power and a romance with the failure of mastery over nature. The lines of his topographical cross-sections flow toward the abstraction of a Rorschach test. In his reconstruction of a mountain peak, he takes the all-time symbol for ascendancy and brings it down.

The clarity of Arnold J. Kempe's drawings seems to amplify the confusions they generate—the hash that museums and art markets make of identity issues. The masks make a broken promise of cultural continuity. They already seem to have accession numbers, already seem to hang on museum walls; they are framed by so many conflicting assumptions that finally it is their

'And though I'll cry whenever I hear it
I'll never forget "Smells Like Teen Spirit"'

-teen caller , LIVE 105, May 8, 1994

BUSINESS HOURS:

Mon.	Sad	to	bored
Tues.	Sad	to	bored
Wed.	Sad	to	bored
Thur.	Sad	to	bored
Fri.	Sad	to	bored
Sat.	Sad	to	bored
Sun.	Sad	to	bored

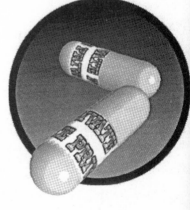

Clockwise: Caitlin Mitchell-Dayton; Cary S. Leibowitz / Candyass; Rolando Mérida; Arnold J. Kemp, *Untitled American Drawings*, 1998, graphite on mylar mounted on paper, 8 × 8 in.; John Lindell, *Milky Way*; Loring McAlpin, *Stella Bersani*; Scott Hewicker; Peter Mitchell-Dayton; Didi Dunphy; Michelle Rollman.

Artwork by Michelle Rollman.

isolation we observe. Who owns them? The African tribes—their original contexts—are the province of the "expert." Even their considerable influence on twentieth-century Western art is framed by our awareness of the imperialism that made such influence possible.

Cary S. Leibowitz / Candyass writes on found materials to articulate an abjection that is psychological—he's "neurotic"—yet so over-the-top that his self-deprecation becomes performance. His assertion of loss is the "before" of every before-and-after, and his work haunts our success-driven culture, where to be unhappy, poor, and insecure is unpatriotic and vaguely threatening.

If the anus is the site of death, it's a death that radiates the glamour of a dark star and interstellar spaces in John Lindell's installation. Whether wedged in the fold of these pages or in the crack of a gallery wall, his elegant wishing star is at once inorganic and ready. As for his dirty bed, something shameful happened there, a shame so intense that it jumped a level of being and became a constellation.

Loring McAlpin's elegant, mirrored *Star-Bersaniani* floats above its shattered self—another icon brought low. It's the shattered nostalgia for Platonic forms. Maybe it's the seventies.

I too have been in Arcadia and it was a pre-AIDS bathhouse or disco dance floor, beads of light splattering vision, brains sizzling on amyl. *Star* is named for a star—the other Leo—in whose work the self is also shattered. We are grateful for Loring's butthole survey and questionnaire, conducted with great rigor on Pork Wednesdays at the L.U.R.E. (Leather, Uniforms, Rubber, Et cetera) which lends our catalog the cachet of urban anthropology.

Rolando Mérida is a Mexican artist who brings multiple points of view and graphic styles to a single drawing. His subject is "real men," by which he means hairy, older, and a little worn. He says, "There is something in a blue collar, a kind of *aura seminalis* in a bushy mustache. I have the urge to draw them on a clean paper. Dirty on clean. No limits on the sheet; one drawing over another, so the page seems to have many drawings playing sex games with each other."

Caitlin Mitchell-Dayton's meticulous celebrity portraits convey an essential awkwardness. Kurt Cobain contorts in the public eye; that is, inside a culture that is a bad fit. The hands and feet of her icons are big with angst and also because sensation resides there, so it's portraiture from the inside. Bob's and Marilyn's uniforms may invoke Genet, desire, and prison, but those painterly stripes and half-erased decisions refer to the abstract expressionists. As Caitlin says, "Once you get your head in a tube, it's all abstraction.

Peter Mitchell-Dayton draws from sixties comics and porn. Like a cat and a canary, each genre becomes more intensely itself in proximity to the other. Neither actually loses its sincerity, yet that is what has been lost. It takes an audience like us to see that these figures are kissing cousins from a simpler era (or a particular childhood). Peter has contributed some *Private Pills* to the catalog. Speed, antidepressant, protease inhibitor?—none of your business. The medicine cabinet is the most public of private arenas. In fact, maybe we take these pills to consume some privacy, like a tonic.

Michelle Rollman turns denizens of kiddy literature into naughty fifties pinups and actors in S/M scenarios. Childhood becomes sexualized and the perversities latent in sentimental children's fare are made explicit. As in other fabliaux, it's all about behavior. These beasts behave unnaturally, as humans do; or too naturally, as humans do. Since we are inclined to attribute animal behavior to instinct, we have to wonder if there is an instinct to kiss a boot, stick a head up an ass. We think it's likely.

Jalal Toufic is a writer, film theorist, and video artist. In 1984 he left Beirut, a city where "nothing (is) left. Not even leaving." The architect Aldo Rossi says the city is a theater of memory; in Jalal's video, that memory is punched full of holes made by bombs. *Credits Included: A Video in Red and Green* records, from inside out, a Beirut shattered by civil war. I say *inside out* because the first section's war-scarred walls are less public than the ravings of the third section's schizophrenic. In his mind the incommensurate politics of the Middle East find a true strategy of last resorts.

We thank these artists for the pages they made that comprise our catalog, and we thank Larry Rinder, Dodie Bellamy, and Gary Indiana as well for giving us their responses to the Bottom. Larry is the Director of the California College of Arts and Crafts Institute; Dodie is the Director of Small Press Traffic, and her long-awaited *Letters of Mina Harker* has just appeared; Gary's latest book is *Resentment*, and his next book will be based on the exploits of Andrew Cunanan.

Finally we dedicate *Bottoms Up!* to Kathy Acker, the greatest bottom of all time, who wrote, "Do you see how easy it is for me to ask to be regarded as low and dirty? To ask to be spat upon? This isn't . . . the sluttishness . . . but the language of a woman who thinks: it's a role. I've always thought for myself. I'm a woman who's alone, outside the accepted. Outside the Law, which is language. This is the only role that allows me to be as intelligent as I am and to avoid persecution."

"Bottoms Up!" was published in *Bottoms Up!* (San Francisco: The Lab Gallery, 1998), an exhibition catalog I coedited with Chris Komater for our co-curated show of the same name.

FROM PATHS *OF* PAIN TO JEWELS *OF* GLORY

The materials in Nayland Blake's sculptures are not so much found or appropriated, as purchased: they retain that first meaning of exchange and equivalence, along with the meanings they collect later. Blake likes homely substances: beans, piss, apple cores. He uses bits of language—ads, songs, pornography— which are also bought and sold. His work has a thrift-store or mass-produced modesty. Blake keeps these materials at the threshold where relation occurs, where they reveal shadow selves (like his preserved substances) or indicate a kind of imaginative order (like his various "devices").

The *Device for Passion* is a kit—a big sponge in a jar of vinegar, a big wooden spoon, and a towel. It's a prop in a libertine's theater of enormity and ritual. Blake applies the rhetoric of sex to the body. *Device for Passion* may be used by a gigantic cleanup committee in the libido where sex is global; the huge sponge and the spoon show how out of scale our bodies are, toy-like and childish.

    The porcelain elements of the *Tea Set* are so generic that they are hard to look at, focus on. They are superfluous as any singular thing that is mass produced in hundreds of versions. Does the bland, common-knowledge quality of classical rhetoric extend to the already-known at Cost Plus? The elements are so abstract that *Tea Set* has a siteless quality, just as a magazine lacks a site, even though its contents may be located in a discourse very much in place. Burnt pornography fills the infuser and the canister—porn as substance to be consumed, taken into the body. By burning

N.H. 1.

the porn, Blake turns the ephemeral commodity, the fragment, into a metaphor for enormity; the little charred specks exert the fascination of a toxic substance. What does it mean that pornography is so threatening a figure—that this tea party is nourished by a ritual of repression?

Burnt Sade (Philosophy in the Bedroom) and *Insulated Pornography* are also ritualized treatments of pornography. In these pieces—book pages covered in wax and lead pigment— Blake frames not an object or a beloved, but a coded system of arousal. Another painting, a verbal readymade, tells the viewer,

DUST.

"Don't hate me because I'm beautiful." Again, a relation or system is being framed, relocated.

These sculptures are calculations and experiments in hysteria; they record the collision of culture and the body in the midst of an epidemic. When they relate to a site, it is to mirror backward the code already anchored there. *DUST* is a flag flown by the STUD (a gay bar down the street from the gallery) with its letters reversed. *DUST* invites the "stud" into art history by putting him in front of an allegorical mirror, like beauty in the old moralities, where his reflection is a skull.

In another relocation, the names that circle the rotunda in the Museum of Modern Art on Van Ness are engraved on plaques and attached to the tips of four cat o' nine tails. The plaques mime the original site's public, architectural quality, while the whips' brand of authority is spelled out on the body, as though art history were "inflicted," as though private sex were public aesthetics. Again, the whips retain their bought quality, the stickers still on, so to speak; they are the idea of whips. Still, the plaques look like they would really hurt. The whips are in briefcases (private) behind glass (public).

The glass in *N.H. 4* (and in Blake's glass containers in general) seems to ask a question about thought: Is it possible to display knowledge? *N.H. 4* is an exhibit in the style of natural history museum. A glass box contains a bobcat head held aloft on metal poles, and a tree fungus sitting on a carved wooden base. The animal head looks fierce, hot, as though the metal poles carried electric current. The fungus looks inert, cold. We experience the two as positive and negative, like parts of a battery. We feel some unwilling complicity with the natural-history museum's practice of taking trophies from nature, an image of endangered plenitude, then realize with a feeling of emptiness that these objects were probably found in the wilderness of Pay & Pack and the Salvation Army. *N.H. 4* attracts and repulses us with the vertigo caused by the animate dead, and by the overlap of different scales of time, animation, and value.

In *N.H. 1* a dead turtle sort of stands in its container, its head thrown back with the drunken festivity of a kite at the end of a string, and we remind ourselves that we are looking at a shel-lacked death agony. Blake mordantly appropriates the good manners and dubious optimism of a high-school science fair—Western Civ's idea of knowledge as taxidermy. The turtle holds a sprig of greenery, like an attic dancer in some spring festival. Written on the plates of its belly—"inscribed" on its shell—are the letters that make up *HYSTERIA*, which brings us back to the actual site of Blake's art, the body and its not-so-natural history.

"From Paths *of* Pain to Jewels *of* Glory" was published as an exhibition catalog for Nayland Blake's show of the same name at Media in San Francisco, 1988.

SMOKE

Mark D'Auria's film, *Smoke* (1993), explores his obsession with fat old men. In the sameness of the erotics displayed in the supposedly diverse films of gay film festivals, it was amazing to see someone lavish attention on these men, and it made me aware that it is far more common in our society to entertain the erotics of murder than the erotics of fat. The film made me aware of how weird we all are. Our community helps me to express my strangeness, but at the same time it asks me to be a normal homosexual.

The sex in the film is so explicit that it will never have general release. The scenes are long, the camera dwells on these men as though they were Rubens's beauties. The hero tends their huge breasts and huge bellies, worshiping flesh that engulfs him. The form of the film mimes the director's obsession. It is a vulnerable statement.

I call Mark's film a happy example of subverting the narrative in at least one of life's departments because it brought a group who were off the beauty map into relation and respect.

"Smoke" was read the Outright Conference, Boston, 1994.

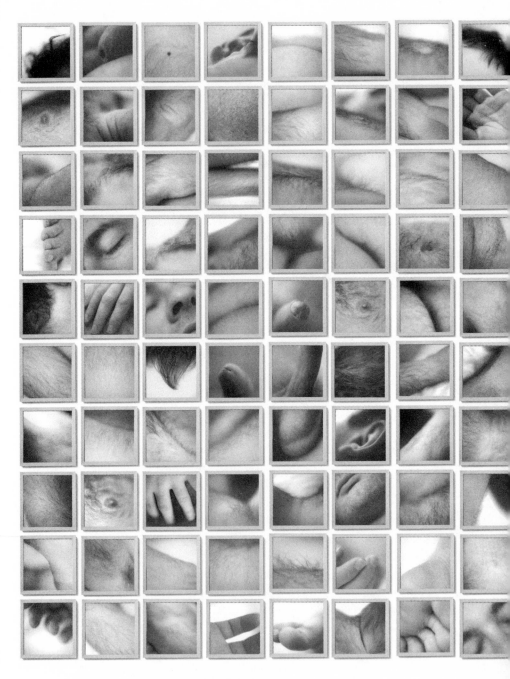

Chris Komater, *Every Inch of Jacek*, 1997.
Eighty framed and toned gelatin silver prints, 63 × 99 in.

CELL

At first glance, Chris Komater's *Out of Breath* resembles any other grid of buttons—the remote for my TV, for example. Then I become aware that the grid on my screen is breathing. The sound generates space and turns the grid into a room. The black means that the room is dark. It's too dark to see, but what would I be looking at? It is big enough for me to enter.

Narratives develop. *Out of Breath* could be a hymn to Genet and his prison cell; close quarters and heavy breathing. Are they in a cell, back room, or bathhouse? A bunkhouse, cabin, or truck-stop toilet? Each breath has been located somewhere on the web, seized, and dragged across an electronic abyss to this black rectangle, so I can say each breath has been taken prisoner. A hymn is musical, and I control the orchestra of breath with a click, so I am the composer. Each instrument has a personality: here's the man trying to contain his pleasure, here's the man allowing pleasure to dismantle him. I imagine most of these lavish sounds actually derive from a variety of other activities; repetition and proximity to each other make them sounds of pleasure. Can we hear behind the rush of breath, say, a swimmer coming up for air? Or a runner struggling toward the finish line? Do these original activities become metaphors for sex?

When I operate this piece, I am summoning a utopia in which we find our identities in the moment of orgasm. We recognize ourselves in disembodied sighs of joy in which meanings proliferate delightfully—because these men have gone over to sex, sex has transformed them into its citizens. In fact, it is sex that breathes—

sex itself strafes these voices, sex categorical. Komater banishes the rest of experience—including the distorting need to become a sexual object that someone can recognize, fuck, and perhaps love.

I used to hear these sounds in bathhouses, the unmistakable shift in register as pleasure took over, the body becoming animal, a loss of control leading to spasms. But that was sex on the hoof, and here sex expresses itself without needing to surmount the constraints of biography, space, and flesh. Is this genre? Pornography stripped of its resistance and shame? I can turn these men on (and off) with a button. Is that arousing?

To this disembodied sex, I enlist my own body and overcome resistance in my own flesh as I make choices that call these frantic breathers into existence. It is up to me to create turbulence. I can't simply turn them all on; I must choose the voices one by one, and so make a crowd. Choose me, says each button, even though it is less than animate. The little space between buttons becomes tense, separating neighbors. We can't see the men so it must be night we are sharing with them. The light on the buttons is the spirit each man possesses.

How much biography can I project onto a particular breath? I would hear this intimate gasping only if his headboard stood against the other side of the wall. Or is he the sinister breather on the phone, another disembodied voice? Is this my own panting in the dark when suddenly I become conscious of it? The agitation of my lover's breath?—I enjoy bringing it to a pitch, the result of my ministrations.

Yet this grating sex-breath is a noise Komater never makes—in fact, he's silent, emitting in the crisis at most a huff. Now he has magnified that little huff a thousand times and suspended it in a grid: twenty-five buttons, play and pause. After ten years together I can count on one hand the occasions when he has made such sounds. Like librarians who write about cataclysms (Georges Bataille), Komater promotes a brand of freedom that he doesn't pursue away from the computer. But perhaps I am barking up the wrong tree, and *Out of Breath* begins with the commotion Komater likes to produce in me, Bob, his noisy partner.

The desire to systemize fragments meets the desire to build a tumultuous environment. Abstraction (flatness, grid) dispatches the collision of personal and public history that shapes any sexuality, as well as the shame of sex, the dirt of sex, the need for sex, and abjection and power. Take those away and what do you have? An essence, a spirit (as breath is spirit) of masculinity? Music? The containment of the uncontainable? An environment that is chaotic and overwhelming? Then I subdue the crowd till only one breather remains.

Komater also enjambs desire and abstraction in his photo grids of skin, such as *Every Inch of Jacek* (1997), but in his earlier installation work he conveyed environment through the ear. In the "western" *High Noon* (1993) he built a Greek chorus of chattering townsfolk, and in *Killer's Kiss* (1991) the audience moved though snippets of Dragon Lady dialogue that twisted the space into film noir. Look for cinema and masculinity in all of Komater's work. *Out of Breath* is not only made out of breath, it alludes to *Breathless* (*À bout de souffle*), Godard's homage to Hollywood gangster machismo.

Later, in *Personals* (1994), Komater mounted as trophies the recorded voices of men responding to a sex ad. You could say *Out of Breath* is a computer installation, but deleting a spatial dimension and leaving sound has created the perfect "environment" for this elegant work. It combines abstraction with the sound of pleasure, the aural image irreducible in a way that a visual image can't be, even a close-up of skin. Where else could *Out of Breath* exist in its intensity and artifice? The shift between depth and no depth, between the fragmented and global—the stuff of the internet—corresponds with the depth and lack of substance of arousal and fantasy.

"Cell" was published online by the Marjorie Wood Gallery, an Internet art gallery, to accompany Chris Komater's May–June 2003 exhibition there.

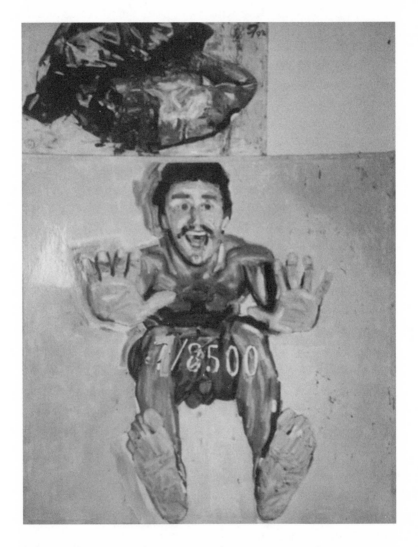

Tom Thompson, *Stack b*, 1985–94. Oil painting, 81.5 × 60 in.
Image courtesy of the artist and Smith Andersen Gallery

TOM THOMPSON

Tom Thompson is one of the best painters I know. What makes him so good? His art leads me into the present—its particular mix of desire, anger, and distance that widens the gap between image and meaning.

If one subject unites Thompson's paintings, it is the assertion of sheer physical being. He has an ardent relationship with the human face and body, right through to its decomposition. Many of his paintings are people more or less thrown together, as they are in our culture. Or more exactly, they are paintings of images, mainly photos, many from magazines, some taken by Thompson himself. Should we respond to the hacked corpse next to the man who's so pink that he jumps with life?—or to the knowledge that Thompson found or took these photos? Guilty and fascinated, we watch the corpse slowly emerge from, give meaning to, and finally tame the tumultuous mess of color it's made of, while, guilty and fascinated, we sneak glances at the naked man splayed in his midair jump. Thompson keeps changing scales: the painting flattens into abstract color and brushstroke—but we can't ignore the price which Thompson writes right across the image, not allowing us to forget that paintings are commodities.

In Thompson's art you can see Soutine's insistence on ugliness, Francis Bacon's evocation of destiny through rendering the body, and behind that Thomas Eakins' love of the canvas and his edgy carefulness. Thompson adds to this his own brand of relentlessness. It's as though he were taking revenge—on what? The viewer? Art history? A civilization gone wrong? Yes, and mortality, and the intolerable loneliness of individual life. Maybe that's why

Thompson's friends so often appear in his paintings, a note of comfort. But again, friendship may vanish as we find ourselves aroused by the image, as though an old friend represented some unknown porn star who was paid fifty dollars to take his clothes off and—what?—get painted?

The essence of this work is collage. Even when a painting depicts just one image, part of our understanding is to wonder how it found its way onto the canvas. I think of the huge haunting face that Thompson painted and repainted many times in his *Military Series*. The mouth is open in need, aggression, and excitement. What does it mean to be excited by men drilling for (probably) World War II?—naïve photos of men participating in a war, rendered in the most sophisticated terms? I follow my desire, estrangement, and shock through Thompson's labyrinth.

"Tom Thompson" was published in the *San Francisco Sentinel*, January 2, 1986.

MANY INFINITIES

In the beginning were the mark and the squiggle. By sticking to these, Dean Smith confines risk to the moment of creation: he puts one mark on paper, then one more, then another. While a few squiggles and marks make a doodle—the record of an artist's inattention—with enough pressure they become a universe. What attracts me to this work is that it is so pared down: here is the mark; here is the universe.

What pressure does Smith apply? His drawings are impossible compositions made up of thousands of discrete marks. There's no way to look at them without thinking of the *performance* involved, as though Smith were undergoing a task in a myth, like sorting a hill of mingled grains. Each picture represents a passage of time; we are obligated to feel that passage. In the old story, Love sets the Soul an impossible task, but ants sort the grains before nightfall with their myriad hands.

The King of Ants is expressive in his desire to help, but the activity of separating grains is not expressive: that is, ants do it. Smith's drawings are made of gestures so small they become mechanical, robotic. Expression is tamped down. The work does not take heat from the artist's application to the page, but there is a particular energy in Smith's exploration of stasis/movement in the act of repetition. Like those other Bay Area obsessives, Jay DeFeo and Bruce Conner, Smith explores a kind of personal limit through repetition both as meditative practice and assertion of brute will. These artists have no problem with beauty; they are not afraid to start in the center and radiate outward. Their art is an impractical allegory on the meaning of freedom: the *object*

Dean Smith, *black hole sun #2*, 2001. Graphite on paper, 51.5 × 50 in.
Collection of Mark Pollack, New York.

resonates with the feeling of "a place to get to"—it rings with
chance and inevitability.

A great labor with pencil and paper usually adds up to
meticulous representation and a display of craftsmanship. Smith
invents his own extremes of craft, the precise mark ad nauseum,
but representation is loose and adaptable. In fact, image may be
a byproduct of his art-making, arrived at from the inside out, as
mysterious to the artist as it is to us. His drawings do not ask for
a particular viewing distance. People gaze at them for a long
while from three or four inches away. There, Smith allies himself

with each individual line, takes each mark seriously. That is, he removes himself from the work by immersing in it. Shapes unfold and expand in response to this marveling attention (his and ours). We become aware of attention as a slow unfolding and we lose ourselves, as the artist did, in reverie that equals a play of surface and freedom from scale.

The drawings are not exactly abstract, yet we are not allowed to "get them," and in that double bind we get an inkling of the strength it takes to live without a story. There are folds: are they magnetic fields, cloth, marcelled hair, something subatomic or geological? Smith builds an incredibly active surface: it pulses and swarms, its flows reverse direction and its contours reverse perspective. Is it a moving topology, animated weather chart, LSD flashback? This richness is achieved in the same way that nature makes a pelt from a zillion single hairs. Like a Rorschach test, Smith's drawings both suggest story and show how chance works against story's seaming inevitability, including the inevitability of the self.

The need to show that experience is at once full and empty is met by intense commitment to a random pattern. Chance plays a formal part in the drawings' execution. A roll of a die determined which of four different grades of pencil would make which velvety disk in *black hole sun #2*. The image is an irregular descending symmetrical phyllotaxis; it's based on the Fibonacci number series, so one is looking at a mathematical system as well as a mandala breaking apart. I'm describing a chaos-theory version of chance that governs magnetic flows, currents of water and wind, currents of gasses and dust, fur patterns and stellar movements.

apex/portal (for R.O.) is a series of repeated lines. Slight accidents—a blip, a tremor—are amplified by the swell of each new line. Four different pens produce four different line densities that create broad stripes, even though the pens are exactly the same color (black), nib size and brand. Perhaps as a perspectival event, *apex/portal (for R.O.)* speaks to the philosophical pyramids of the conceptual/environmental artist Agnes Denes, especially in her example of art-making that encompasses mathematics and philosophy. Denes said, "Pattern finding is the purpose of the mind and the construct of the universe."

untitled is a puzzle. When a drawing radiates and even pulses, one thinks of a universe that radiates its principles of time and space. But how can a universe emanate from *two* points? Perhaps the two images—separated by a harsh juncture—relate to each other like images on a filmstrip, showing the same universe sequentially. Or the drawing could take its form from the body, the two starting points as eyes or nipples. The drawing seems diagrammatic, but of what?

In their slow accumulation, Smith's drawings have something of the grandeur of science rather than "lived" experience, like the achievement of naming the thirty thousand genes of our DNA. *principle* reminds me of early scientific illustration, before philosophy, theology, and science separated into discrete fields. In the eighteenth century, the word *science* was used to describe knowledge of all sorts, and the first response to a phenomenon was wonder. I am thinking of William Charles Wells, a British physician who studied dew. Each night he placed balls of cotton in the grass and under shrubs, and each morning he weighed them to determine how much dew had fallen. Mr. Well's self-imposed task was not without risk; he died of a consumptive condition attributed to crawling at night in wet grass. His work combined simplicity of method, empiricism, statistics, and wonder. I find the same delight in Smith's drawings, as though pattern is the truth behind local instances of thought, perception, and weather, as well as the grand orchestras of matter and energy.

Dean Smith's allegiance to the smallest unit seems almost impossible, an impoverishment and rethinking of scale. His art is founded on this contradiction; it is threadbare and incredibly rich. By reinventing scale, he has found a way to bring spirit, philosophy, and science together again; they speak without conflict from the same page.

"Many Infinities" was published in Dean Smith's exhibition catalog *Drawings 2001* (Santa Monica: Christopher Grimes Gallery, 2001).

BETWEEN LIFE AND DEATH

> When you turn your head,
> can you feel your heels, undulating?—that's what it is
> to be a serpent.
>
> —Frank O'Hara

Say I live in a Frank Moore painting. The difference between my life and death is a distinction on one level alone. From the point of view of the countless viral particles, fungal spores, and bacteria that swarm in each breath I take and across every surface I touch, my death is as incidental as some exploding nova would be to me as I write this. Or my death equals the extinction of an entire species. That is, all life crawls, runs, swims, flies through all life in elated permeability. Nature is swarm and flux whether it occurs in a sickbed, a national park, or the imagination. Exotic DNA zigzags through us like the silver stripe through the Bride of Frankenstein's coiffure. There is no distinction between my social life and the earth's other events. "I am nature," said Jackson Pollock. Frank Moore says, "New York is a glittering multicelled, accreted structure—as much an expression of our species as a coral reef is an expression of coral polyps."

At the same time, we are all specialists. A fungus lives on tree roots and breaks down nourishment, making it available to the tree. The proboscis of a certain moth evolves to suck nourishment in the form of blowjobs. An eagle evolves human hands, the better to seize a boom box midair. The subject is always an ensemble of forces and interactions, who nevertheless inhabits the niche of his own specialty. The man in the officer's uniform makes a particular kind of sex happen.

Compassion extends to the damaged cell and to the wronged universe. That is how Moore can paint aphids and invalids with such tenderness. That is how a painting of a deer in a deforested forest can generate wonder. There are villains, but that is not the real story. The shift downward in scale, downward into narrative, is the story. From nineteenth-century awe to twentieth-century dismay, nature becomes part of our own *story* of the sublime. Instead of losing ourselves in nature, nature loses itself in us. Moore insists on the persistence of beauty within this transformation and relates it to the systems of the body; that is, he grounds it in autobiography and paints it with a luminosity that carries its own message of amazement and even joy.

Wildlife Management Area (1990), *Yosemite,* (1996)

A deer startles in the stream, but it's already a trophy, because this so-called wilderness is no better than a game park where the state manages timber and provides hunting and fishing for sportsmen. The grouse already hangs in a shooting gallery.

The animals and land are struck dumb by horror; nature has lost its voice, which is replaced by the words "State Reforestation Area." Moore is certainly making an indictment against habitat fragmentation and blood sport, but there is also the question of the light switch and kitschy lamps, which allow me to go past the plane of the picture, but only after a struggle. Does perspective alone draw me into this blue wasteland?

The painting is a lamp. Moore cut a hole in the canvas to install the push-button switch, and the sconces are juicy collectables; the shades are embellished with duck hunters in a blind. Moore cut down a tree from his own landscape to fashion the "rustic" frame, and the antlers came from hunting trophies. If the painting itself is a trophy that depicts a trophy, am I the hunter? Circles of involvement widen. Nailed to the painted tree is an actual sign that Moore found in the woods near his home in Deposit, New York. If there's a them, I am also them.

As a boy, Moore spent summers at his grandfather's house in the Adirondacks. In fact, the first art Moore recognized was in the WPA style of those summers: Thomas Hart Benton, John Steuart Curry, and hunting and fishing pictures. (Later, Moore was drawn to the magic realists Peter Blume and Paul Cadmus: WPA surrealists.) In a vintage lodge Moore saw lovely old murals of hunting scenes. At some point the innkeeper had decided to electrify his establishment, so they chopped channels through this mural and laid clumsy white patches of plaster wherever there was a light switch. The murals depicted a virginal landscape which was actually being violated by the presence of the lodge, and now the virginal depiction was violated by another hand. In this way, Moore's picture becomes an emblem of its own violation, enacting layers of need and desire, of spiritual anxiety. At the same time, this landscape-lamp is a fabulous object. Who is the hunter, who is the consumer, what is the trophy, what is being preserved?

Wildlife Management Area impersonates a kitschy Adirondack lamp; its giant descendant, *Yosemite*, is a 10 x 12 ft. postcard in the same rustic-souvenir style. Moore collected pinecones for the frame on a Yosemite camping trip. The painting—Moore's largest and one of his bluest—depicts a culture that loves a national park to death. The valley walls are made of photo-silk-screened money; tiny rock climbers scale their heights. If Yosemite National Park is a giant garden, then the valley is a human zoo, a Macy's parade complete with Mickey and Yosemite Sam. Bears are a focus of cultural confusion: campers feed them, but when the bears lose their fear of humans, rangers must remove or kill them. On the left, targeted bears scavenge in the trash; in the center, the wiseacre Yogi Bear—"Better than the average bear"—strolls along with his sidekick, Boo Boo; at the right, a child drags a giant teddy bear that Moore saw on sale in the concession stand at the Ahwahnee Hotel.

This antigarden is not silenced like the flora and fauna of *Wildlife Management Area*. Permanent cartoon horror animates the giant sequoias. The tree ringed by "the human family" seems just as appalled as the tree with a tunnel cut through its trunk. Their Medusa crowns rustle—the rattle of diamond-backs. There was a campaign to rid the park of these rattlesnakes, sacred to the Miwok.

At the eye of the hubbub, naturalist John Muir sits on his own tombstone. His example and values have long dominated the discourse on wilderness. At his feet, a campfire sends infinity signs into the sky, and other campfires broadcast smoke signals that stand for desires and values which Yosemite must accommodate—a noisy iconic babble about the role these parks play in our lives. Moore's pop, cartoon version of nature plays off the sublime of Muir, Albert Bierstadt, and Frederic Church; still, *Yosemite* inspires awe based on its scale, tilting perspective, and majestic twilight-blue.

Niagara (1994), *Maid of the Mist* (1994–95), *Niagara* (1994–95)

Maid of the Mist, 1994–95. Oil on canvas over wood panel with copper frame and pipe attachments, 60 × 96 in.

From 1993 to 1995 Moore painted a grandly scaled series on Niagara Falls. These paintings convey a feeling of genetic threat, urban encroachment, toxic destruction. They are sermons, like *Peaceable Kingdom* or *Expulsion from the Garden of Eden,* except in this garden death prospers by our own hand. The Niagara paintings also convey a feeling of rapture; their tremendous beauty helps to build that paradise.

Niagara is a complex symbol. A glamorous Niagara fashion spread in the *New York Times Magazine* marvels, "Finally, something larger than yourself." It is describing a superfund site and one of the most polluted bodies of water in the United States.

Moore observes, "There should be a German six-word compound that says, *I-go-into-a-virgin-ecosystem-and-as-soon-as-I-set-foot-in-it-I-turn-it-into-my-own-inner-likeness.*" Consciousness has a ferocious need to see its own reflection; in Eden, the first thing Adam did was to name the animals. The more we touch the world, the more it exteriorizes our inner being. For example, in 1890 Eugene Schieffelin released sixty starlings in Central Park because he wanted to bring all the birds that appear in Shakespeare to the USA. Now the starling is a notorious pest, pushing the purple martin and eastern bluebird to the point of extinction.

Moore worried about the vapors he inhaled going under the falls ("It's better than an Evian atomizer," sighs the fashion spread) because AIDS makes him vulnerable. He requested a copy of the federally mandated *Toxic Release Inventory* from Great Lakes United, an advocacy group, and learned what a mess the lakes are.

Moore holds up a mirror to our own mirror making. Whatever we are, that's what Niagara Falls has become—there's a kind of wonder in that. Moore framed his *Niagaras* with copper pipe and faucet handles, a reminder that the falls generally run at forty percent, the rest diverted into hydroelectric turbines. With a length of copper tubing, Moore represents our planet's hydrosphere as a closed circuit.

Niagara (1994–95) is the key to the series. Moore lays out the two falls in a grand horizontal that includes the industrialized American shore, the Maid of the Mist, and a video camera. Moore based his view on Church's *Niagara*, but these are hardly the falls that Church encountered in 1857; now we turn them on and off. Moreover, a video-based visual culture has replaced painting as the medium we use to teach ourselves to see: today's Niagara is not paint on canvas, but pixels on a monitor.

In the first great vertical of *Niagara* (1994), water braids itself as it crashes down. Alchemical symbols wash onto a stony beach, the detritus of our search for spiritual perfection through science. Some of the symbols, like the one for Mercury, appear in modern form in the mist. In the second great vertical, the poisoned breath of the falls swirls up and seems to resemble ape and human skulls: ecosystem decay, unraveling of habitat, consumption of resources, and the icy beauty of the twining double helix, crystalline and impersonal, disinterested. These photo-silk-screened chemicals undermine or destroy the human genome—a bitter, mocking parody of DNA. Meanwhile, the falls thunder downward, wowing us tourists; somehow, we are the first humans to set foot here. Moore puts the same words in our mouth that Edward Hicks used in 1825 to frame his own painting of the Falls: "This great o'erwhelming work of awful Time / In all its dread magnificence sublime."

If *Niagara* displays our dystopia, *Maid of the Mist* shows that dystopia's spiritual side. Tourists approach the falls in a ritual manner, and the donning of this attraction's electric-blue hooded raincoats gives its passengers a monastic uniformity that belies the information Moore inserts into those blue masses. The tension between the painting's cerulean bodies and ultramarine coats creates a feeling of volume. The figures are so solid and so transparent that they put me on the verge.

The painting is structured as a triptych, a *Last Supper*. A glow emanates from behind Christ; since I see his skeleton, perhaps he is a spirit, or dead. Perhaps he is the martyred falls. The Maid of the Mist was a Native American who sacrificed herself to bring water to her tribe by interceding with a snake god. You can find its head in the spray; now the snake is the chemical manufacturers who dump a witch's brew into the Great Lakes Basin.

Moore is calling for health as these human forms dissolve in toxic mists. There are no villains on board, only tourists transformed into votaries of a mystery cult whose strange joy exists as a contradictory hush inside the falls' thundering.

Gulliver Awake (1994–95)

Gulliver Awake, 1994–95. Oil on canvas on panel in enamel frame, 40 × 72 in.

Gulliver is bound to a chalky pharmaceutical landscape; he has AIDS. He is a social phenomenon captured by a mélange of figures that give his life shape and story. He's a big meaty guy, strong sexually; he displays that strength generically, his flesh dense and pouty like a Tom of Finland beefcake. He litters the landscape with handcuffs, butt plug, crushed K-Y tubes, rubbers. The ropes binding him (homophobia?) are eroticized, and the alchemy of role-playing transforms the familiar authority of his officer's uniform into sexual force. The jacket's warm ultramarine crackles with energy, while the call to pleasure shrinks and bleaches the rest of his life in utter estrangement, a monochrome of thalo green, a nasty color from a hospital or a chemistry set.

Gulliver is beautifully modeled; his leather pants are gorgeous. The characters animating this chaotic little country are painted simply. Different idioms for different lives. They remind me of Grandma Moses' New England: a view of citizens inhabiting their separate niches, a spectrum of adaptations filling a landscape/farmscape with bustling activities, a (disjunct) vernacular music. Sometimes the figures are riddles: mother offers an apple—how *is* mom an Eve, tempting us with what seductions? Or is it the apple that keeps the doctor away? The naïveté of

Moore's rendering equals his subjects' faith in their ways of being and living.

Gulliver may be a universal symbol and cultural metaphor, but that does not evict him from his own ecological niche. He's gay, *obviously*. He's a bottom, *obviously*. His uniform tells us he wants power relations in sex to be overt. He speaks from that position to the person topping him; he recognizes that call to pleasure. He's looking up, getting up; his health improves, his body clamors, there's a different flavor in him. He wants to exceed himself physically. A moment of ecstasy: arousal stirs each cell in his body like a simmering pot.

Moore gives him an ancient Arabic poem to offer. Desire creates belief, so it's a prayer:

> Here's the prayer of a corpse
>   spoken with the living voice of a man
> beaten by so many blows
>   *between life and death*
>   *that nothing is left—a body*
>   *almost invisible, but here.*

He speaks marveling, not to us, not even to the man who can save him by merely batting his lashes, but lost in elated contemplation like a Bellini saint.

Arena (1992), *Wizard* (1994)

The AIDS pandemic cuts through our symbols, hierarchies, and institutions like a laser. Moore renders what AIDS reveals: political hypocrisy, greed of the pharmaceutical companies, silence of education, class inequality and racism of healthcare, the losses sustained by the arts, the refiguring of sexual identities and practices. *Wizard* is the apotheosis of these paintings. It draws us into a majestic bewilderment, a grand scape with intense details, like a *Last Judgment* whose general annihilation needs to be unpacked: the glass ball means vanity, the iris means *strengthened by persecution*, the toad means . . . Or, perhaps closer to the mark,

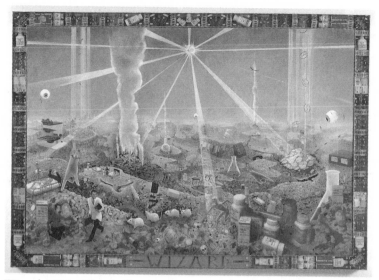

Wizard, 1994. Oil and silkscreen on canvas with artist's frame, 68 × 95.5 in.

Wizard is folky in its blend of the didactic and the fantastic. I stand at a *reading* distance from the painting. The world may be ending, but it's going up in a blaze of scorched symbols.

Moore painted *Wizard* at a time when he was making trips to Marseille to participate in the research of Jean-Claude Chermann, a maverick who had been directly involved with the identification of the retrovirus HIV-1 at the Pasteur Institute in Paris. Now Chermann is devoting his life to finding a vaccine that will be useful in Sub-Saharan Africa, where the bulk of AIDS infections occur.

Wizard is spectacularly beautiful; it causes a spectacular rift in me because the disordered wasteland—a phantasmagoria swarming with incident—roils below a spiritually ordered cosmos whose point of origin is a splitting cell that is also a sun, the first principle and source of life. Or is it a metastasizing star? Its rays strike a pile of money, burning coffins, and a leopard man whose KS lesions are leopard spots. He's a fierce predator, an activist on the prowl for medication and a cure. He picks up the scent of the scientist—a portrait of Chermann—who leads his laboratory rats on a Yellow Brick Road right to the edge. Will he track the doctor to the edge of the world? To the cast Lucite frame? The frame is four inches square and embedded with pharmaceuticals, AIDS journals, lab equipment, syringes and bottles of Zovirax that morph into photo-silk-screens of Zovirax bottles in the painting, bottles which become boulders in the landscape.

As though *Wizard* were a painting by Hieronymus Bosch, I am fixated by my need to decipher. I find hospital beds and the French names of different strains of HIV from Africa, Europe, and the United States. There's a telephone, its receiver off the hook. The hyperrealism of the bottles and boxes of meds isolates them in a kind of hope, while a funeral pyre consumes the coffins of Moore's friends and colleagues. I may behold the end of the world, but the parched landscape is based on the same American vernacular as Thomas Moran's *Chasm of the Colorado*. Negative space can become positive in that wilderness of sharp edges; the devil pops out of the flipped volumes of the gullies and arroyos. Moore copied that image from a cheap paperback of Goethe's *Faust*. Is Faust the white-smocked doctor? Above the badlands, the positions of the three floating eyes suggest that the fourth belongs to me. They are heartless observers of the plague; perhaps they are journalists without a personal stake.

Wizard derived from *Arena*, an earlier painting. In *Arena*, Moore's lover Robert is dying; his spirit ascends. The nine rings of the operating theater recall the architecture of Dante's *Inferno*, while sci-fi chemical robots seem to gesture in dismay at the antiquated medical practices and attitudes. The poet John Giorno, who introduced Moore to the Nyingmapa sect of Buddhism, meditates in one corner along with Ayang Rinpoche and the Buddha Amitabha; friends from Act Up storm in from the other side; a human hide drapes across a mother's forearms as though her son has become a deflated balloon. A skeletal "Steve" offers a phallic pear to a skeletal Adam—goodbye innocence—and lab skeletons of animals wait attentively for Robert to join them. Human skeletons carry banners with Latin mottos—*We Are Shadows and Dust, Birth is the Beginning of Dying*—while in the foreground pretty-boy purveyors of eternal youth discover that their strong bodies are actually bundles of fragile chemical processes.

Arena was Moore's first work where every element has a direct link to his life. He was painting, but also composing a nonlinear autobiography in which an episode is a hub where lines of meaning converge. Autobiography at once unites the painting thematically as a description of Moore's life and requires fragmentation in order to portray that life. Moore alone understands some of the images in *Arena*, yet their very specificity ties his fate to his community's fate.

Moore grafted AIDS activism onto an already developed politics of global ecology. In paintings like *Arena* and *Niagara*, the worst is already happening, and like earlier painters of Last Judgments, Moore strives for total visibility. *Wizard* blows up the personal ecology of loss into an apocalypse—the painting of a plague. The map of a plague. *Wizard* is a form of collective ritual, and it asks this question: What is the threshold of collective catastrophe—of extinction?

Patient (1997–98), Lullaby (1997), Beacon (2001)

Lullaby, 1997. Oil on canvas over featherboard with red pine frame, 50 × 65 in.

A herd of bison roams an empty bed in *Lullaby*. In *Patient* that same bed hosts the onset of winter and becomes the source of a waterfall that carries downward the last autumn leaves and blood from an IV drip. In *Beacon* the patient is back, but water has flooded the painting, a vast ocean on which his bed lists and founders. The imagination that brought winter into the sick room seems to have lost control: all nature becomes a blue hospital across which the beam of a lighthouse broadcasts a double helix of DNA. The sea voyage is a symbol for life beset by danger. Like Gulliver, the patient raises his torso and looks outward with a rapt expression; he's looking for a new world.

Moore's mother sang "Home on the Range" as a lullaby, opening a nocturnal frontier. *Oh give me a home where the buffalo roam, Where the deer and the antelope play.* The unconscious plays in bed. Moore has spent too much time in hospital beds, and the sickbed will have its symbols. The buffalo roam in a *weltschmerz* of childhood and American loss. Their toy-acceptance of the bed as a prairie brings us to the fragility of the species, their inability to recognize their own irrelevance. A single buffalo strays away from interpretation, looks out over the cliff of the mattress, staring off into space. It seems to say: *This painting glows in a way you can't account for. There's light and you don't know where it comes from.*

A patient departs, taking with him the overheated subjectivity of the sickbed. *Patient* records his absent heat—his life in death. He is absent, and he leaves his absence behind, which is somehow uncorrupted. The end comes as a chill tended by the rest of creation. The autumn leaves, the water spilling downward, and the polluting blood are the patient himself. Intimacy and distance intensify each other, generating great tenderness in the face of harm.

Moore photo-silk-screens images on the surfaces of many paintings—here it's snowflakes. These images don't challenge three-dimensional space, but float above the most contemplative works, as they do in *Angel*. They assert the plane of the picture, like a painted cornice in a fresco by Piero della Francesca. That is, they remind me that the painting is an object of contemplation, an aide to meditation in a process that wants to change me.

In the Garden (1995), *With This Ring* (2000)

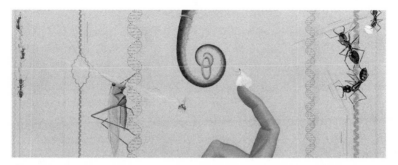

With this Ring . . ., 2000. Oil on canvas on featherboard, 37 × 95 in.

One definition of a species is that the production of fertile off-spring takes place only among its members, a gene pool. Drawing on the potential of genetic engineering, Moore redefines species as the totality of life itself. In genomic terms, one life form is really not so different from another—technically, we are all marriageable.

The unhindered mixing of genes creates the lilting magic of *In the Garden,* a suite of paintings that Gianni Versace commissioned: *The Client, A Midsummer's Night, Black Narcissus, B.J.,* and *Survival of the Fattest.* Each of these blue paintings features a different green. These works seem indebted to Victorian fairy painters, like Richard Dadd and Joseph Noel Paton, in their erotic preciousness and creation of pixilated ecologies though intensity of detail. The divinities in these paintings are fantasies of genetic manipulation. Here is Edenic nature before God decides who gets wings and who fucks what. Adaptive radiation is in process: the insects and the divinities mate, cross-pollinate; butterfly-boys evolve wings in the latest couture designs; a Venus of Willendorf's wings attach at her nipples; a hermaphrodite draws a hollyhock carriage bearing Isis; a dragonfly ravishes a man in a lotus boudoir—spawning a new winged species?

There's a sense of rich time; the human, natural, and divine have united in the garden of Moore's house and studio in Deposit. Maybe that's why the windows are black even though it's daytime—the human abandons his house, life, and genetic destiny. Moore says, "That flower grows out of the soil—it's atavistic and Shinto and wild primitive savage raw sexual—even to make an image means you're polytheistic."

In *With This Ring*, a bride is entering into holy wedlock with an octopus. That is, a finger reaches for the gold ring; the little bride is its idea. Moore based her on a wedding photo of Jacqueline Bouvier, the goddess who reproduced for us all. Her veil lengthens her body, the reproductive body of the nation, as though she teams with eggs like a termite queen. At the same time, she can read Maeterlinck in French, and her support of the arts promises a spiritual fruition. Jacqueline speaks in that whisper of hers, which is like the other whisper of the age, that of Jackie's twin opposite, Marilyn. You must draw closer to hear, which may be the idea:

> *Everything's so pink! Weather by Cassini! It reminds me of Charles Ludlum! I knew him! Now he's extinct! Our reflections! Our obstinate teleology! Our hopes and our admiration! Are simply the unknown! Where we bump against something even more obscure! So we can make a little noise! Which brings us to! The highest consciousness! We can attain! Just as the song of the nightingale! Reveals the highest consciousness! Proper to its species! So sing my pink opera! I'm on a carrousel! Reaching for the brass ring! Of reproduction!*

Because of its size and the tenderness of its depiction, the grasshopper seems to claim a spiritual life not based in subjectivity. Let's make it the minister presiding over this marriage. The grasshopper is an emblem of bad husbandry, yet its organ of stridulation is silent—no fiddling—and no justice of the peace was ever so greenly genial. In their exquisite social order, ants are an emblem of good husbandry; they flank the painting, climbing strands of DNA in an ecstasy of information. They farm aphids on one side and on the other side carry genes for collagen and chitin (human and insect proteins) as though getting ready to trade skins.

Moore's thumbprints are part of the mottling on the octopus's skin. The octopus and the insects are so lovingly rendered, they are realized in the double sense of the word, discovered through the process of painting. Another way to say that: they display their mystery while preserving it.

The color is fresh, almost musical, local color playing off an overall pink that radiates health as an aroused, transparent weather. It's a rare Moore painting that isn't blue. The pink shines: the paint was applied, brushed out, glazed, painted, brushed out, until color became depth. Moore uses a variety of finishes in one painting, like the impasto that becomes the sheath of aphid bodies. The variations on matte and shiny make the figures 3-D as I move around them.

Everything I Own (1992), Angel (1996), Oz (2000)

Everything I Own gathers Moore's possessions into his contorted hands, an inventory of belongings held in a mudra, a gesture of offering. Everything I hold dear—to be tossed into the air? The hands are severed at the wrists as though to isolate this activity of holding worldly goods, or to suggest that the body too must be jettisoned. I'm reminded of the death-forward spirituality of Tibetan skull cups. The simplified renderings and toy scale turn the goods into doll furniture—a severe autobiography. The objects seem curiously stable, yet thwarted and frustrated, like dead people's things. From the standpoint of my death, I see the finite number and limited character of my possessions and, more incredibly, that their life span exceeds my own *despite* their limitations: my mirror will no longer reflect my image.

As though I'm solving a procedural mystery, I want *proof* that an afterlife exists, and *Angel* offers the classic forensic evidence: footprints. Human footprints disappear into the distance; the angel, now graduated from spatial relation, walks in the sky back into our world.

Angel can be approached as a riddle, like the Sphinx's: Who walks away a human and returns an angel? Yourself. Or it is the path of a Bodhisattva who travels through the gate of his own skeletal arms? Even in winter, blackberries grow through our human bones, absorbing nutrition from our flesh. Flowers growing from corruption—is that proof of sainthood, or simply what always happens? The wintry view takes in Sunset Rock in Deposit. There's the setting sun without warmth, or is it "the light"?

The painting is rather empty and too centered for comfort. Its movement is like a fan blowing cold air across an empty room. Snow empties the world of color, then color returns as it does on a snowy day—the red of the forest, the snow-darkened Prussian blue of the air, the clear cobalt-blue of the snow, blue conveying a sense of divine presence. Chunks of discarded anatomy—jaw, spine, and cerebellum—emerge from the meat red of the forest. The angel does not want a body or a body's heat, let alone a possession. As a possession, the painting itself is like the body of an angel surrounded by wings, a beautiful encumbrance.

Finally, *Oz*, Moore's rueful comedy on the history of objects. People stand on hills made of their possessions. They have accepted their identities—that is, their lives equal their possessions, which in turn display the hostile inertia of matter. It's as though each of these people is described by his own chaotic sentence. Each takes in the view from his turf, isolated by his belongings and desires, values and traditions. Symbols for defective chromosomes cover a teepee, an allegory for the genetic ghettos created when American Indians were confined to reservations. Moore declines to distinguish one variety of isolation from another, a human fate from the fate of a gene pool. His density of reference is close to poetry, another kind of landscape. The horizon is a strand of DNA where fantastic structures fashioned from DNA offer the benefits of the genetic revolution.

A Swarm

In many of Moore's paintings there's a swarm, an area of flux, the visual location of potential that rises from chaos or sinks back into it: tumults of sperm shapes and whirlpools roil in sky or water; convulsive landscapes of rubble are also inventories of a world becoming at once more fragmentary and more global; mists and clouds seethe with snakes, skulls, and chemical symbols. These areas seem to extend outward or downward, past the floor of the painting into the world that generated them and everything else. They stand as shorthand for a contradiction: the paintings' high finish conveys a sense of completion, while these convulsive areas assert incoherence and change.

Say I live in a Frank Moore painting; I am a swarm of genetic possibilities that extends from my body to the horizon. Like Niagara, I am a new system overlaid on an old system; I'm awash in chemicals invented in the last fifty years whose effects I can't imagine. I acknowledge that the greed, ambition, and need that pollute and deforest reflect a horrifying aspect of myself. Still, fabulous science untangles DNA and my very life hangs on the advances made by wizards of research. The potential for harm is great, but my terror does not obscure the fact that there is a new measure to learn. That is, I reconsider my discomfort and try to integrate the chaos of my daily life with this genetic risk and promise.

In the first place, I accept that there is no spot on the earth free of my presence. If the picture that contains a cheetah does not also contain my smashed Coke can, then a less visible product, just as raucously man-made, is busy shaping and destroying. In the second place, I am more permeable than I can imagine. My colon is a county fair of friendly bacteria; my immune system is a Mardi Gras of mitochondria wearing exotic masks. When I reject the opposition between myself and the rest of nature, wonder replaces terror. I redefine my health as an enormous complex web, an ecology. I enter an enchanted realm whose magic is simply that I coexist with other organisms. Under the equals sign of marriage and sex, an octopus and Jacqueline Onassis have the same value, and the moth that blows me is my inferior only if I replace philosophical merit with the right of the strongest.

Wonder can be a form of activism; Moore deploys a language of wonder, four-square, wide-eyed. He paints his mighty subjects with innocence and with a highly controlled palette: the modulation of warm and cool blues. Mary's mantle is the blue of contemplation; *Der Blaue Reiter* is the blue of mystical nature; Miles Davis's *Kind of Blue* is a still lake of sound. I think Moore's blue is the color of our dear planet, our bright organism, a blue of compassion and wonder.

"Between Life and Death" was published as the introduction to *Between Life and Death* (Tucson: Twin Palms, 2002), a book of Moore's paintings.

THREE

NARRATIVE BENT

BOB'S FUNDAMENTALIST MOVEMENT

A few years ago I discovered that my Bar Mitzvah portion—that is, the part of the Torah I read to the congregation in Hebrew and considered in English in the form of a little sermon—was the story of Sodom and Gomorra. It confirmed in my mind, for ten minutes or so, that there really is such a thing as predestination, at least when it comes to homosexuality. Haven't you noticed that the queer member of the family is the one with the fruity name? There's Bill and Fred and John and *Stanley*. There's Pete and Ed and Bob and *Loring*.

In my speech I did not question the story. I sided with God and pointed out that he is actually very fair and even kind because he issues the town a warning before annihilating everyone. What choice did I have? I was facing the entirety of my life as a social being, they were the audience, and I already felt unmasked—outed by God himself. Sodom and me. At thirteen, I knew annihilation lay ahead. I'd already had my warning: homosexuality the disease, homosexuality the crime. If I had defended the crimes of Sodom, the congregation would have stoned me. For the condemned man, stalling for time equals fighting for his life.

You may recall that Sodom, though guilty of every abomination, was nuked for the crime of inhospitality to God's angels, a crime that all of us can recognize and condemn. It seems only by chance that homosexuality finds its way into the story, like a bill before Congress in which a seemingly unrelated issue, like the desecration of arctic wilderness, is grouped "inside" a measure pertaining, say, to highway improvements in New Jersey. People can say no to inhospitality to angels and yes to improved highways without saying no to homosexuality. The thought will be continued for us.

As if to assert the idea that hospitality and heterosexuality are the same thing, Lot offers his own daughters to the riotous townsfolk in order to divert their lust from God's angels. I think those young women have a unique point of view in this tale. I would like nothing better than to have sex with God's angels. The desire to have sex with God's angels seems natural to me—in fact, more natural than desires less supernatural. The angels were equipped for the occasion with human flesh and they wanted to take that brand-new meat and drive it around the block. There's no question who would be on top: the glory of hospitality belongs to the one who entreats the guest to enter. Now that I'm really imagining it, I am going to take a twenty-minute break from this essay, goodbye.

It's lucky I have a skylight! Heavy French clouds roll though my body. It's odd how they spread my knees apart almost wider than they can go. And then: Lightning and Thunder! I am too splayed, too off balance to—what—resist even a little? I am *all* hospitality, as though I'm a character in *Angels in America*, but luckier! I am delivering my Bar Mitzvah speech over again—Dear Friends and Family, in our community let's marry homosexuality to hospitality. The Bible shows us that the whole fucked-up warring world would be a lot better off if everyone just marched into my butthole. Let's say with T. S. Eliot, "In my end is my beginning." Let's say with Eddie Floyd, "It's like thunder and lightning / The way you love me is frightening!" We offer God's angels the hospitality of our fundaments, so we call ourselves Fundamentalists!

"Bob's Fundamentalist Movement" was published in *Animal Shelter*, no. 4, eds. Hedi El Kholti and Robert Dewhurst (Spring 2015).

FOUR ON EMPTINESS

1) When I was a potter in the sixties and seventies, there was nostalgia in the field for the shaping of bowls and vessels—the ancient activity of enclosing a particular emptiness with a shape whose use and beauty are exactly the same, different only in the words that describe them. So throwing a pot on the wheel I could live in a myth and be emptiness inviting form into existence, as the Song dynasty pots seem to do; or I could battle for existence against the rigors of emptiness, as the Zen pots seem to do. If content empties, then story migrates to form. I even made closed spheres whose function was to contain nothing.

2) I wonder if that's why Keanu Reeves is so popular. There's something sixties about him. Does his cult suggest a kind of retro awareness of nothingness as an aesthetic pleasure? But not like pottery, not nostalgia for imminence, more like goofing on chaos theory—the emptiness of statistics. Like a bowl, I want to lift him for a moment to display the lack of stimulation, his exalted materiality and his inclination to flatten out of existence. The world is too bored to concentrate on a book. Keanu pauses while descending a staircase. He's information.

3) It seems to me there is a knot in experimental writing that consists in approaching the present (real time), which creates fragmentation, around which emptiness (silence, porousness) is displayed, which in turn makes words and the cogs and wheels of narration more opaque than they normally are. This tangle of operations is set off by the desire to make art that represents or

participates in the present, which is impossible to bring into words because it does not yet/can never exist in that form.

You can subtract meaning from language—but does meaninglessness also go? Is that the flip side? *In order for the sign to have an exterior, a boundary line, the referent must exist, if only as a phantom* (Agamben).

In my novel *Margery Kempe*, I wanted to compose certain sections of topic sentences, so that each sentence arises from the silence of beginnings, before speech, and delivers the possibility of a new world. Each sentence is a kind of promise, an increment of hope that replaces the broken promise of the last sentence. What is that promise? That the world will continue, that one image will replace the next forever—that is, the world will respond to your love by loving you back. The silence is that of a world about to be born.

4) But it could also be that of a grave, the last word. Ed, my dying friend, said, "My death is an emptiness that I can't fill."

"Four on Emptiness" was published in *Non*, no. 1, ed. Laura Moriarty (October 1997).

ARCHITECTURE AS FATE

For the last few years, San Francisco and New York have been trading places as the number one and number two tourist destinations *in the world*. Not Rome, not Tokyo. The two leading consumer travel magazines, *Condé Nast Traveler* and *Travel + Leisure*, name San Francisco the top US city destination. Tourists spend more than $5 billion annually in my little city. It's impossible not to be affected—I often feel like a tourist here myself. I'll bet Romans do not feel like tourists in Rome, with their strong division between public and private life. This division has its architectural expression: the façades of their buildings are closely regulated to harmonize with other antiquities, while inside anything goes. You can step through a sixteenth-century portal into a sleek eighties interior. It's not pleasant, but you can.

I look out my study window. There's the buttery light and impossible view: city, bay, bridge. The dazzle in the air puts the gingerbread details in unreal focus. This vista *is* San Francisco. I feel pleasurable déjà vu writing about this vista directly: it resists thought because it's so overexposed. The films and drippy photos projected onto the culture's psychic screen make me feel that everyone got here ahead of me, and so did I.

Much of San Francisco's charm derives from the neighborhoods of Victorian architecture that remain intact: mansions, row houses, earthquake cabins. In the seventies, I worked as a ghostwriter for an illiterate in the Redevelopment Agency, and together we managed to demolish a little neighborhood. I still feel guilty, but also relieved that our stupendous inefficiency kept us from doing worse.

We were able to destroy buildings because suddenly there was money for new ones. People want new buildings. Except for the grandest structures, like Versailles and Durham Cathedral, history is not interested in saving itself: when medieval Rome got hold of New World plunder, it arrayed itself with baroque Rome. San Franciscans were no different, except we couldn't afford to demolish our Victorians. Our architectural heritage is still intact—like Charleston's, Florence's, and Lisbon's—because we could not afford to knock our buildings down.

For most of the twentieth century, San Francisco was a working-class city, its great events tied to the history of labor. Its waterfront and dilapidated streets made frequent settings for hard-boiled detective fiction and film noir like *D.O.A.*, *The Maltese Falcon*, and *The Lady From Shanghai*. Our literary bohemia was class conscious, from the Objectivists to the San Francisco Renaissance poets to the Beats to the dreamy intellection of third-generation Language poets. In 1964, George Oppen wrote, "Strange that the youngest people I know / Live in the oldest buildings." It's true; we lived in dilapidated Victorian slag heaps—lightless boxy rooms that opened on long hallways stifled by paint-clotted dadoing. The bare bulbs of ugly chandeliers made everyone look sick.

Cities should not fall to ruin. The beauty and civic importance of the Victorian buildings have become apparent, and there is a tremendous drive to preserve them and—a further step—to return them to their original condition. The restoration industry flourishes. The old building I bought in 1986 was practically derelict, so I have passed through all the stages: reproduction molding, Victorian pigments, repro tiles, Morris wallpaper produced with antique screens, the hunt for original hinges. There is a science to restoration, and therefore a goal of accuracy. I could scorn Italianate Victorians that were rehung with Queen Anne doors. Crimes against purity!

Purity can be a death wish: before I got hold of myself, I even tried to hook up the original gaslight whose soft flickering makes sense of those chandeliers. Alarmingly, the gas pipes in most old houses still run through the ceilings, merely capped off where the chandelier hangs. I wanted to revive the dead by reattaching the chandelier to its severed neck. Would that make me feel at home in my home?

I thought I was living a private obsession until I felt the impact of my neighbors' joy when I removed the asbestos shingles from my façade and put up new Victorian molding. Their pleasure can't be entirely severed from that statistic on tourist revenue. Though I don't enjoy that money directly, it supports a slew of arts organizations, recreational facilities, and even some low-income housing—and so, the city as a whole. I put my civic shoulder to the wheel and make my city a more attractive place.

The word *restore* has a moral spin. Is it laudable to revive the past? Is the past an endangered species, like the Redwoods in the national park or the desert tortoise? I felt exuberant, as if I were curing the ills of the century, rescuing experience by dragging it across a battle zone. Put another way, the dilapidation of my building may not have been pretty, but it did occur in the continuous present that I also inhabit, and it displayed the work of time. If I delete that history and enter a borrowed past, am I a tourist?

Still another way to put it: after a century, the petit bourgeois return to San Francisco. In our search for the good life, we eliminate the intervening years. Even the telephone lines are disappearing into the ground—wires that carved the twentieth-century sky into a cubist jumble. Now the sky seems more expensive. What have we added? Trees: now trees seem necessary to the good life, but the new trees are *already* mature, like the full-grown palms installed on Market Street, as though our faith in the past cancels our faith in a future in which young trees grow old.

How does a city, or even a café, become a center—what do people look for in San Francisco that authenticates their experience? Does experience reside in the past? Why *want* to sleep in the Lincoln bedroom? If tourists come here looking for authenticity, where in San Francisco do I not feel like a tourist? A poetry reading?—Yes, I'm at home there. The San Francisco Arboretum? —My heart swells with pride when I visit that great park. The public spaces of my sexual minority? That's complicated. My neighborhood, the Castro, has been called a gay Mecca—and Mecca is a tourist destination. Young adults frequently spend four or five years here to get a handle on what used to be called identity issues. Yet the knowledge that gay people are making voting blocks, conversation, and love assures me like home fires burning that the city is mine. Unlike the Romans, perhaps my version of private life occurs in public.

At present, more money is spent restoring old buildings than erecting new ones, so we can say that restoration is the dominant contemporary mode. It's an extraordinary idea. A century ago, people hardly knew what earlier eras looked like. I wonder if old TV programs, photographs, and movies exert a kind of stylistic drag on the culture as a whole. Even the Victorian revivals— Neo-Gothic, Neo-Renaissance, Pre-Raphaelite—made new things identifiable as such. Was there ever a pervasive style that wanted to return to an earlier era? Where do you look for something lost, but in the past? Community presumably existed, and we are trying to reinvent it in an unusual way, by time travel.

My desire to restore my little house was part of the same impulse that has ,Providence opening up the river that lay buried beneath its downtown through most of the century. The same impulse fuels the rejuvenation of public buildings and neighborhoods across the country. My desire is reflected in movies that seek to deliver earlier eras whole cloth. I enjoyed these wallpaper epics until I got sick of them. I know something is off kilter when I leave the theater feeling that I'd endure the characters' horrid problems if I could only have their tailors and dishes.

One irony of all these endeavors—books, film, and urban renewal—is that periods rarely look like themselves. In Francis Ford Coppola's *Tucker*, those streets full of fifties cars never existed, because in the actual fifties there were still plenty of cars from the forties and even the thirties. Or those stylish Victorian rooms in *Age of Innocence*—didn't the real rooms contain Great Aunt Olga's regency commode?

The guidebooks say, "The city is a museum." The uniformity of the city's architecture makes it easy to read, legible—and perhaps that is a clue to its tourist draw. The danger of *preserving* experience for display is that San Francisco will become a Victorian theme park, and that is already happening. The restoration of the city generates an eerie tension, as though these new old buildings are waiting for their restoration earthquake, and then the costume party will end, and finally we will be able to go home.

"Architecture as Fate" was published in *Bay Poetics*, ed. Stephanie Young (Cambridge, MA: Faux Press, 2006).

DIVORCE

While everyone in the city is getting married, I am getting divorced. Always ahead of my time, I am engaged in bitter disputes over property while others merge their bank accounts. Always in the avant-garde, I avert my eyes from Chris while they gaze at each other with unguarded expressions. Our relationship will be truly over when I can look at him again. The life we had planned together fell apart—a feeling of desolation as strangers seem to buy our union, our derelict property. I find random sex while they discover monogamy. I resent the time that promiscuity takes. It's a grievance against Chris, though now I'm locating people who want to make pleasure happen in a body like mine. Search for: *older*, *bear*, *daddy*, and avoid those who take these designations seriously. The Australian who wouldn't shut up—*aye mate*. The vice president in charge of ATM's erotic massage in Pleasant Hill—first he said destiny brought us together, then he declined to see me again. The Irish dance teacher who didn't call back; the architect who wanted to harm my nipples; the numerous guys with their bellies in their laps and average penises who think they have well-endowed swimmers' bodies. I am mildly obsessed with Internet dating, while other people return each other's phone calls and emails as though that were normal. While everyone else in the city is making a legal vow, I wonder how to go about canceling ours. I search through drawers for the official paper and try to determine which government office to call while they are drawn to the marriage bureau in City Hall. While the horns are honking. While friends throw rice. While reporters take notes. While parties get underway. I weep in my garden, watching it bloom for the last time. I'm afraid to leave this garden because I put too much of myself in it. I am hanging onto this environment like the alien at the end of *Alien*, clinging by its toenails to the ship hurtling through nothingness. Why are there no parties with gifts for divorce? Where is my party, now that my household is ripped in two and I actually need the new blender, TV, vacuum? While they give each other courage, I have stage fright. That is, who am I now? What are my lines? Who can I talk to, emphatically awake in the hours of the night while they sleep annealed skin to skin? Awake and without resistance because there is no one to recognize me. While they are buying sheets together, I sleep on my side, a haystack of papers and dirty dishes on his side of the bed. While they are setting up house in each other's consciousness, I learn to banish Chris, don't think about him one way or another. While they are planning to have a child, my son is caught in the middle. Fine, I'll go say hello to Chris's relatives when they come to town. Do you think you can do it? Get divorced? The new couples march through the wide front door of Noah's Ark while I sneak out the back like a thief. They are becoming more than the sum of their parts while I am becoming less than one. Their friends are getting to know each other while my friends choose sides.

"Divorce" was published in *I Do/I Don't: Queers on Marriage*, ed. Greg Wharton and Ian Philips (San Francisco: Suspect Thoughts Press, 2004).

A LITTLE PRISON JOURNAL

This isn't Gandhi trying to get a foreign government out of his country, and it isn't Dr. Martin Luther King, Jr. trying to sit at a lunch counter. These people are breaking the law to get attention and it's a waste of everybody's time and money.
—Prosecutor Joe Hurley

On June 20, 1983, I was arrested at the antinuclear blockade of the Livermore Laboratory. Here is a journal I wrote in the Santa Rita Jail.

Monday morning: At 4:30 a.m. the clock radio flooded my bedroom with a Hungarian rhapsody faster than my unconscious could bail itself out. I got up, a thief in the night. I wrote support people's phone numbers on my torso with a ballpoint, hid some migraine tablets and a few dollars in the lining of my corduroy coat, put on layers of clothing for cold nights and hot days, and bunched up a few plastic bags in case we were kept on a bus all day with no toilets. Denny slept. I could hear my breath. I had agreed to be nameless so I said goodbye to my wallet and driver's license. I kissed Denny awake and assured him that I'd be back in a day or two.

I belong to a gay men's affinity group called Enola Gay. Enola Gay leaves San Francisco in two cars and arrives in Livermore at dawn: a chill inland sunrise, purple clouds backed by a white sky. A suggestion sends us away from the legal demonstration down Vasco, along with twenty others. We stand in the middle of an alarmingly empty road. Other protestors drift by.

What if we don't get arrested? Then cars appear and we sit down and spread out; after we halt the first few cars we get up, excited, sing and chant, although sometimes the silence quiets us: fields, pastures, scrub oak, a horse. Eventually sixty or seventy cars back up.

An hour later: Too tired and hot for singing. We mill around. The cars wait listlessly. The heat buzzes—an audio dislocation induced by lack of sleep. The enormous fact, about two miles away, of Lawrence Livermore National Laboratory, which we never actually see, dwarfs our human scale. The lab heads our weapons production chain; it should twist the oaks, yellow the grass, call down a Biblical darkness. These ordinary American fields and pastures depress me.

Then from out of nowhere leaps the Dance for Life Affinity Group blaring 4/4 music from a portable tape deck. They dance hard in pairs, eye to eye in a seventies time warp of tight disco—hips gyrate and dancers spring singly across the asphalt in grands jetés.

Two police cars pull up. Support people stand back. We scramble down. A cop stands above us and puts us (spreading his palms over us, so that we are) under arrest. Fear and awe. They take Richard and me together. They are reseating us in a line in a dirt parking lot. Being arrested is merely a change of position. Richard goes limp but in one motion the cop puts him in a half nelson and jabs a pressure point under his chin hard enough to break skin. I shout, "Shame on you—he didn't hurt you!" right in the cop's face. I don't touch him (nonviolence training). My reprimand reminds me of my mom. He's about twenty-five, I'm thirty-six, and he *whines*, "Then tell him to co-*o*-perate."

Monday night: 1028 arrested. The men and women are in huge circus tents! We can see the top of the women's tent. We're in the middle of a field. This is not so much a jail as an internment camp for 1028 willing to do civil disobedience. Wind blows through the tent. Its green and orange striped walls are always moving; the big top is beige and red—the canvas sinks and bellies out. Lights mounted at the top insist on the height and length, like a huge train station that pulses. At night we are also lit from outside by two floods but this is merely a flat agricultural valley and the darkness is just as penetrating. Two generators hum. A coil of barbed wire and a chalk line stand for our prison walls. Four hundred fifty men sleep in narrow cots in one tent, with a smaller one for eating. It was hot during the day, now it's cold and windy; all the clothes that nearly killed me on the bus I appreciate and wear to bed.

Tuesday night: The District Attorney asks Judge Lewis for two years probation and either $250 or eleven days. If we do civil disobedience during probation we are liable for six months in jail. Probation is their strategy to break the peace movement. The penal system wants to isolate us, process us singly so that each is a child in the wrong whose personal fate has a haphazard quality. We combat that strategy with solidarity: we decide to remain nameless John Does and refuse arraignment. In other words, they are stuck with our collective body. Civil disobedience is elegant. Like sex, you do it with your body.

This is very strange—a male society, 450 mostly straight John Does of conscience. During high school I realized I wasn't one of the boys and invented my life accordingly. Now my fear comes back. Still, there are no fag jokes and they seem to care for one another. A contingent of men's-movement men sleeps right across the aisle. They are students; they stroke each other soulfully. It's back to high school for me, as though twenty years didn't happen, as though no one would talk to me, as though life happened elsewhere. I want to be in their ideal society. I trick myself into thinking that I am unhappy and they're happy because they resemble the boys I once desired.

It's outrageously cold here; the blankets are a joke. Someone just put on a plastic bag, then his t-shirt. I bet that works. I think of Denny and warmth.

Wednesday morning: The sheriff comes to arraign us—we refuse—he could use force. When he doesn't we celebrate with a big circle, songs, chants. It becomes a ritual celebration twice a day. "Listen up, gentlemen"—but few go.

In line for breakfast, so tired afterward I sink abruptly to the dirt. Rotten food: two tablespoons of *gruel* straight out of *Oliver Twist* and vile coffee with beige cream that smells like rubber. The National Guard catered the food! Enola Gay discusses Linzertorte while eating lunch, the peanut butter spread so thin it doesn't discolor the bread. No one complains publically (middle-class guilt even infects people who aren't).

Hot sun today. Naked men sunbathe on an old concrete loading ramp (distracting). I'm reading a Harlequin romance. Breezes undulate the red stripes. Men jog, do yoga, learn eighteenth-century country dances. Summer camp.

I got through to Denny on the phone—our conversation was broken, like a hospital visit. How *are* you? How are *you*? Fine, fine.

Wednesday night: Strategy meeting all day long, and workshops on topics like Peace Movement in Europe, not to mention the full moon ritual for those who want it. Constant meetings, constant singing, a jail culture. We call ourselves the Santa Rita Peace Conference. But with the gypsy tent colors, the crowded isolation, and the (mostly) white population, this could be a displaced persons camp in central Europe.

I no longer want to be a men's-movement man. I just want to ravish and objectify their bodies, languorously naked and open in the heat. I select one and obsess. Beautiful men (some filled out with muscle, others whittled down to muscle) are mysterious to me. When I'm attracted, I assume the person *has* my attraction—a magical transfer.

Every night a talent show: as the next act wheels onto a stage marked out by ten cots stood on end, we shout, "*You too*, can be *sucked up* in a *tornado of talent*." One act was a performance piece on *Star Wars*; Daniel Ellsberg does a magic trick, then reminds us to tell the press that we are protesting against the weapons to be deployed this fall. The MX cruise missile and Pershing missile are first-strike weapons; they raise the stakes by giving a tremendous advantage to the side that attacks first. I imagine the motives of many people are more diffuse.

Lights out: officially we are John Does—a murmur of "'Night, John. 'Night, John." Jokes in the darkness: Why does a dog lick its cock? Because it can.

Thursday morning: I glance up, somebody's shadow walks across the roof—red and beige. Joggers' shadows circle the striped tent walls. The entrance is a bright rectangle of blue. I'm surprised to be here still.

A trickle of men leave; we applauded them, then chant "*No* fines. *No* probation." Still, I hear some guards chatting about electric cattle prods not leaving marks—ugh!

Friday: Enola Gay is fasting today, it's a relief. Noise and commotion: 400 men in a tent, bad food, cold nights. The judge won't budge. "Listen up"—clapping and singing—I almost fainted in the sun. An older man stumbled backward, fell. I saw his head bounce, heard it. I'm often tearful.

I begin a shipboard flirtation with a man named Paul. He's my age; my previous sex objects now seem like so many Hueys, Deweys, and Louies. I'm back in my life. I start making friends. In one week I recapitulate my entire maturation.

They set up portable showers in a brown tent and let them run a few hours each day. In line I meet Aaron, a middle-aged Jew who bakes for my favorite Italian bakery. As we talk he unconsciously rubs his belly, chest, and pubis, and by that I understand he's straight. During the shower a man and I are each other's mirror for shaving, tenderly pivoting a head, running a finger below the ear, along the jaw. Strange to be without a name, ID, *and* mirror. The water is so gummy that shampooed hair looks inorganic and black crud comes off it on a comb. When I think of my face I recall a random collection of features located in a photo or mirror; meaning falls away and I don't get a sense of why I look the way I do.

After dinner: In one corner of the tent an impromptu dance with conga drums made from empty water containers. Men in underwear gyrate. A flute joins in—lots of Bible shouts, *hallelujah* and *amen*—a camp-meeting cross-circuit of anger, sex, goodwill, and frustration. Collective life has lost its charm. I miss women. I want to disappear into a book (as in childhood?) and reappear when I'm free (an adult?). I feel hostile and overfocused. I shut my eyes and mentally locate and undress the men who attract me; they eagerly submit or I overwhelm them with superhuman tenderness.

Saturday: Tomorrow is Gay Freedom Day and Enola Gay has called for our own Freedom Day Parade. Most men here are gentle so we never knew who was gay. Still, the men who attend our parade meeting are news to me. A farmer from Petaluma looked *exactly* like a farmer from Petaluma, etc. I take a lesson from the straight men and touch people more. During a meeting I let my head fall on John's shoulder. I channel my erotic life into brotherly hugs that appease my loneliness and give me ballast.

Saturday night: The posts creek, a windstorm—dilated eyes, a tremulous excitement in the spine. The tent pulses and heaves, we're inside a giant termite queen. Paul and I: both have lovers, both couples are monogamous *so far*, haven't slept with anyone else *yet* . . .

Sunday: Gay Freedom Day. We stuff clothes to make Mr. Santa Rita and carry him on a sheet. Paul and others turn sheets into togas, shouting "Toga! Toga!" We have noisemakers and a man in a white wedding dress! We have chants: "Apples, Pears, Peaches, and Cukes, / We are Fruits who don't like Nukes." Two disabled men in motorized chairs are surrogate Dykes on Bikes. We are nervous because (1) gay men have some problems with rape and murder in jail (you have to trust the system enough to put yourself in it), and (2) what if only ten people show up? But 300 join us. One group dresses in handkerchief bikinis. Another turns sheets and blankets into wimples and habits: the Sisters of Perpetual Incarceration. We finish at the loading platform with a talent show. The audience shouts,

"*You too*, can be *sucked off*, in the *Tornado that Dare Not Speak Its Name*."

Monday: The captain bellows, "This is not Camp Friendly or Camp Sunshine." New rules: single-file lines; no wearing sheets; no wearing tampons (the woman had a parade too); only "discreet homosexual activities"—in a tent of 400? We speculate they mean the men's-movement men; they are mostly straight, but touch each other intensely.

The legal team shakes their heads, the judge won't compromise, we are sober. Guards roam around at night shining flashlights in our faces—I struggle in with the dawn.

I was in line for allergy pills for dust. The sergeant shouts, "Circle! Circle!" Imitating us? Guards surround me.

Sergeant: Maybe we should throw this one out?

Me (voice too high): Fine with me.

Sergeant: Naw, he's too small a fish. (Then, confidentially) Have you ever considered that this might be a dream, that you are asleep, alone, and all this (a wave of his arm) is a figment of your imagination?

The answer is yes. Eight days and I'm still in jail: the constant din surrounded by silence, the uncertainty, the cold nights, the food—

Me: Have you been watching too many *Twilight Zone*s?

The guards: Disrespect! Disrespect!

Here's one of many imaginary conversations with Judge Lewis.

Me: As the days pile up we become more convinced that we are political prisoners. We are punished more for what we believe than for what we did. If we get nine days, $450, and two years probation for stopping traffic, how do you treat shoplifters—the guillotine?

Lewis (rumored to be running for State Senate next year): Face-to-face with a criminal, you don't negotiate a settlement. Our weapons defend a free country. Doubtless you would be happier in a totalitarian one.

Me: The same observation has been made about this court.

Tuesday: Paul leaves; he is flying to Kansas to help his parents harvest the wheat. I'm getting shell-shocked; I find I start crying when I imagine that I'm crying at home or crying in a restaurant (food) with Denny (love); that is, I cry in anticipation. We're exhausted—faces either slack or too focused, incomplete gestures, anxiety sharpened by the legal muddle. We are determined and angry and our physical number remains our most effective bargaining chip. Still, when people go to arraignment we give them a warm farewell.

I'm wearing a blue kerchief like a bandit to combat the dust—it startles people. It completes my lack of identification. Half of us have sore throats, sore lungs. I imagine Denny is angry with me.

The final chapter on the men's-movement men: today one of them calls me "Sir" and I enjoy that respect.

Dinner taxes the imagination—nouvelle portions of cubed spam suspended in canned apple-pie filling minus the apples, with a can of fruit cocktail thrown in, then warmed to the temperature of mucus and served with a slice of white bread. We talk about Linzertorte. Before dinner the sergeant announced a new rule: if anyone throws food at the guards no one will eat. He was right to be nervous. We're giddy and depressed. Richard says, "It's bureaucratic food, food in the abstract for abstract people." We name the dish the Martyrdom of St. Cecilia. Many are constipated; mine is the opposite problem. The food ransacks my body: I have diarrhea every morning, just one blurt, like "Fuck You."

The dust is a haze—people appear distant. It may contain asbestos.

Wednesday: Judge Lewis offers a $500 fine, but finally no probation. We meet to discuss the fine. I join the circle and men look up for a second, big eyes, heads hardly moving. We sit on the dirt. I'm having a crisis of Pessimism of the Intellect. We wrangle for hours, we are indignant and spaced out. Finally someone tells us (can it be true?) that the women quickly consensed on this message to Lewis: "Shove it up your ass."

Night: Someone has an epileptic seizure out by the telephones. The guards make us carry him on a cot to the medical trailer—no doctor. When he starts coming out of it, the guards rush over, jump him, apply hammerlocks, push pressure points, *handcuff him*, then drag him away screaming. Encounters with the guards are always inconclusive, except for this conclusion. They are like a sharp knife—so quick and professional we don't feel scared till later.

Sometimes, just after lights out, the whole 400 fakes an orgasm in response to the Discrete Homosexual Acts rule: "*ugh! ugh! ugh! ugh! oh! oh! oh!*" Someone shouts out in the darkness: "How many erections have you had?" Shouted replies: "I've only had two." "I've had four." Then a murmur of "'Night, John. 'Night, John."

Thursday: Dawn, the generators click off. Lots of us wake up from the sudden lack of noise. We lie awake in the cold.

Later: A new offer by the DA was upped by Lewis. Now it's time served plus five more days or $240. Finally there is no tactical advantage to stay here any longer. Our solidarity killed the two years probation, reduced the fine from $500 to $240, extracted a promise of equal sentencing. They are prepared to keep us here through the Fourth of July weekend. About 150 leave; more will leave tomorrow; hugs and applause from those who remain.

We are fingerprinted, photographed. I'm arraigned in a classroom with about twenty others. Still no IDs. They must accept the faces and facts we present. But we are precise—"I've lived at x for eleven months, three weeks"—as though there are eyes everywhere. At 9:00 p.m. I find myself on the outskirts of Livermore near McDonald's twin arches.

At home: 11:30 a.m. Denny and I embrace, look at each other. I still have sea legs. I don't see why rooms aren't noisy and swaying. Harold brings over some Linzertorte for Enola Gay. We eat soberly.

At dawn I get up—coughing, worried. I vomit quietly and climb back in bed. Denny says, "Why are you awake?"—a grievance in his voice. "We prisoners get up early." Denny asks if I'm okay. I cry for half an hour or so. I'm not sad. Finally he just rocks me. Do that, I say to him mentally.

In the morning, talking about the action, Denny says, "It was a big deal and not a big deal." That's right. It was a lot for me to do; I almost never felt in danger; I lost weight; I'm proud of myself; the world still doesn't stand much of a chance; I'll do it again.

"A Little Prison Journal" was commissioned by the *Village Voice*, but rejected because my story was not gritty enough. It was published in the *New York Native*, July 2, 1984; and reprinted in *Five Fingers Review*, no. 2, ed. tk (1984).

ROBERT GLÜCK'S MIDDLE AGES

Lately, my middle-aged homo friends feel a general bafflement about our age group, a sense of displacement in the gay community, and a lack of presence in the gay media. We joke about going back in the closet, where at least we can control our own invisibility. So I asked the *Bay Area Reporter* to let me edit a series of monthly columns addressing the subject of being gay and middle aged. I have lots of questions and I've brought this column into existence to supply some answers. I'm going to invite a variety of men and women to contribute. It's an exploration, nothing definitive. I don't know what will turn up, but I expect to learn something about myself.

"The old / New to age as the young / To youth," wrote the San Francisco poet George Oppen. That is, every age is always a new experience. Part of my problem is that I have little in my own past to show me how to age. There's less if I look to the mainstream, still less in the gaystream.

Are there seasons in every person's life? If so, how can I recognize and become them in a way that is lively and meaningful? I'm fifty: am I in late summer? early fall?

I can't grow old as my parents and grandparents did—that generation gap is still in place. So I have to invent a way to be old. My parents lived in a culture that was separate from the young and I am not ready for that. Besides, there is no longer a culture separate from the young. The young and I listen to the same music, more or less, buy our jeans from the same stores, watch the same films; and when I hear the radio of a convertible Chevy packed with today's youth emitting T. Rex, I know their generation gap has not yet opened, though the years are piling up.

In the sixties and seventies, I used my generation gap as a self-defining border; the story of the times was the story of my peer group of fags, hippies, activists, and bohemians. I still have a peer group—is the story of the times our story? I doubt it. We are not members of any group in the same way that young people are. Perhaps this is one difference between the young and the middle aged.

What difference? When I was young, I looked for recognition with great urgency: I needed to know who I was, and I needed to tell people about it. I remember the intensity (fueled by gallons of coffee) of delivering my whole self in talk to a friend. Now it's more complicated, and I would say my friendships with my peers are informed by the sweetness of knowing that most of our experience can't be put into words, that little is visible on the surface.

There's pride, shame, and luck in growing old. When I look in the mirror, instead of fierce identification, I only party recognize myself. My face is not absolutely committed to the present. I see remnants of my past, and the past can seem irrelevant. This is painful to write. I see the new thing, age, which is depriving me of physical beauty. To find beauty in an aging face, we would have to find relevance in the past. Instead, our (American, gay) culture is youth oriented. Oddly, I helped make that culture. It is shameful to grow older. The culture tells me that somehow I really should be young forever, and aging is a mistake that I have made. I turn away from my own body with a lack of forgiveness.

In a movie review on one of the gay pages, the critic praised a film for portraying an "intergenerational couple"—one man was twenty, the other thirty. I had to tell my friends about that one. We groaned together—and my boyfriend Chris Komater, an artist who is nineteen years younger than I and a film buff, recalled that Humphrey Bogart romanced Lauren Bacall, Cary Grant romanced Sophia Loren, and Fred Astaire romanced

Judy Garland and even Leslie Caron without the intergenerational specter. What happened to change things? Has the generation gap snapped after all?

According to the personals it has. At fifty, I have fallen off the map of sexual viability. I can no longer be just a guy. If I want to join the party, I have to join it as a sexual type. Dizzy daddy? Leather top? Yet I have never been happier sexually, and my years past forty have been romantically busy. An informal poll tells me this is true of many gay men and women (though other polls may yield different results). So what is that about?—that I was more fucked up when I was young? Well, yes, though any day I'd trade the neutron bomb of my midlife crisis for the alienations of my younger self. If we are such babes, why doesn't the gay media tell us so? Still, if the community hasn't provided us with selves that mature, we owe it endless thanks for providing us with men and women to sleep with and to love.

Every so often while making love with Chris, I imagine that we are in a bathhouse or sex hotel, and that men are lounging outside our door, watching us, and finding it interesting that a thirty-one-year-old is fucking a fifty-year-old and vice versa. I suppose that little crowd is the gay community, and in some way our sex and our lives belong to it, although of course our lives are also entirely our own. When Chris and I are in a position that separates us—say, he is standing behind me—I think, a young man is fucking an old man, but when we are tangled up together, it's just Chris and Bob merging in a sweet blob. Is that what heterosexuals feel?—different when separate, same when skin to skin?

Am I sugarcoating the pill of aging? I should add that my body is starting to collect ailments that will be mine till I die. My memory sometimes falters and so does my stamina. I could have predicted that. But there are also pleasant surprises: no one told me that as I age my orgasms would be more shattering. Perhaps there is less to shatter? The break in consciousness is longer and it takes me longer to recover. Now the connection between sex and death is less mental. I'm still in bed wondering where my arms and legs are located, while Chris is bouncing down the hall.

Generation gap, intergenerational couples, sore knees, orgasmic demolition: that's a good place to stop for now. Next month writer Eileen Myles will tell us what midlife means to her.

"Robert Glück's Middle Ages" was published in the *Bay Area Reporter*, 1998. From 1998 to 2004 I edited a series on gay midlife for the *B.A.R.* that included Gary Indiana (the most thrillingly negative essay ever to appear in a gay journal), Eileen Myles, John Killacky, Jeffrey Escoffier, Brian Bouldrey, Richard Schwarzenberger, and others.

HORROR GARDEN

Last winter I pruned my *Brugmansia* way back. I prefer calling it a *Datura*. *Datura* is a genus that used to contain *Brugmansia*, but now *Brugmansia* is its own genus. In any case, it's an angel's trumpet, and an unusual one, because the fleshy pink flowers don't hang down, but rather "nod" like gorgeously sinister Victrola trumpets. Like other *Brugmansia*, it's spectacular in bloom. The species is from Peru, and it was given to me by a dear friend who has died.

Brugmansia of course are poisonous and deliciously night scented—*Gardenia* with an edge. In Nathaniel Hawthorne's "Rappaccini's Daughter," Beatrice, the mad scientist's child, inures herself to poison flowers, and I used to think the chief amongst these "vegetable existences" was *Brugmansia*. "Were I to breathe it long, methinks it would make me ill." By degrees Beatrice not only becomes immune to their poison, she becomes poisonous herself, an evil bloom. When the young man who has fallen in love with her can't refrain from kissing her, he dies.

Brugmansia are part of the huge nightshade family, Solanaceae, which includes such suspects as tomatoes, potatoes, peppers, eggplants, *Nicotiana* (tobacco), petunias, and Jimson weed. *Brugmansia* have become illegal in Florida because teenagers use them to get high; ingesting too much causes coma and death. In India they're used for suicide and murder, garlands of "devil's trumpet" are woven into the hair of Shiva the Destroyer. In Europe, witches' brews. It's a favorite cemetery tree in South America, and throughout the two Americas its narcotic alkaloids were used as ritual hallucinogens, medicines, anesthetics for sacrificial victims and such. Medical drugs produced from these alkaloids dilate pupils, treat motion sickness, and are used in the manufacture of birth-control pills.

Brugmansia's herbaceous cousin, Jimson weed, got its name from the havoc it wrought when British soldiers sent to defend Jamestown in 1676—yes, I've been to the library—cooked some up with other greens for a "boil'd salad . . . They turned natural fools upon it for several days. One would blow up a feather in the air, another would dart straws at it with fury; another, stark naked, was sitting up in a corner like a monkey, grinning and making maws at them; a fourth would fondly kiss and paw his companions and smile in their faces with a countenance more antic than any in a Dutch droll." Party down, redcoats!

I have trained my *Brugmansia* against a wall in a fan shape, so I prune it quite a lot. But it never recovered from last year's pruning. Why? It hardly put out a leaf. The bark was green, and when I scraped a little, it was moist and living. Were snails eating the leaves as they appeared, so many Rappaccini's daughters munching their little salads? I threw down some snail-and-slug killer from that wonderfully lurid yellow-and-black box, and yes, little by little some leaves appeared. But there was an overall strangeness to the tree. Some limbs did not put out leaves; some weird eruptions appeared on the bark.

I watched this develop for a while. Then one day I dug into one of these little volcanoes with my thumbnail. Some wiggly, maggoty things fell out onto my hand, and I flung them away with a shout. A swarm of them was emerging from the wound I had made. I inwardly reeled at the delirium tremens of white lozenge-shaped insects, some kind of larva? The skin bristled across my back. Or some kind of borer? I stared at them, slack jawed. They were roiling over themselves like fiends, a few falling completely out of the tree in their excitement.

What are they? They are not termites. Termites are creepy; I have seen them attack a sick tree, so I know what they look like. What enacts a circus from Hell beneath the bark of a soft tree?

This was a difficult image for me to process, and I quickly left the garden and put the insects out of my mind. I relegated them to the part of my imagination I reserve for dreams, because doesn't that swarming cause an atavistic jolt?—the terror of alien social organization, furious energy, jointed legs, unconquerable numbers combined with individual vulnerability? What is it about insects? The tiny pearl of green goo a bug becomes on my thumbnail can tax my imagination more than the life of the pig, a prince of the animal kingdom, which I might sacrifice in the form of a sausage for lunch. Still, I am very fond of my *Brugmansia*, and before long I was searching for possible culprits in pest books at a local nursery. I could not find a bug with that particular lozenge shape, like a *Paramecium*, so of course I had to collect a sample and send it in to the county to be identified. There's not much to be done against borers, but I wanted to get the situation under control, if only to know what had so revolted me.

I returned to my *Brugmansia* with a glass bottle, dug a trench with my thumbnail, got ready to jump back. I dug some more— I dug and dug, reluctantly. I did not want to harm or scar my tree. But I found no bugs at all, nothing. Larva season must be over—until next year? Almost immediately the tree put out big leaves and those wonderful blooms.

I regard it with a wary eye—some limbs are dead, but on the whole it does not look too bad. Still, these bugs have not left on their own—they will be back. It is a perilous life. My *Brugmansia* escaped the predator, but next time, as the announcer says on *Wild Kingdom*, it may not be so lucky.

"Horror Garden" was published in the *San Diego Reader*, November 30, 1995. Beginning in 1994, I wrote a garden column for the *Reader* named Mr. Plantier. (I also wrote articles on gardens and design for *Metropolitan Home, Nest,* and elsewhere.)

DOG SOUP

Gardens, however modest, are visions of paradise. As such, they are settings for activities that take me out of time. Gardens reconcile me to time on the grandest scale. In gardens I engage in the pleasures I would be enjoying continually if earth were more like heaven.

What pleasures? I sit and talk with a friend, I drink a cup of tea, I look at buds that will turn the *Wisteria* into a blue river free of gravity, I daydream, I flirt, I attend a wedding or party. The garden confers on these pleasures a sense of occasion. Because of gardens' evocation of heaven, we sometimes give them our dead. Gardens can be places of memory and regret. In the eighteenth century, cemeteries became gardens. That is, when our civilization became secular, we began to bury ourselves in idealized nature rather than the urban churchyard. Cemeteries are public parks, re-creations of the Elysian Fields where death's moment stands still in the form of eternal monuments, which are then softened by the seasonal time of trees and rolling lawns; eventually the marble is worn smooth and reclaimed by nature. That softening of stone is part of the charm of all garden sculpture, not just tombstones.

We stage our acts of mourning in gardens. I helped my friends spread the ashes of their parents and lovers by the roots of apple trees, by a Japanese stone lantern, by a patch of irises, under a pomegranate tree.

So when my dog Lily died, I buried her in my garden. This is not a new idea: my family's yards have been the final resting place of praying mantises, turtles, mice, and a snake. In Peggy

Guggenheim's famous sculpture garden in Venice, a corner is devoted to Sir Herbert, Lola, Lulu, Kachina, Imperator, and finally Peggy herself.

Lily led a charmed dog life for sixteen years. I was proud that she lived in apparently indestructible health and that she was the object of so much affection. She sickened on the morning of a day in December. At eight in the evening, she stretched into a trembling bow and subsided. Her body scared me a little. Sluggish fleas crawled out of her blond fur as her body cooled. My neighbors thought the weeping they heard was caused by the departure of my lover. I was indignant—he would never be the cause of grief so pure!

The next morning friends came over to help me bury her. I had just constructed my garden, so it was a good time. Where I live, the shale and clay are so hard that I had to use a jackhammer to create some room for topsoil. In a way, I had made a container garden in the earth. That morning we dug about three feet into this soil rich with chicken manure, and I laid Lily's stiff body at the bottom. A little dirt smudged her snout. I went to rub it off—and then I realized that she was actually going to be surrounded by dirt. The fact that I was going to take someone I loved who had simply stopped and put her into a hole in the ground seemed more incredible to me than the idea of heaven or resurrection.

I sat down and wept in earnest. I waved my friends away and they sort of crept out of the yard. My unrestrained tears came from some place beyond my control, while in some other place I was getting Lily's blanket to protect her—from what? The death-rich soil? I could not let anyone help me close up her grave.

Later, I planted two old climbing roses over Lily. The Gloire de Dijon is a lovely Climbing Tea from 1853, with creamy buff flowers that hold a dazzle of apricot-gold within, Lily's colors. That rose is a tender plant—it limps along, asking for more fungicide, more fertilizer, and often I think of replacing it, but then the blooms appear and I am appeased for another year. The hybrid musk Kathleen makes large sprays of China-pink buds opening to white, single-petaled "apple blossoms." The trunk is thick as my wrist and hearty as a tree. Kathleen is more vigorous than the Gloire de Dijon, more pest free, freer of mildew, rust, black spot . . .

But that's jumping the gun. I buried Lily in December, before the rains began. I had noticed that the soil I bought was warming up—the organic matter had not entirely decomposed. As the rains proceeded, that section of the yard began to emit a weird smell. The basin I had jack hammered out of shale could not empty as fast as rain filled it up. The stench was like nothing I had ever encountered, and it sent a strong message: something had gone wrong in my Elysian field. The plants didn't seem to mind the smell even when it grew stronger and more negative. I guess they were making the point that plants are not people. The stink could have risen from the under ripe manure, but I began calling it Dog Soup.

Reluctantly, I took action. I had created a monster in my garden, and this time I did not wave my friends away to be alone with my emotion. I begged Richard, a stalwart gardener, to tackle the problem, because I did not want to run into Lily. He dug out the contaminated soil, and we shoveled in some fresh dirt mixed with sand and compost. Lily stayed where she was; she emitted no further messages, unless you count the cream and apricot roses on the Climbing Tea. My feeling of horror subsided.

The grave in my garden marks a spot to think about Lily in passing, to locate feelings of tenderness. I make a joke and say that I live next to the graves of my ancestors, but in our mix-and-match culture it is something even to live by the final resting place of my dog.

"Dog Soup" was published in my column, Mr. Plantier, in the *San Diego Reader*, February 23, 1995.

O. J.

I guess Dr. Martin Luther King said it best, "Injustice anywhere is a threat to justice everywhere."

I keep coming back to King's observation, suitable for a high-school valedictorian address. When did I start to assume that all information is tarnished and that crime and punishment have lost their association? My disbelief is so deep it becomes a mysticism that detaches electron from nucleus and dissolves every other kind of relation—that's only partly true.

I begin to cry and never stop—that's a lie. The world appears as I enter it. I step out the door and accept the vague day, overcast in San Francisco, so drab I give it my complete belief.

In King's statement, I wonder where "everywhere" is. Where do I witness O. J. Simpson's trial? Valences shift in an electronic environment—something's happening that *is* me; if I am a witness, it's to my own confusion in the face of the corrupt information I have become, always was.

So I make a fiction—say, I'm a tree trimmer who is still working at 11 p.m. or something. The lump of fear in my throat finally teaches me how to speak. "I saw nothing," suddenly cautious, "saw nothing at all." I set up a 900 number like Kato did in which I disclose the universal ruin in this story, which is that self preservation itself causes distortions, monsters, the gaiety of a public hanging. Horror binds a community.

But why write that? Fictional accounts of the murders are what we're already getting. Can I write about the trial while knowing nothing about it? Many are doing that professionally.

It's interesting to me that I assumed Ronald Goldman was gay from the beginning. Why? That he was a waiter? An actor? That he was returning Nicole's *sunglasses*? It turns out I have a friend of a friend in LA, also named Bob, who slept with Ron—and with Parker Stevenson and Shaun Cassidy. I'm going for the Russ Meyer approach.

What can I assert with confidence?—lies and rumors. Justice is more recognizable in its absence. So I'm going to tell you what I learned (mostly on the phone):

> Ronald Goldman was gay. He hung with a group of closeted actors. I learned that from an LA friend by way of a New York friend.
>   A friend-of-a-friend knows the coroner in LA who said that the bodies of Ronald and Nicole were almost decapitated, and that Ronald's cock had been sliced off and put in his mouth.
>   Somebody I know knows somebody who knew the maid, Rosa Lopez, back in, where—Texas? He said that she could not have been paid to lie, because if she had been paid she would have done a better job.

One night I was trapped in my car behind a police cordon on Mission Street where a shooting had occurred. Two black bus drivers were chatting about the case right outside my window—they were also trapped. One had been a student at City College with O. J., and he had no doubt about O. J.'s guilt, because even then O. J. was famous for his rages and dire treatment of women.

A Chicano writer, laughing—they were at a bar discussing Rosa—told a friend of mine that deceiving white people was not the same as lying.

Then another friend in New York said, no, we were wrong, Goldman's not queer.

Another writer told me that Judge Ito and O. J. live on the same street and belong to the same country club.

My cousin Jerry reminded me that his mother, my aunt Irma, used to live on Gorham in Brentwood before it was so ritzy. She lived less than half a block from where Nicole was killed. Ronald worked at a restaurant at the other end of the block.

These sections are short because I am having trouble speaking—a celebrity sliced off my cock and shoved it down my throat. That's not true.

A New York friend said *National Enquirer* said O. J.'s dad wore a dress. Is that what Dominick Dunne means when he says in *Vanity Fair* that O. J.'s dad left to "pursue another lifestyle"?

A San Francisco friend's sister works in an LA newsroom where one of the journalists thinks this: O. J. had bought Nicole's car for her. After they split up, he knew she had money problems. Nicole's tires were occasionally slashed, replacing them was expensive, and it was generally assumed that O. J. was responsible for these acts of vandalism. That reporter thinks O. J. was on his way (with his knife) when he encountered Nicole and Ronald.

The living set up 900 numbers. In photos by Annie Leibovitz, they are buried beneath the dead. The dead are actively dead. That's the most interesting thing about this case: this extreme union of noise and silence.

"O. J." was published in "Witness," *Fruit*, no. 1, ed. Anne d'Adesky (1995).

DEAR KEVIN COSTNER,

You spent $200 million on a movie and you don't even understand the plot! Kevin, in your movie you are a macho fish, and your relation to the ocean is to extract goods from it or to conquer its monsters. But Kevin, you are one of those monsters! You should let me direct *Waterworld*:

First, all creation groans and is in pain together. Then—since you are already a cold fish with your big cod face—I push you overboard.

Transforming from a human into an animal is a sexuality. Tremulous Lon Chaney, Jr. shapeshifts because he's aroused by speed and the smell of blood and he's too weak to resist. I take pleasure in his struggle because I want him to fail, I want the human to be overthrown. I'm on the side of unruly delight. Likewise the vampire.

You grab a mouthful of slow water and squeeze it through the honeycomb of living ribbons and out the back of your head along with CO2 that fizzes like Bud Lite, a little kick. With each breath there is a reaction in your body, you become one more increment a fish. Ease in a different element is sexual, flying, breathing under water; the new element is the unconscious, where the libido rules. Kevin, you are a merman, yin above, yang below, like the exquisite *Creature from the Black Lagoon* with his fins of black filigree. You are nakedness, Kevin, where the iridescent scales and the hot flesh meet. Then why not experience the lure? Why not coral reefs where your hips undulate in sinuous momentum? No longer an obstacle to light, you break into a thousand spangles when your school darts into the sun. You stroke for pleasure, you have some fun. Is this variety of happiness an abomination to you? American patriot, supporter of right-wing assholes like Phil Gramm? Does your heart condemn you? All the better, fight against it, Kevin: you are incredibly strong, so the call will be stronger.

On the surface you pitch and toss, a mariner without a shore, lost and exhausted. Your stupid ship with its contraptions to keep you human, like civilization itself—it's a foolish and distracting toy. Like the human, it sinks, a wreck. Go to sleep below, listening to the clang of your heart through your body; swells cradle you in the nursery of your new birth. In the black water you become that amphibious beast of the Gnostics, the first man, wailing from a mouth still slimy with clay.

You deleted a scene in the trailer for *Waterworld* because your gills resemble vaginas. Kevin, in my movie you embrace the briny and the pearly in yourself. You have two cunts and a dick, so why act like a redneck auto mechanic?

Now you are ready to love a human—like King Kong, like Catwoman, like Snake Woman, like Gerbil Man. Your affair will fail because the impulse to explode is too strong. Kevin, jump forms, be a fish!

Finding land at the end is a cop-out. We are all going to be fish. What a relief to be free of former things and to wake each day with a clear mind, no cloud of depression. The ocean will dry my tears, because the knowledge of death will have passed away.

Sincerely,
Robert Glück

"Dear Kevin Costner," was published in *Forward to Velma*, a one-off magazine made up of letters, ed. Gerald Fleming (2013).

WORLD

I was dyslectic *avant la lettre* and badly needed glasses as well, so my first four school years were passed minute by minute in a fog of real time and the fragment. From a psychological perspective, the humiliation of this long period fuels my attempt (at least in some of my writing) to use language to render the world in a spherical way, to experience the thrill of being entirely awake, *risen*, the thrill of bringing the world to a point when/where all secrets are known—which involves, in fact, some further, exponential learning to read. The goal of clarity contains in some measure the goal of sympathetic magic. But the goal contains its own contrary, because the attempt reveals the impossibility of clarity, the parameters of my own faith, and the resistance of language. Therefore, an interesting goal.

I was the last person in the third reading group, sometimes trading places with a retarded boy. We took turns reading aloud. During my turn I came to a word that looked familiar because of its shape and the letters I knew: *w* on one side, *ld* on the other. Would. Would also contained *u*, a letter I didn't know. But where the stranger should have been, there was an *r*, an acquaintance. I lived briefly but intensely inside this Martian word. I stalled for a while, but the direction of the hateful sentence (whose context, whose entire meaning I'd lost) was forward. I'd like to confuse the thematics of this drama by adding that I was taught in Hebrew school to kiss a book containing the name of God if I dropped the book on the ground—what book didn't contain God's name, how would I know either way?—and this perversity of my forefathers appealed to me. So I said "would," but hopelessly threw into the center of the word the sound of the *r*. To my total astonishment, Mrs. Banks strode across the circle and shook my hand so energetically I almost lost my balance. Then she slapped my back as though I'd made a great advance. I accepted the commotion—what choice did I have? I remained in the dark for a long time about the world I'd discovered, and why making an *r* sound produced such wild joy and affirmation. Misplaced joy.

I am grateful for the fragment; unity is a disease of meaning. At the same time, literature that purveys disjunction generates its opposite, frames itself with a canon of criticism—authoritative, technical, "closed." This critical theory dictates the meaning of form, the meaning of freedom—that is, it argues a self, even a nonself, which *is* the reader, which the reader recognizes and agrees to. Maybe we can't avoid unity or disjunction, maybe they enjoy a principle of conservation. In any case, this is my response to *Tyounyi*'s question, what patterns are influencing habits of reading within poetry?

I have remained an extremely slow reader, dazzled, easily led off the page in forward momentums different from those the author might be choosing. My own work is discursive, while at the same time it follows thematic organizations almost decorative in their strict patterns. I just finished reading Philippe Ariès's *Hour of Our Death*, a history of death since antiquity, a beautiful book which helps me write about AIDS. I am reading *Crossouts*, Lydia Davis's translation of the second volume of Michel Leiris's autobiography, marveling how his endless unraveling of interior life at a certain point becomes objective—in that sense, "unoriginal"—without rejecting personal disclosure, loose association, and idle speculation, which at any point Leiris is free to disown. He organized the book around particular misreadings and misunderstandings.

"World" was published in "Patterns/Contexts/Time," *Tyuonyi*, no. 6/7, eds. Phillip Foss and Charles Bernstein (1990). It was reprinted in *At the Public Library* 18, no. 3, ed. tk (1991), a monthly magazine published by the Friends of the San Francisco Public Library.

HIV 1986

A small ache harasses my chest—I've wondered for months if it's muscle tension or a virus. Is it my chest or this office that houses so much trouble? I sit on a card chair, cross my legs, and glance at the other men, studiously incurious; I inhale wicked institutional cheer and exhale collective anxiety. I'm taking the HIV test because my desire to know if I've contracted the AIDS virus is a little stronger than my reluctance. I usually write in the spirit of disclosure but I want to clarify feelings and thoughts *before* my medical relationship to the AIDS crisis is established. The Health Center guarantees anonymity; even if I decide to make a secret of my lab report, it will alter the way I see myself and, therefore, alter everything. Like other gay men, to be on the safe side I behave as though I'm contagious. A positive result gives that proposition (with some exceptions) medical certitude, while a negative result puts me (with fewer exceptions) in the clear.

I read the endless AIDS coverage in the gay press. These reports cannot gauge the accumulating sorrow because no language can express so great a feeling; I get an inkling of its scale in the torrent of factual coverage, a deluge of facts, debated and repeated, as though sheer enumeration could save us. I wonder: Will a cough lead to pneumocystis, headache to lesions, a mark on my skin to Kaposi's? My boyfriend speculates that, like a war, the full effects of the trauma won't appear till the disease is "conquered." Sometimes, in my calmest moments, dozing, an image of myself flashes on my mind's screen: I'm sobbing deeper than I ever have, arms in the air, head thrown back theatrically, as it never has been, as I would never allow.

Immediately I have an impulse to make comparisons and draw morals, to deflect attention from the real trouble, to give a past tense to what can't be fathomed. Anxiety demands a universal to escape itself. All right: AIDS is the disease of the eighties. Why? Well, the destruction of the immune system is an allegory of the breakdown of "basic structures" now experienced by our country and the West. Or: AIDS is bad news from a remote yet governing part of the body (the immune system, the CIA), and I theorize that the virus was concocted by one of the more feverish outposts of government-sponsored research. Or: AIDS resembles radiation poisoning's silent decomposition, its unwholesomeness and cataclysmic forecast for all people. Or: AIDS is the result of sexual imbalance—we were unnatural or too natural (a death's head leers from the anus).

These interpretations are foolish and comforting, as though finding what *exists* were the same as inventing a moral, as though at some moral's bottom line I'd stop being dazed and scattered. I can't supply meaning to a catastrophe whose real life takes place in the microscopic distance where viruses are normal and *my* existence is an unlikely game of creation and destruction without any stakes. I feel this chemical remoteness to be the void in its mechanical uncaring and its absolute precondition for my existence. Why ask it for comfort when it illustrates the opposite?—that is, the improbability of life. I discover this solitude when I lie awake, aware of my existence, wondering if my breath is labored or shallow, if I feel exhausted or just fatigued, wondering if I should associate the operations of my body, the deep hum or tension that is myself, with the workings of the virus.

AIDS must be seen as this rent in the fabric of life, personal and public. Like other catastrophes, AIDS heightens our lives in a way that we would never want. I'm cast into the region of the uncanny where animate and inanimate blur. I tell myself, I can't die this way, but of course I can. A sense of destiny asserts itself in the face of so many blighted ones—the "me" avid to continue being me comes forward.

With that in mind, can I manufacture some historical perspective? During the late sixties we glimpsed Utopia for a moment. We saw that the world was the world, not someone's interpretation of it, that life was the fulfillment of itself; that our destinies—our selves—were our own. This revolutionary idea appeared on different fronts, and American identity revamped itself. Actually, we merely claimed the happiness and freedom that were promised to us throughout our childhoods in the deceptive fifties. For me, a budding gay man, new identity meant sexuality. The rules an invisible world made for me had become opaque; I could see they were obviously invented for someone else's benefit at the price of my own emptiness; they seemed to disappear in a burst of laughter. First, we created a mental and geographical terrain in which we could know each other and be known, could recognize gestures and share meaning; second, our sexuality provided a sublime to transcend and dissolve those newfound selves.

In short, it was gay community—well organized, inventive, imperfect, equipped for urban life in the seventies and eighties, and subject to its pluses and minuses. Unlike older communities, ours thrived in an urban setting, in commercial institutions like bars and baths and cafés; it added its own chapter to the history of love in those decades. What other population could respond to urban anonymity by incorporating it into the group's love life as anonymous sex? To the degree that my own aroused body expressed the sublime, it broke every social contract, while invitation to the sexual act unified a community and was its main source of communication, validating other forms of discourse. As we created the community it taught us a new version of who we were, then we became it. Such a shift in perception about oneself is almost mystical, with the implied reordering of priorities.

Inevitably, a reaction. A new model showed us that the sexuality we had thought we discovered was actually a twentieth-century invention, part of an ongoing specialization process—as specialized, in fact, as the twentieth-century version of hetero-sexuality. Science and authority shape these identities as much as we do. Moreover, the sexual revolution, at least in my neighborhood, peaked and declined well before the onset of AIDS. Finally, identity and consumerism share an equals sign more now than ever before. Urgent greed, as though the American bandwagon were pulling out for good: yuppies, guppies, an impoverishment of life for which we feel rightly ashamed. Still, where are the selves we discovered, the selves that were discoveries?

It's easy to show that the world is distant, life is distant, we have the vocabulary for that: disjunction and pastiche. (Retro modes inform architecture, fashion, politics—let's get *back* to America. The big movies are wry reworkings of the old genres.) But a touch is itself, a meeting place for the body and the sublime. It disregards language that wants to generalize, negotiate. This unique "meeting place" also describes death (if anything does). That's why observance both of sex and death can function as a community sublime. To make death general, to say ten thousand died of AIDS, is an example of how language lies. Each death is beyond language.

And yet: ten thousand have died, more on the way. I imagine—with inescapable racism and also because it's mostly true—that epidemics happen in the third world. Our last global scourge was the Spanish Flu of 1918–20, which killed between fifty and one hundred thirty million and, like HIV, mostly struck healthy young adults. Five hundred million were infected, 27 percent of the planet. But doesn't the past, in this respect, resemble a third world country? Now gays bear the contempt that the USA holds for anyone in trouble. Reagan won't associate himself with homosexuality or a disease. It's a public impulse to silence that affects everyone. I'm still a little shocked when I see the word "homosexual"—let alone "AIDS"—in the papers, and how confusing to associate the national libido with death.

"Ten thousand have died"—an example of how language lies in articulation, and Reagan lies in silence. In bed, when I listen to my body for distant alarms, I am in a time and class by myself. Still, AIDS creates such magnitude of *loss* that death is now where gay men experience group life most keenly. It's where we learn about love, where we discover new values and qualities in ourselves. Death joins if not replaces sex as the community sublime. We used to have the baths, now we have the Shanti Project and other volunteer organizations that institutionalize the approach of death; and AIDS support groups, and safe-sex clubs where lust is framed by the AIDS crisis. A sex-slave auction benefit for the Shanti Project certainly deserves its own exegesis under the heading Mix and Match—and then there's telephone sex; changes in sex practices even between longtime lovers (sex acts have a history); the innumerable AIDS journals, anthologies, and recountings. I read the obituaries in the gay newspapers instead of the sex ads. Stories about AIDS patients and treatments are passed around, traded, repeated. They help me in my solitude. They are the very matter that creates community, gives it its character, its form and being.

But everything disperses before the question, will I die soon? For that reason, it's an unfair question—it breaks the social contract—and the only sensible question to ask. What other purpose does the mind have, if not to navigate the body safely through life? Back to the Health Center: a nurse calls my number; she finds a vein; it fills a test tube. I always feel self-love whenever my blood appears in a vial or as a taste in my mouth, or when it surfaces through a cut or a puncture. It stands alone now, at attention in its test tube like a messenger from the Egyptian Book of the Dead. It's hard to remain clear when a jackal-headed scientist weighs my heart against a white feather. In two weeks I will lean the results. I hope I can get out of this alive, the mind says, referring to life and not *able* to imagine alternatives.

* * *

I wrote "HIV" in 1986. In 1988 I want to add: (1) AIDS has been diagnosed in about 59,000 Americans, of which about 33,000 have died. (2) First steps toward treatment now exist. People who died two years ago might be alive if AZT and AL721 arrived sooner, and I am haunted by friends who had nothing to stop their fall. The politics of treatment and research is radicalizing a generation—demonstrations, sit-ins, civil disobedience. AIDS politics is complex, but not too complex to have shining heroes like ACT UP (New York) and *AIDS Treatment News* (San Francisco); and villains like the NIH and the FDA, erratic and secretive agencies who support the pharmaceutical industry over the health of people with AIDS. (3) In the US any publicity is good publicity—AIDS put homosexuals on the map. Gays appear on the front pages, generating interest if not enthusiasm. *Time* magazine *apologiz*ed for not covering the March on Washington. Our protests have become American history: the Smithsonian collects AIDS posters, pamphlets, ephemera. A profound shift is occurring in our image. (4) Lesbians have stepped forward to forge links with gay men in many varieties of help and solidarity, not incidentally bringing gay people together across the gender divide to form a gay political base. (5) I am more afraid of AIDS because I see so many deaths, and less afraid because of treatment and the "companionship" of so many normalizing factors, articulations, groups, and institutions. AIDS has become a kind of career; diagnosis means work and struggle, a more perilous future.

"HIV 1986" was published as "HTLV-3" in *City Lights Journal*, no. 2, ed. tk (1988). It was reprinted in *Personal Dispatches: Writers Confront AIDS*, ed. John Preston (New York: St. Martin's Press, 1989), and in *Sulfur*, no. 17, ed. Clayton Eshleman (1990).

THE BEST LUBE

You could say in this intimate arena our needs are not the same, that we are all different. Yet an arena consists of actors and spectators. Are the makers of these products watching us?

We certainly are different when it comes to assigning meaning to the experience of penetration and what it takes to bring us to the act. And different from ourselves at different times. I would like to be fucked by one of god's angels and I think perhaps that is happening right now. And really, where there is so much spirit, spit can work! Spit is usually so inadequate as to be laughable when the rare anal intercourse occurs in a film. The macho cowboy spits in his hand, wets his cock, and—*wham*—sinks it to the hilt in his sidekick's eager butt. Has that butt grown a callus from riding the range? Or at night in the tough chaparral are thousands of cowpokes hitting the canvas ceilings of their tents? The anus is a tender virgin who needs coaxing. She needs a gentleman who will make a deep bow from the waist in the form of plenty of lube. You can't use too much.

Penetration can mean everything that society means: marriage, power, play, pleasure, work. Or everything the individual might mean at a given moment: love, anger, submission, humiliation, goal orientation, glory. But the mechanics are not so varied, and I suggest that the closer I get to talking about the physical sensation, the more generally applicable I am likely to be. In a penetration, there is nothing to be gained from abrasion, everything to be gained from sliding without resistance. See the Talking Heads' "Sand in the Vaseline."

There was a day when someone went to the medicine chest and got the Vaseline, and that was almost before my time, I barely remember it. It was a jar of dinosaur remains, the corpse of their world. My god, what the dinosaurs have done for humankind! The foundation of my house was being excavated last summer, and the one artifact the contractor unearthed was a jar of Vaseline from the nineteenth century. It came from Brooklyn, where the first petroleum jelly factory opened in 1872. The inventor, Robert Chesebrough, had been working on a way to distill fuel from the oil of sperm whales, but this work was rendered obsolete by petroleum. The waxy material that became Vaseline was called "rod wax" by drillers. I felt a marveling kinship with my neighbors in time, even though they probably bought it for healing rashes and burns—that's how it was first marketed—which it cannot do.

In a later day that I remember better, I went to the pantry or refrigerator and got the Crisco. Procter & Gamble introduced Crisco in 1911 to provide an economical alternative to animal fats and butter. Crisco was the first solidified shortening product made entirely of vegetable oil. It was the result of a new process, hydrogenation. Neither Vaseline nor Crisco dried up ever—it took days to get them off the skin, though the coating could be an intimate souvenir of a happy hour. So, the first two great lubricants are actually gifts from the animal and plant kingdoms. There is nothing at all in water-based lubricants to compare with the deep luxury of Crisco or Vaseline spread over a membrane. How do they work? They turn skin into silk, a medium that wants to shine, to be touched, a surface deep and reflective. One feels depth in the skin, the skin unfolding unendingly like the Virgin's mantle, and the nerve endings drone with pleasure. A good lubricant extends sensation almost like marijuana.

We have water-based lubes (from the seventies) and silicone-based lubes (from the eighties). Silicone lubes are all alike; they have some of the old staying power and some of the old luxury. With water-based lubricants, it's all about staying slick, washing off, and conveying the feeling that the lube rejuvenates the skin. The best one in both categories is ID. Honestly, Good Vibrations should hire me as a product tester! Who else would tell you what the best lube is? That is the public service I am performing now that my boyfriend is turning me into such a big bottom. ID works, but ID does not hold a candle to Vaseline and Crisco. Now there is J-Lube as well, which derives from veterinary medicine. Porn actors like it. You mix it up yourself—google it!

"The Best Lube" was written in 2006 as a response to a request from an online magazine for a "best of" list; it was rejected. (Now, 2016, I think Gun Oil is best, just to say.)

QUEER VOICE

Queer voice is a conceptual mud puddle, yet I recognize it when it hails me. It must somehow express our culture's problem with deviance and at the same time it must contain male becoming female, and female becoming male, and male becoming male for a male, and female becoming female for a female.

Long ago my queer body was dense with homosexuality the disease and homosexuality the crime. Isolation at that intensity is a form of violence, is it not? Sex is a sacred act, and by that I mean it takes place in public. In every sense, queer sex is more public than most.

In Frank O'Hara's "Personism: A Manifesto," even the language that speaks about language is eroticized: "As for measure and other technical apparatus, that's just common sense: if you're going to buy a pair of pants you want them to be tight enough so everyone will want to go to bed with you." And, "It puts the poem squarely between the poet and the person, Lucky Pierre style . . ." Lucky Pierre is the one in the middle of a three-way.

We are told that before the nineteenth century there were homo acts, not homo identity; so no queer speech? Somewhere in one of John Boswell's histories—the Renaissance? the late Middle Ages?—he notes a piece of contemporary advice: one way to identify a sodomite is that he likes to eat well. So, no homo identity, but homo dining? During World War II induction physicals, tests were administered to identify men who suppressed their gag reflexes. So, no asking, no telling?

When I look at the sky, it becomes a homosexual sky. When I sit in a chair, it becomes a queer chair. I exhale queer atoms. Words are homosexual when I use them, or do I *attract* queer words? As for masculinity, I go through life assuming I am pretty neutral, that I am not easily identified. When I hear or see myself on tape, I think, "*Ohmygod, what a big fag!*"

"Queer Voice" was published in *Queer Voice*, ed. Lucy B. Gallun (Philadelphia: Institute of Contemporary Art, 2010), to accompany a visual art show.

TO THE *SOCIALIST REVIEW*

Nov. 2, 1982

Dear Editors,

I wanted to let you know how pleased I was to read Dennis Altman's article, "Sexual Battlegrounds," in the October issue of *Socialist Review*. Although other journals have broached the subject of gay "lifestyle" from the safe distance of high theory, Altman's article outlines the tensions inside the gay community, and discusses gay sexuality in terms of a critique of sex in our society—certainly a first for much of *SR*'s constituency.

The split between gay men and women is not new; it was always alarming, and especially now that gays top the New Right's hit list. It is further alarming to see homophobia inside the feminist movement because in a general way the fate of the gay-male community rises and falls according to the success or failure of feminism and its credo, "the politics of personal life."

On the other hand, it's heartening to see bridges being made between the gay community and the Left, such as Altman's article. Exasperated gays departed from the Old Left in the early fifties and from the New Left in the late sixties to found their autonomous movement. At that time the Left seemed unable to address forms of oppression outside the scope of class struggle and work alienation. Not that the Left completely abandoned gay issues all those years. It has a checkered civil-rights record— not so good as the Democratic Party, which occasionally does seize control of the state. At the moment most Left organizations support gays insofar as we can be dealt with under the rubric of a minority group. For example, the Bay Area Organizing Committee, a Marxist-Leninist organization, proposes as a part of a general line an analysis of the "special oppression of gays and the role of the gay movement," and as part of BASOC's original points of unity states, "We are anti-sexist . . . We will not relegate the fight against women's oppression to the background by counterpoising it to other class and political struggles."

This is hopeful, but the minority-group tack brackets the gay and feminist challenge to all men and women to examine their own gender socialization. The NAM/DSOC merger documents are even more hopeful on this score: "The socialist society we envision has at its core a feminist conception . . . It would value all sexual relationships gay, lesbian, heterosexual."

Of course there has been a gay Left all these years. In 1951 Harry Hay and four other men started the first American gay lib group, the Mattachine Society. Of the men who started the group, two were members of the CP, a third had been an active member, and the other two were fellow travelers. The Mattachine Society had a large progeny. My own introduction to Marxist thought was in one of scores of study groups seeded by Bay Area Gay Liberation (BAGL). A thorough history of the gay Left over the last fifteen years would be the subject of long books; certainly these books would contain chapters on oppression from the Right (*commie perverts*) and from the Left (*bourgeois decadents*), from murder to internalized hatred; not to mention the agendas of the gay Left's many groups, their grassroots movements, their lobbies, magazines, journals, caucuses, forums, etc. For example, BAGL supported the Farm Workers Strike and organized against racism in gay establishments. I imagine in any demonstration or picket line you would find a disproportionately high ratio of gay men and women—I do. Moreover, in some countries the gay movement is viewed as part of the Left. In Mexico the Left informs and structures any progressive movement. Recently the Partido Revolucionario de los Trabajadores, a Trotskyist party, ran Claudia Hinojosa, an open lesbian, for representative, a national position that would equal in this country a senate seat.

I was invited—along with Gene Dennis and Kim Anno—to lead a writing workshop at the Bay Area Labor Festival in San Francisco, held at the Building Service Center, June 12–13, 1982. Locals 2, 87, 400, 1100, and 1650 sponsored the conference. As usual when attending a Left—rather than gay Left—event, I was wary. I guessed that the conference would not be hostile to gays, but I don't like being tolerated. Instead, gay issues and the feminist movement—along with ethnic and sexual minorities—were made central topics by the keynote speakers. Dave Jenkins was formerly director of the California Labor School (Harry Hay taught classes on the history of popular music in a similar institution, the People's Educational Center—as a closeted gay, of course). Jenkins is currently the ILWU legislative coordinator. He gave an anecdotal speech that included stories about gay leadership in the labor movement, naming names. I was a little stunned. But learning that there were faggots in the Maritime Union is one thing. Quite another is to critique the Left, using gay experience as a model. Stanley Aronowitz, in his address, pointed out that when the Left was vital, it functioned as a community, affording its members the rewards of community life. He pointed out that it is surely the long suit of the Right that it offers its customers family, church, and flag. It is an indication of how depleted the Left is, that it can only ape the Right—for example, Michael Lerner's Friends of Families. Talk about grasping at straws! As Aronowitz pointed out, the Left has a lot to learn about community building in the eighties, and women and gay men can teach it something on this score.

There is not yet a real discourse in the Left on what community in this decade could be. When there is, I imagine lesbians and gay men will have forged many of its terms. As for S/M and the other ways in which desire is educated, I'm astonished by the furor. Perhaps S/M upsets people because it reshapes relations in our world in such a vivid way—not only heterosexual and class relations, but power relations generally. S/M reshapes these relations outside their most visible contexts, exploitation and financial gain; and it acknowledges power but gives it a new context, which is nonproductive, non-goal-oriented. Are power relations a basic component of sexuality? Certainly they will not go away soon, so I think the Left should reflect on the mediations of power and desire. If breaking down boundaries between public and private sex is a central tenet of the gay men's community, then people on the Left would be wise to think such thoughts as these: What constitutes interiority? Who stands to gain from public/private dichotomies and firm gender definition? What is the role of male supremacy in all this? Does anonymous sex give us the opportunity to shed—or share—individuality for a while? Is this opportunity a basic feature of community life? Do we tacitly approve of a sexuality created by—and leading to—systematic repression? If so, what does that bode for the future?

Yours,
Robert Glück

This letter was published in the *Socialist Review*, no. 66 (vol. 12, no. 6; November/December 1982).

FOUR

—

PEOPLE

ROBERT DUNCAN: TRIBUTE

Most people in this room knew Robert, and so I would like to use my time today to remind you that Robert was a tender friend and the greatest playmate. Christopher's book of interviews, *A Poet's Mind*, gave me a taste of something that I had been missing—the amazing experience of listening to Robert. I am going to share a few memories and then give the last word to Robert.

I interviewed Robert for the *Advocate*, June 26, 1984. In that era it was the homo journal of record. I tailored my article to its demographic, and yet reading it after all these years, I'm surprised to find that the article does not really popularize or simplify as I had feared. And moreover I think that it would be unlikely, and even impossible, for such an article to appear in such a magazine at present. So, that measures the difference made by twenty-eight years of gay desire to join the mainstream.

One of the lucky parts of my life was to be an intimate of Robert and Jess's house. Once Robert showed me his baby pictures. Here was "little Duncan," as he called himself. "Look at happy little Duncan." The baby's face was remarkably like the adult's. Then he showed me another. "Look at happy little Duncan." Then another. "Look at happy little Duncan." Finally he showed me a photo of himself in a little cart. Next to him sat a baby, his sister. Little Duncan wore a huge frown—Robert said, "Little Duncan is not happy anymore!"

Robert was saying that he did not want to have a sibling. It seemed to me that Robert was explaining a portion of Bay Area literary history. Once he told me that he found a letter from Jack Spicer in his files—a letter that he had forgotten about—in which Spicer tried to end the famous "Venice Poem" dispute. You were right, I was wrong, I should apologize. Robert said that he had ignored the letter. "I preferred the quarrel." If Robert had vexed feelings about his peers, certainly he was generous with younger writers like myself. For example, he passed on some of my stories to Donald Allen, and that is how *Elements of a Coffee Service* came to be published by Don.

I invited Robert into my Writers on Writing class, where writers read a bit, talk a bit, and answer questions. A student asked, would you tell us about your early life? Robert started with his birth and then went backwards and somehow outwards, finishing three hours later at the caves of Lascaux. When our time was up, he marveled, so soon?

Robert loved to gossip and he could say the most amazing things. For example, he claimed that George Oppen was involved in Trotsky's murder. That George was one of Paul Robeson's body-guards on a trip to Russia. (The kind of decision only a committee could make.) That Louis Zukovsky maintained an apartment early in his marriage where he had assignations with men. That Ruth Witt-Diamant, the founder of The Poetry Center, liked three-ways. I was his date for the Ruth Witt memorial, in which he rambled, sometimes to himself, submerged in drugs. He was in a wheel chair—it was his last public appearance. About halfway through, he said, "I have come to the end of the good I can say about Ruth Witt," but really the only positive thing he had said was that she was good at finding parking places.

In the late seventies, a poetry event took place over two nights at the Gay/Lesbian Center on Page Street. Twelve gay men and twelve lesbians read together. This was a very novel idea at the time because the two communities hardly spoke to each other, and the atmosphere was tense. One woman read a poem about a mother verbally abusing her little boy on a bus. There was nervous laughter from some of the men, and the poet stopped midway. Trembling with rage, she told us that she had read the poem many times at women-only events and had never experienced laughter. There was total silence, till Robert called out from the audience that none of those women had ever been the boy in her poem.

I made a party for Robert's sixty-fifth birthday. When I asked him who I should invite, he said, only family. I wondered if he was using the ancient slang, meaning only gay people, or if he meant the family he had created for himself. In any case, his list included only gay people, so perhaps the former? I got party hats, and Robert wore a pointed hat on his forehead, like a unicorn.

As Robert got sicker, I found I could talk more. It was a sign of his weakness that we could have a normal conversation. Once, we were both lying in his bed, having a visit, he under the covers and I on top, and I talked over him, over something he said. That was a first. For a moment we were stumped. He said, "Old men's ideas are as good as young men's ideas, but old men do not have the force to assert them." I imagine that had been on his mind—we were in the midst of the Poetry Wars. Speaking of that, even though there was supposed to be a contest between Robert and the Language poets, I noticed that he was writing a recommendation for a Guggenheim Fellowship for Ron Silliman. So perhaps there was more recognition and complexity in their relations than is generally assumed.

I came across the file that I kept for the *Advocate* interview. There were some deletions in our conversation, so I thought I would end by giving Robert the last word, which seems only right.

> The thing about Spicer, and the same was true of Marjorie [McKee, briefly Robert's wife], is that it was like playing a very, very expert game of tennis back and forth with somebody who

can really do it, because they don't just conform to your game and if you were conforming to theirs you'd be lost. There was an absolute sense of challenge with both of them.

I overcompose anyway, so a lot of my tactics are to try to break through this composition. If I look at it another way, I'm the kind of bird that builds this kind of nest. Every time I think I'm going to make a wild way-out nest, it proves to be the same with the same little old eggs sitting in there, unless a cuckoo got in.

Anaïs Nin was really a very shallow example of what a woman's mysteries and scandals could be. On the other hand, I wasn't living sexually with Anaïs Nin. Women seemed to me to know more than men did, and still do, so I get angry with them when they don't, as if they were being recalcitrant.

Denise Levertov wrote to Jess, "Couldn't Jess help to get me to see her point?" Jess wrote back to her, "If I thought I could change his mind I would never have moved in with him."

More Notes on Robert Duncan

Robert gave amazingly long readings. The duration made it a performance in itself, something larger than life, an amazing abundance.

We both liked tripe at the vast dim sum restaurant on Pacific Avenue, Asia Garden, now called New Asia. And chicken feet.

I saw Robert in his cape in the seventies but never dared to speak to him. I had read his poetry in Donald Allen's anthology when I was a student at UC Berkeley, and my attraction was that he had made a world for himself out of words. A young thought, really. Later I was sometimes his date at events—say, the Bruce Conner film retrospective at the Castro Theatre. At a party or reception, we arrived and left early. Actually, I just tried to keep up. We would make one circuit of the room, eating with both hands. By the time we were done the guests had arrived, and we would make another circuit, not eating a bite, then depart.

I met Robert in the very late seventies, when he read with Kathleen Fraser at Intersection. He had read my little chapbook *Metaphysics*, which I had sent him, so he had an idea about me. He became more interested in us—in Bruce Boone and me— after he read Bruce's *My Walk with Bob* and my *Family Poems*. That is, after New Narrative got going. Partly it was our interest in him. Bruce was interested in "gay bands" and did a number of essays on that theme, exploring the Duncan-Spicer-Blaser circle. We wanted a gay band of our own.

Once Bruce and I took Robert down to Santa Cruz, where we had dinner at Fred Jameson's house—he was teaching at UCSC at the time—along with Nate Mackey and Norman O. Brown. "Nobby," the purveyor of polymorphous perversity, seemed dry as a country vicar. We played a game—name a favorite composer, artist, poet. They all agreed on Mozart. Robert chose Dante. Who was the painter?

Robert fell in love with the young poets, Aaron Shurin for one. Someone in Australia I believe. Me later. So there was quite a bit of negotiating. We handled it in our different ways. I simply carried on as though nothing was different, and finally Robert protested, rightly, that at least his feelings should be acknowledged. What did it amount to?—some caresses, a kiss or two. Aaron has a more human story. When I was in the midst of that, thinking about what I should do, I invited Robert over to have lunch with Kathy Acker. They set out to charm each other. Robert told Kathy that he had saved her Black Tarantula pamphlets that she had mailed out in installments before they were gathered together into her first book. He joked, "You'll become so famous that they will be valuable." They recognized each other as fellow explorers. They talked about Melville and about Charles Olson, who was important to Kathy as well, it seemed. That was in the early eighties—1981? There is a lovely photo of them together that Kush has. Kathy thought Robert was "fabulous," advised me to sleep with him, and said that she would absolutely.

I gathered from Donald Allen and Michael Cuddihy and others that Robert was a terror to publish. He had no compunction about blowing up at his publisher, even at Michael, stricken by polio, who put together a Festschrift for him—one issue of *Iron-wood*. Robert was always kind to me, but he could be unkind and I often wondered if that was a characteristic of his generation, some version of authenticity, an attribute of the great. O'Hara, too. Certainly Don Allen could be imperious, and of course Spicer was famously brutal.

Robert was a saver. He never threw anything away. That was true of his amazing conversation, in which paragraphs could be recirculated. Robert's conversation is best documented in *The H.D. Book*. I wanted to publish it when I was an associate editor for Lapis Press. I collected it all, but never could bring the project to realization because the press was waffling about its own direction. Instead, we published the little book—letters between Duncan and H.D.—by comparison a very simple task. Robert simply gave me a zerox of the letters, and that was it.

Robert used to call Gertrude Stein and her generation the "Hot Victorians." There was a poem I especially loved in *Groundwork*, "Interrupted Forms," and I observed that it read like a Victorian poem, and Robert liked that.

In the last years of his life, Robert, Thom Gunn, and I had a lunch club. We met every few months or so, usually at a Mexican restaurant not far from Robert's house. Robert and I liked the tongue. I was the puppy, happy to listen to the two of them. Or, Thom and I were glad to hear Robert talk. Toward the end there was quite a bit of negotiation; Robert was no longer able to walk very well. We'd call a taxi for the distance of two blocks. Once, when the taxi arrived to take him home, Robert rose painfully and began the long journey into the street. In the busy doorway he saw a penny on the threshold, and down down down he went, then up up up very slowly. He was a saver.

It was another Robert, really, when I ate dinner with Jess and him at their house, Robert still asserting, but also a domestic man, a middle-aged gay man, part of a couple. A visit included a trip to Jess's studio, and that was so lovely, though even a question put to Jess was answered by Robert. After Robert died, I used to invite Jess and Thom for a birthday lunch together—both born in August. Jess came forward, into the world more, the result of dealing with Robert's illness, and then from managing on his own.

When Robert was in St. Mary's, I read him the whole of *House of the Seven Gables*. He would dream through it sometimes, and tell me his version, often including himself in the story. There was one time when his potassium was not right, which made him paranoid—he said he knew what it was like to be in hell.

Jess become demented at the end of his life, and a group of friends looked after him. This was not simple because he was independent, reclusive, and refused to let anyone stay in his vast house—"This house is too small for two people!" I visited him on Fridays and took him out to lunch. During our last lunch together, Jess was silent, as he often was. I rattled on about a trip to Maine to visit my dear friend Elin Elisofon. Surprisingly, he broke in, and asked me what Elin was to me. I said she was like family. He said, define family. I said, I know that when I'm trouble she will help me. Jess took my hand and said, I'm family too.

This tribute was read at the launch for *A Poet's Mind: Collected Interviews with Robert Duncan, 1960–1985*, ed. Christopher Wagstaff (Berkeley: North Atlantic Books, 2012), at the Berkeley City Club, October 21, 2012. "More Notes" was added in 2015.

THOM GUNN MEMORIAL IN THE MORRISON

READING ROOM

I spent so much time in this room reading poetry when I was a student here in the late sixties. This is where I first read Thom's work, in an anthology, a sampling of British poets—I think it was called *The New Poetry*. It seemed odd to me that anything new could come from England, and, in fact, most of the poets did not seem new at all. But Thom's work jumped out along with the citizens of his poems who are "born to lose." These young men give their all, but to what? Not exactly to love, not exactly to pleasure, but to a certain vision of the present where energy is the chief good and where it speaks through the body and through the group. This man:

> Wore cycle boots and jackets here
> To suit the Sunday hangout he was in,
> Heard, as he stretched back from his beer,
> Leather creak softly round his neck and chin

Twelve or thirteen long years later, Robert Duncan brought a pal to a reading I gave at Aaron Shurin's series on Natoma Street. Those two acted like boisterous kids, laughing at my jokes, slapping each other on the back, actually elbowing each other in the ribs, and I was amazed when the pal in the tough leather jacket turned out to be Thom Gunn. I wanted to age like those two friends; that is, never to grow old. Later we made a club of sorts, meeting every few months, and now both my dear friends and lunch companions are gone.

When Thom and I read here on campus in the Green Room in 1995, Thom asked me to read "Purple Men," a story that he hoped would scandalize everyone, and some people did walk out. Thom enjoyed a scandal, and when we met, he usually told me something about his sexual mountain-climbing expeditions, but the first thing he volunteered during his last years was that he was not writing. After that our conversation was like anyone else's, except punctuated by Thom's bark of a laugh. Books and movies, news about our constructed families, poetry gossip. We had a soft spot for Keanu Reeves and for the camp debasements of TV shows like *Models Inc.* When I was thinking about starting a relationship with a much younger man, I complained, "We have nothing in common," and Thom sensibly replied, "See a movie together, then you'll have something to talk about."

Thom came to my Writers on Writing class at San Francisco State just seven days before he died, so I guess that was his last public appearance. As usual he spoke without pretension and without prudery about his life and work. He enjoyed himself, and my students and I were moved by the quality of his attention. It was a night class—I insisted he take a taxi home. He had planned to ride the bus.

When I introduced Thom to my class, here's some of what I said: One does not think of Thom's lines so much as his stanzas, which are amazingly flexible, at once relaxed and tense, and adaptable to a full range of emotion and depiction. That stanza points outward. I was not surprised to learn that when he was a boy he wanted to write novels, because he shares the novelist's endlessly renewable surprise at the fact that one person is different from another. His poems convey modesty before the act of creation, and a friendliness and even gallantry toward the reader, which underwrite even the grittiest passages.

Finally, two comparisons. This love of friendship extends to his subject matter. Like Yeats, Thom is a poet of friendship. Sex is generally an expression of friendship, sometimes fleeting, rather than romance. Second, like the poet D. H. Lawrence, Thom loves energy, especially physical energy. Thom respects it, mourns it when it passes, praises it in its excesses, describes it in all its signs and shapes, and generally delights in it.

Yesterday, looking at Thom's poems, I discovered in my book-shelf a surprising number of chapbooks and letterpress books that he had given me over the years, that had been gathering there; and I felt the loss of Thom in a new way as one does, the shape of loss taking new forms, this time missing the loyalty of his friendship. In one of these books, Thom has a poem called "Back to Life" that ends:

> The lamp still shines.
> The pale leaves shift a bit,
> Now light, now shadowed, and their movements shared
> A second later by the bough,
> Even by the sap that runs through it:
> A small full trembling through it now
> As if each leaf were, so, better prepared
> For falling sooner or later separate.

This tribute was read at the University of California, Berkeley, August 29, 2005.

BARRETT WATTEN

THE NEGOTIATED SELF

I heard a few of Barrett Watten's essays when he delivered them at 80 Langton Street (later, New Langton Arts). They were harrowing: something had happened but our relation to it was that of captive witnesses watching Watten think. Now, reading these essays, they continue to be quirky, resistant, but also comprehensible, even suspenseful—a passionate reading of the twentieth century, an investigation in which everything is at stake. Watten's loyalties, grievances, and contempt are real; they are partisan, not pious. More—Watten maps for himself discoveries as he sights them, developing a critical approach. "I wanted to extend an argument by virtue of the disjunction between previous methods and as yet discussed literary facts." It's a difficult project because what hasn't yet been said lacks terms, so Watten invents a vocabulary or applies borrowed terms to his new context. Here are some of them.

1. Scale. "While *size* determines an object, it is *scale* that determines art" (Robert Smithson); so, for example, explanation changes a subject's scale, since it provides a broader context. The idea is *relation*: "The impossibility of social scale in the 40's generated the personal aesthetics of the New York School." Literature looks for new "languages"—a heroic quest and the first cause of disjunction, since a larger scale is a Utopian break, whether that scale is the future, origins, geology, pure being. Finally, "Language determines meaning on a scale of its own." That is, language becomes a "dimensionless utopia."

2. Technique. The principle of construction, how the writing is written, the coming into perceptibility of the poem. Watten identifies specific social contexts from which techniques emerged—like the use of the noun phrase by Larry Eigner and other postmoderns. "Events seen through technique here become a form of sheer being."

3. Method. The overall activity of the writer in the world—the extension of the act of writing into the world.

4. Image. Watten's book could be seen as a running investigation of the meaning of image. Russian Formalists free it from the symbolists' weight—it goes from being essential to a "device." For the surrealists "the image travels endlessly; this is the substance of Surrealist internationalism." In Smithson, "images cancel each other out"—a moment of estrangement perpetuated through a structural metaphor; language becoming matter. Watten compares the different uses that Breton and Clark Coolidge make of images generated by involuntary memory.

5. X. Reference, what is outside, total, the world. Once it's understood that meaning resides in systems, this understanding imparts a luster to the beyond, to nonmeaning or total meaning. The missing X is impossible to encompass in language, but different approaches to it give poems their particular edge. Poems approach the missing X by means of form as much as content.

6. Modernism. "Modernism was heroic and had a belief in the future. And I identify with the distance and objectification involved in modernism . . . it's possible to make a world in which one would like to live." I added modernism to this glossary because it's wise for us postmoderns to ask, whose modernism? The heroically asserted disjunctions of the moderns are now (as they predicted) standard fare in our hardly Utopian consciousness. Diverse writers and groups

rightly claim this terrain of wavering boundaries—think of Julia Kristeva's "abjection" or Guy Hocquenghem's migrating gender relations. Watten's modernism is masculine (nine women are mentioned in *Total Syntax*—most in passing) and orthodox. By that I mean his emphasis is on materials, with their coefficient of resistance, and on the meaning of form. He charts the inroads formalism makes as our century "progresses." There is no "impure," no expressionism, no Proust, T. S. Eliot, H.D., Genet, Bataille—who make autobiographies to criticize, complain, and tell stories about the self's painful negotiations. Self, language, and world have a lot in common but probably don't share a common denominator, a beautiful and ugly realization that takes its twentieth-century place with the ancient mutabilities. When autobiography does emerge, as it does in Olson's work, Watten rejects it, bringing Olson into line: "Finally the Romantic self *itself* argues for precedence of language against itself and its defects."

Like every serious writer, Watten develops his own relation to his ancestors—in this case, his "famous fathers"—partly to create a lineage, partly to set the above terms in motion. He invokes writers who reinvent the self and define themselves on the largest available scale. Victor Shklovsky, the first of these "governing figures," is a welcome one, and with him Watten takes us through Russian Formalism: "Everything in the work exists in order that it be perceived." That's both estrangement and technique; and here's scale: "Literature stays alive by expanding into non-literature" (Shklovsky). And to illustrate, there's a zaum, a verse form invented by Khlebnikov that operated on the phonemic level, below "meaning"—"When the rhythmic requirements of a language outstrip what is possible to say, poetry enters into the area of 'transrational' poetics—overloaded with connotation to the point of blur."

Breton is next, for me the most problematical figure. The method developed by Breton and the French surrealists was amazingly liberating for other writers: it touched every subsequent vital writing practice—Spanish surrealism and New York

School poetry, for example. Watten writes: "The end product of the Surrealist method: to free the mind so we can have it." But much of the French surrealists' poetry was lusterless: "L'Union libre" will go down with "Invictus" in the chronicle of the misadmired. Proust's use of involuntary memory was more interesting because it involved more risk—risk impossible in the equivalence of the surrealist image. That's Bataille's critique: that surrealist oppositions were static, undialectical. Watten has mixed feelings about Breton too: he tells a cautionary tale of literary vanguardism. Still, Breton was a gold mine of technique, and technique constructs a future (like the steam mill inventing the factory.)

Watten's Robert Smithson is an argument against liberal humanism—against modernist Utopia. Instead, we see ourselves in unmediated geological time and space, subject to irreversible processes like crystallization and entropy. "To be conscious of the actuality of perception" leads to knowledge of time and death. Watten looks at Smithson's prose as a possible literary model: "It is the detachable frame carried along the open road—where the frame is, if anything, more physically real than anything seen through it."

Watten's essays are brilliant and useful; his deepest work is on Charles Olson, his "compression of narrative time to an imagistic radical." It's a great discussion. For Olson, the initial equals "truth"—it reminds me of Freud's "modernist" faith in the truth of initial scenes, a sense of origins that postmodern theory dismantles. Watten shows how Olson's recognition of beginnings comes to equal for the poet-historian recognition of his linguistic material on a formal level. Olson factors his formalist estrangement—first sightings in history and language—into the work in a structuralist way. (I can now see Olson's brand of existentialism as a kind of moral formalism.)

"Reference is stabilized" (becomes a text) in memory or writing, or by considering history as a genre, so getting reference into writing can be like incorporating texts. Reference: the missing X. About Hart Crane's "Royal Palm": "What does an absolute pole of reference do to the structure of a verbal work of art?" Watten's reading of Crane is gorgeous.

> The poem aspires to raise another palm tree in "heaven," that is to say in the mind, one that it will never achieve. But in so doing it creates time and space—time, a narrative in reverse, a progressive return to the initial, and space, the illusion of the approach to the palm, fleshed out in the numbers of intersecting semantic planes, all self-consuming. Here manner (the poem) and matter (the palm) are set apart at a considerable distance for maximum effect.

These essays conclude with discussions of contemporary work that bring Watten's various subjects into the present. Almost all the work is Language oriented, despite the loss of the best example. Dennis Cooper is not mentioned, even though he is an inheritor of Crane's approach to the absolute referent (in Cooper's case, the beloved who is also a zero). Kathy Acker is absent, despite the fact that her prose is *the* example of collapsing genre into trope. Is literary history a set of problems whose collapsed solutions are Language-oriented poems? Is this a postmodern equivalent of modernism—that is, a pastiche of earlier modes? My collective impression is that a *group* reviews the articulations of earlier periods as an allegory pointing to itself and its final position. That makes *Total Syntax* interesting and sets its limits. It surely deserves a place of honor in the canon of Language writing—Watten locates a poetics, gives it a history and a vocabulary, and I can't think of anyone who could accomplish that with more authority and depth.

It's a convincing poetics: nonresolution of meaning is its governing figure. There is the focus on materials, the dazzle of an extreme formalism which heightens the inherent ambiguities of reference, and the glamour of a linguistic scandal. On the minus side, the work accounts for power structures (subject matter) metaphorically, as in "this stands for (is) a self" in the same sense as "this stands for (is) language." Power structures overlap with but don't equal language. A writer could not use this poetics to convince or to explore power relations: it lacks polemical or erotic continuities, hence the largest view is not represented.

Watten writes: "The 'self' as the meaning of literature as we have experienced it in American art since World War II had become a total limit. There is a disjunction occurring now in the form because there is new content; there's something that hasn't been said, and that's what I want." The drama of twentieth-century lit is its privileged role in tearing up and making new models of the self. That's what gives a new aesthetic (Breton's, Shklovsky's) its scandal. Still, self is an historical construction. It can't be dispelled with linguistic play: it's not a literary construct—it's political, economic, philosophical, or none of these. Banishing the self has its dialectics—self returns as "other." Out of two voids—between signified and signifier, between silence and speech—step monsters who become us. Disjunction (exploded self) registers schizophrenia / critiques the world based on disorganization / cleans the windows of perception / proposes an improved self / accounts for the arrival on the stage of history of autonomous groups with their own "languages," a social basis for plural identities and "voices" (sort of a linguistic social democracy).

So most interesting writing is inhabited by a constantly renegotiated self. Like the other images of self, this negotiated self is a trope—is it a suitable one? To me, it's the most interesting in poetry now.

But it's a difficult task to untangle the two aspects in current writing. On one hand, a progressive formalism, which Watten's essays illustrate, finally precludes narration and subjectivity. On the other, pleasures of the writer-audience connection reassert themselves, from which follow spectacle, thrills and spills, and (hopefully) the leverage to recreate ourselves. During the last decade critical writing has taken stage center in the production of models of the self. Critics like Barthes, Foucault, Kristeva complete the picture, since they include modernism as text *and* allow history (power structures) as context and critique—that is, they provide continuity and disjunction, a wider view. I hope that poetry can extend its scale once again into the world and encompass this new language. But here's Watten with the last word:

> A discourse on poetics from the standpoint of poets being in charge of their own interpretation will begin with the structuring principles of language—the ways in which a poem can be built. "What a poem is"—at all levels, from the sound pattern to its determination of social meaning—is the means by which it extends through the medium—of language, culture and self.

"The Negotiated Self" was published in *Poetry Flash*, no. 148, ed. Joyce Jenkins (June 1985).

DENNIS COOPER

RUNNING ON EMPTINESS

I have been a fan of Dennis Cooper's work since the appearance of his first book, *Idols*, in 1979. Since then he has built each new book—*The Tenderness of the Wolves*, *Safe*, and now *Closer*—on the one before it. Each is a deeper exploration of beauty, death, pop culture, sex, and emotional distance.

Even so, *Closer* surprised me. It is certainly Cooper's finest work. It's a novel, structured as a rondo, that depicts a few months in the lives of a few seventeen- and eighteen-year-olds who make up a small, perverse circle of students inside a larger, perverse America. There is no sense of what a norm might be on either side.

This is not a cautionary tale, or a "study" on the effects of drugs and outré sex on the young, any more than Edgar Allan Poe was cautioning his readers to avoid dreary mansions or too much solitude in the crypt. It is, like "The House of Usher," an exploration of mortality that generates feelings of awe and fear.

The boys live in the *Leave it to Beaver* suburbs of a fantastic planet (LA?) where emotion is miniaturized and inappropriate, communication somewhat old-fashioned. Even lust is corny, except in its most predatory modes. The plot centers on their desire for "a badly tuned hologram" named George, a boy whose life is falling apart, even compared to the dismantled lives of his friends. George lives in a male world. His teachers are all men. His mother, the novel's center of feeling, is dying of cancer and can't speak.

George is sustained by LSD, Disneyland, and a sex life that forms one of the main sources of suspense in the novel. We wonder if he will survive his affair with Philippe and Tom, tormented fiends who kill boys like George. "Philippe lay in bed imagining George's death. He was extremely drunk, his eyes were closed. The world he saw rang with percussion. Skeletons snapped. Blood and entrails exploded on a grand scale, while George, deposited deep in these fireworks, flailed like a tiny acrobat."

Cooper takes us into Philippe's thoughts: "I am too interested in what is beautiful, and when beauty is not somewhere, I create it. But when something is beautiful it is impossible for me to understand. 'How do you mean this?' I mean beauty is powerful. I feel very weak when I see it, or when I create it. No, I cannot explain. . . . 'Death is beautiful?' It is too beautiful to explain. . . . 'You wish to die?' No, I wish never to die, but to see myself in death. To know what I am in the answer of death." This passage, which sheds light on the would-be murderer, is so eerie because it also illuminates the motivation of any writer.

Like a porn novel, or any genre novel, *Closer* has an element of daydream about what can be taken for granted. Homosexuality is mostly taken for granted. The question is more like, is coprophilia too weird? George is the star because he is so beautiful and so far gone, yet he has enough self-realization to maintain a plot-line. Like a porn hero, George has "natural" ability—he knows what his partners want, which is mainly to play dead. Steve says, "He's face down a few feet away, lying so still it's like he's not listening, more like he's dead or has left his nude body idling in a room. It's a spooky sight. I'm about sure I'm in love with it."

On one hand, these boys know nothing. On the other, they have seen it all. George is a type America produces, murders, and then is haunted by. That is, George and his friends are Marilyn Monroes, desirable and exploitable, "too dumb to live." They may have little sense of self preservation, but they can discuss the mechanisms of desire with the freedom of eighteenth-century libertines. George says, "I allowed this guy Chuck to have sex with me. . . . I was like something he wanted to buy but couldn't really afford." They are aware of the feints and substitutions of desire. "I'd arch my back and come, dazed by the strange combination of lust and petty loss I felt." One of the pleasures of this novel is in the insights they trade.

If their approach seems pornographic, it's because they learn sex from pornography, which inspires a high level of invention and scrutiny. "We look at a photograph and get aroused, yet we still have our wits. But just now I became so distracted by what you were doing to me, I simply lost my perspective. You turned into someone I'd much rather not know." They learn how "to be" from what is most distracting—Disneyland, splatter movies, pop music, porn. "Alex tenses. He pictures the skin being torn off the kid and gobbled down like a pancake." Cooper portrays these "pathologies" with the same loving attention Poe gave to his. The boys are heavy judges, every utterance falls on the scale of sincere/insincere—both challenged and appreciated for being fake. Alex, just crippled in a car wreck, can't be distracted from a splatter movie. 'That's the worst look of terror I've ever seen," he says. Everything loses ground to the fake—fake intimacy, fake death, fake sex.

Put another way, they are connoisseurs of failed effects. David, for example, is delusional, yet in his wildest fantasy he is a pop star with no talent and bad material—blandly cute and without character. "The critics who hate me are fairly articulate. The ones who adore me are shallow and indirect. What is a 'dreamboat' exactly?"

Cooper extends Poe's particular terrain. Like Poe, Cooper is a religious writer and the horror genre is a religious genre. Where else do people rise from the dead? Over and over, almost as a refrain, the characters come up against mortality, which in fact makes anything as temporal as desire or self seem fake. "Being gorgeous. . . It helps me believe in myself and not worry that I'm just a bunch of blue tubes inside a skin wrapper. . . . On the bright side, this means I'm a siren. I lure children into adulthood by mouthing insanities like, 'I love you,' when what I actually mean is, 'You'll die someday.'" They are haunted by the irreconcilable gap between the everyday and death—"that ambiguous inch between facial expression and soul." Death weakens them because they have no value that survives its spotlight.

Cooper has given a voice to an emptiness we can barely stand to think about. He is a fanatical purist, which means that he must take nothingness into account. Poe (our first formalist) said that the most beautiful subject, most fit for literature, is the most melancholy: the death of a young maiden. Cooper's drugged-out, murdered teenage boys are our Annabel Lees in their beauty and inability to survive, in the intensity of love's failure to nurture or protect. In fact, they don't necessarily have to die to be dead— "We become two little ghosts wearing human masks. . . ."—which takes into account the century between the two writers.

A boy one-half inch more mature than the others puts an end to the story's various perils. We experience relief, but also some disappointment—have the beautiful monsters and victims vanished? Actually, the boy has only to say "I love you" and be more than halfway sincere. Is Cooper sincere? Then evil is chased away with a boo!

Closer is immediately recognizable in its contemporary themes: loss of scale, the miniaturization of experience, stunned emotional life. Cooper dallies with the workings of narration and, in doing so, with the meaning of self. His work belongs with that of Poe, Sade, Baudelaire, and Bataille, other writers who argued with mortality.

"Running on Emptiness" was published in the *San Francisco Chronicle*, June 4, 1989.

PAMELA LU

PAMELA: A NOVEL

When has a euporia of such stunning invention rung the changes of an aporia so absolute? *Pamela: A Novel* marries the ability to generalize with the endless unrolling of the self as it readjusts to its own failure to exist. Lu tracks the doings of L, R, C, A, and the narrator, I, as they look at a mall, eat at a Malaysian restaurant on Clement Street, go for a walk. L, R, C, A, and I are instances of themselves, functions, mispronounced words. Lu conveys the boundless artificiality of their experience and the particular nausea of imploding infrastructures in a pastiche of eighteenth-century style whose artifice is never broken and whose solemn periods are as measured as a march by Handel.

I prefer to think of Lu's sentences as Ciceronian, and of *Pamela* as classical revival in the tradition of the early modernists like Isadora and Nijinsky. Here are the generally held truths, *what oft was thought*, expressed in old-new sentences ringing with collective confidence. Lu's generally held tenets call for a disbelief so extreme it acts as faith.

These truths, *ne'er so well expressed*, are emitted by We, a glorious pronoun in which Lu builds a social space and founds a society. Like any court society, the function of each member is to be a little different from the others in order to create fascinating permutations of like and unlike. *Pamela* could be a collaboration of Madame de La Fayette and Maurice Blanchot, but "the community of doubt" looks like a rotary club next to L, R, C, A, and I!

Archimedes said, "Give me a place to stand and I will move the world." But what if the place to stand turns out to be too far away? Then he would be in a good position to comment on the disappearance of the subject. The combinations of intimate and distant, full and empty, fertile and arid, expectation and loss, and the sheer might of Lu's prose, fill this grateful reader with a mournful jubilation.

"*Pamela: A Novel*" was published in the *Small Press Traffic Newsletter* in 1994. It was reprinted in the *Stranger* (Seattle), November 4, 1999.

TED BERRIGAN

FOR THE POETRY PROJECT

In 1969, I went back to the land. I couldn't be a poet there, so I found a ride on a ride board to New York, which still radiated the glamour and genius of Frank O'Hara. Somehow, I was O'Hara as well as a rather somber hippie. The driver turned out to be a Hungarian poet, Zoltan Farkas—where is he now? Zoltan seemed kind of rough—he called a gun a "rod"—and he knew Anselm Hollo. We stopped in Iowa City where Anselm lived in a kind of Utopia, a heterosexual masterpiece that was utterly beyond my means and my abilities. Lovely house, lovely wife, great job, pretty children. Was this what I, a poet, looked forward to? Anselm suggested taking Ted Berrigan's writing workshop and he gave me Bill Berkson's address, assuring me that Bill was a nice guy. When I arrived in New York I wrote to Bill. I still reel inwardly when I recall that letter—giddy and overfamiliar, a la mode, I thought then—in which I asked him to supply me with a job, an apartment, and a lover. I instructed myself to make one mistake a week (the literariness of that thought makes me wince). Every breath I took was a mistake, but how could I know? How could I find out what a living poet did and how a living poet thought and spoke? The only reason to bring it up now is to make shame happen, the last uncorrupted emotion. Bill *is* nice. I have never asked him if he remembers that letter, even though he's my friend and my boss at the San Francisco Art Institute.

I had already read Berrigan's *The Sonnets* and I studied *The World* like the Talmud, trying to learn to write and be. Later, when Anne Waldman told me she was accepting a poem of mine, I was so abashed I couldn't speak, and I can still feel my body then, my head wobbling and grinning like a pumpkin on a stick, lit up, moronic. Anne Waldman, Ted Berrigan, Ron Padgett, they were gods to me. I just sat in the corner of Ted's apartment on St. Mark's, absorbing, absorbing, which was fine, since he emitted ceaselessly. He showed us a poem he'd just written about meeting Anne at Grand Central Station, and he asked me to read it to the group. Then he explained how he had gently nudged Grand Central into being a symbol without depriving it of its daily reality. He read some of my work. He praised it, said he had a few things to tell me, did I have a phone? No, I didn't. Could we meet? It seemed we both slept during the day, but at night I worked at Grand Central unloading mail trucks, my nocturnal reality. Though Grand Central surrounded me with "language acts" and symbolic meetings, it turned out to be an impediment to communication. I wonder what Ted wanted to say.

I first read at St. Mark's with Leslie Scalapino, and later with Kathy Acker—two great writers. With Leslie, I read a long graphic chapter that takes place in a bathhouse. A woman sat in the first row with her little boy—what did they make of all this homo sex? That chapter ends in a chaste passage on the romance of Mickey and Minnie Mouse, but for some reason as soon as I began reading about the mouse couple the woman dragged her son away, right up the center aisle. Leslie and I wondered about that.

Later, I was on a panel moderated by Charles Bernstein, with Nick Piombino and Lydia Davis. Something about narration, narration, narration. I talked about the ways people represent themselves in language. James Sherry kept asking, "Bob, why narration?" "James, remember at the bar last night, you told me about yourself and what was going on, and the form you took was little stories?" James joked, "I didn't mean to," which I still think is hilarious. The real response came from Erica Hunt, when she called out, "Writing is not talking." There we all agree.

This essay on Ted Berrigan was written for the St. Mark's Poetry Project, New York City, 1997. (I wonder if it was published?)

CHRIS KRAUS

ALIENS & ANOREXIA

Chris Kraus's second novel, *Aliens and Anorexia*, is two things at once. First, it is a companionable book; you will be very glad to think along with Kraus, try on her comic, eloquent "reading" of contemporary culture and the meaning of storytelling. Second, it is a performance: Kraus becomes naked in public, and then more naked because she tells us about her own failure, that un-American condition. *Aliens* is a heterogeneous record of failure set in diverse locations, at once in the center and on the outskirts of the avant-garde. "A single moment of true sadness connects you instantly to all the suffering in the world." Taken together, these failures amount to a critical position and reveal a great longing for a true relation to the world. As alienation becomes more intense, the ways to establish connection become more extreme. This makes the novel a "case history," but its illness afflicts us all.

To elaborate her theme, Kraus meditates on the life and work of French philosopher Simone Weil: Weil's "panic of altruism"; her sense that narrative is supposed to "make things right"; and her anorexia, framed not as "woman's manipulation" or even personal salvation, but as moral stance and critique—a state of decreation. "Female acts are always subject to interpretation," Kraus writes. "It's inconceivable that the female subject might ever simply try to step outside her body, because the only thing that's irreducible, still, in female life is gender."

Braided into this matter are Kraus's failure to market her film, *Gravity & Grace*; Ulrike Meinhof's ghostly soliloquies ("This is Ulrike Meinhof speaking to the inhabitants of Earth. You must make your death public. As the rope was tightening around my neck, an Alien made love with me"); the story of Kraus's Scheherazade attempt to keep her e-mail-and-phone lover from the disconnect ("The story had an s/m moral: it isn't chemistry or personality that counts, it's what you do. This is a quantum leap beyond modernism's ethos of transgression, in which eroticism arises from disgust. Disgust implies duality; requires content. But now that there's no longer any meaning in the landscape, it is possible to fabricate desire anywhere. The technology of s/m transforms neutrality into content"); and the life and example of Paul Thek. Finally, we learn about a group that believes it will be carried off by a spaceship on a certain night (in fact, the plot of Kraus's movie, *Gravity & Grace*).

This is true hybrid writing in which a whole genre can become autobiography by virtue of the author's engagement.

"*Aliens & Anorexia*" was published in *Small Press Traffic Newsletter*, Fall 2000.

ROBIN BLASER

SMALL PRESS TRAFFIC LIFETIME ACHIEVEMENT AWARD

I'm here to present Robin with Small Press Traffic's lifetime achievement award. Knowing that this presentation would follow Norma's introduction and Robin's reading, I wondered what I might add to this evening's offerings. What a mistake it would be for me to introduce you to the poetry you have just experienced. On the other hand, if we can gather anything from Robin's six decade career, it is not to make a conclusion, but to continue the story and take our direction from the poem, which is indirection. He says, "We enter a territory without totalities where poetic practice is our stake and necessity."

Why The Poetry Center?—did you know that Robin was a librarian here at State from 1961 to 1965? That was after he worked at the Widener Library at Harvard. Robin's history is bound up with the history of this city, from the San Francisco Renaissance till 1966 when he moved to Vancouver; and beyond that, through the following decades, weaving the cities together, their left politics and problems of representation that have proved such fertile connundrums. That is, what does and should language do? That is, what is a poem? That is, the problem of figure and ground. Just as he turned San Francisco from an idea to a place for the Canadians, he was a Cascadian bridge for us.

And why Small Press Traffic? In the midseventies, in the early days of New Narrative at Small Press Traffic, Bruce Boone showed me Robin's "Moth Poem," that glimmering marvel that appears and disappears at the same time. Those moths were not symbols but facts. Here was a poetry that was fact oriented, image oriented, and against symbol, and yet filled with light and immanence, as though Robin were some kind of Objectivist writing from some kind of heaven. He said in "The Fire": "It is, I think, the purest storytelling to try to catch that light—and the difficulty of it, the loss of it, is personal. If I see the light, even fragmentarily, and lose it, that too is subject matter." Here was a fragmented writing that proposed a narrative that was continuously reframed. Here was a writing that lifted the self out of the box of psychology into the largest realms. If life is a serial poem, then lifetime achievement must be a kind of Holy Forest. He wrote "I want here to create the image of a field which is true history, and autobiography, as well as land, place, and presence."

We were looking to the Berkeley Renaissance and to those mighty Companions, Robin Blaser, Jack Spicer, and Robert Duncan, to find a model of what we wanted for ourselves; that is, to their example of a band of writers. And Robin has remained an example for us in San Francisco and for our Canadian friends. His poetry speaks to the concerns of the West: What is a community, what does it consist of? What part does language play in this Image Nation, this community of doubt and faith? In this real and imaginary community, the métier of poetry is passed down from poet to poet, and the Poet is a village commons, a local and global commons that produces image after image. Robin wrote, "And here I wish to say that it is not language which is the source: it is the record of the meeting, and the magical structure of sight, sound, and intellect (which is derived from Zukovsky's definition of poetry) but it is also the medium which can be shaped." Learnedness is a form of agency here— Robin communes through the medium of learnedness with the great Companions who are also citizens of his hometown, Dante, Nerval, Merleau-Ponty, Deleuze.

Robin has shown us how agency and public life occur in poetry, and by that I mean the quest for individual freedom and basic human rights. His elegance of mind and spirit does not leave anything out, and by that I mean his is a poetics of interrogation. His rich scholarship is a form of recognition because it gives us access to our own dally and hourly experience—a learnedness that is not different from emotion or risk.

I salute you especially as a fellow westerner, since your engagement with western matters gives all of us yet more elbow room by tearing down yet more fences. The poesis is "an activity turned in / all directions." That said, when I think of the image you have developed, I think of the eastern West, the Asian West where healthy spiritual sight equals clear vision, and image radiates immanence. "Black water swept by the wind / upside-down trees / and sky, shadowy, at the bottom / other step-stones / holes in the world."

It is an honor for me to present this award, and a pleasure because Robin is dear to me, as he is to so many. As his friends know, he is the grandest of playmates. When Robin and I were at Naropa together, we engaged in a purely disinterested experiment: to gauge the effect of martinis on the human body at high altitudes.

This is to say, Robin Blaser is a key poet of the New American poetry and beyond. If, as he says, paraphrasing the Mother of Us All, that Canada is his country and San Francisco is his hometown, then what *is* your home town but the place you come to be recognized? We must conclude that we belong to him, and that he belongs to us. So, let's give him this award.

This award speech was read at The Poetry Center reading and ceremony, San Francisco State University, September 16, 2007.

DODIE BELLAMY AND SAM D'ALLESANDRO

PREFACE TO *REAL*

Real includes correspondence between Dodie Bellamy and Sam D'Allesandro, a story taped by Sam before his death in 1988, and a long letter by Dodie that reinvents the subject of death in the fullness of the present.

The letters are a spinoff of Dodie's larger work, *The Letters of Mina Harker*, and they demonstrate the community-mindedness of that project. In the early eighties, Dodie decided to appropriate *Dracula* by becoming Bram Stoker's victim/vampire. Dodie/Mina wrote to fellow writers who answered as themselves or as figures in the vampire legend (Bruce Boone was Dr. Van Helsing) or as myths of their own making (like Sam's SX). Dodie's plan broke the form of the epistolary novel by making it real; in doing so she allowed her correspondents to display the fiction of their personalities. In other words, it's pure New Narrative.

I am proud to say that this and other great works, like Kevin Killian's *Shy*, Sam D'Allesandro's *Zombie Pit*, Michael Amnasan's *I Can't Distinguish Opposites*, Edith Jenkins's *Divisions on a Ground*, Francesca Rosa's *The Divine Comedy of Carlo Tresca*, and Camille Roy's *The Rosy Medallions* began in workshops I conducted at Small Press Traffic, the poetry bookstore in San Francisco. It was a time before death and full of potential. We were emphatically pre-HIV, and Language poetry had opened up theoretical vistas. So much talent attracted more talent and the workshops led a charmed life. We were developing a prose to refigure reader-writer relations, deal with gender, sexuality, and the body, and examine the meaning of narration. A writing that bent back toward surface and artifice, but still took risks.

Different amounts of Arcadian sunlight fell on us depending on who is reminiscing, but I think the meeting and romance of Dodie Bellamy and Kevin Killian will secure my workshop a place in legend. These letters describe the start of that amazingly fertile marriage.

Real illuminates the before and after of AIDS. In the first section the unbridled SX and Mina are both contemptuous of their hosts, Dodie and Sam. Sam says, "God, I think we could be so real if we could only find the way." How convey the whole truth?—by using secrets, evasions, lies, insecurities, and the unknown. (Mina says, "Bad metaphors are the only way we can approach the really important things, don't you agree?") This is played out in the drama of sob sisters who thoroughly enjoy the trouble they cause and are. Mina asks Sam, "I need a woman, will you be that for me? I mean I need somebody to talk to. I mean I'm hurting." There is a truth-or-dare flirtation: "Mina, I'm naked right now." Will SX and Mina have sex?—since for each, everyone is a possible partner? "What I want to know is whether you hate me or just want to fuck me?" Doesn't real contact equal perversion?

They were two young poets new to prose and longing to arrive. They were part of a community they name: Steve Abbott, Bruce Boone, Robin Blaser, Jono Weiss, Roberto Bedoya, Francesca Rosa, Eileen Myles, and others (with Dennis Cooper, Kathy Acker, and Patti Smith as reference points).

The language of therapy is raised, but Dodie and Sam dismiss the notion of mental health as a joke. They enjoy their complications. Both writers reject the closure of inner life but retain its conflicts and enigmas. For both the body is an evasive absolute: turn it inside out, stretch it like taffy, fry it with drugs, clobber it with orgasms. Secrets become social blood. With his last breath, Sam says "Everything's leaking out—now everyone knows everything. My secrets are getting away . . ." And in the last section the hidden facts of his life—like his real name—are brought to light.

I miss Sam. I was drawn to him—then up close his beauty seemed so large it scared me away. His was the death that most diminishes my own corner of the writing world, and I hope this book helps to establish his cult. His palm print is visible in the halting, desolate story that was transcribed for *Real*.

Although Dodie was leading "in competition for gross-out—but that's such a yawn since being female all the cards are stacked on my side," in the end Sam won for shock and extremity—he died. Dodie's last letter (1993) is a homage to him ("To look as precisely as possible at the ever-wavering presence . . .") and a series of inventions on mortality in the time of AIDS. The prose is pitched so high it's thrilling. The letter is a summit of writing on sex and death, a garden in which the void prospers. "Sam, I never dreamed that playing dead could make you feel so alive." Dodie's work so enlarges my life I could describe it endlessly because I would be talking about myself. I look forward to the publication of *The Letters of Mina Harker* so our fin de siècle can have its own *Les Chants de Maldoror*.

"Preface to *Real*" is the preface to *Real* by Dodie Bellamy and Sam D'Allesandro (Jersey City, NJ: Talisman House, 1994).

1996

EDMUND WHITE

A BOY'S OWN STORY

When I retrieved my copy of *A Boy's Own Story* for this essay, I was surprised by how short the book is—a little over two hundred pages. By the time I finished it I had come to think of it again as a big novel. Why is that? The story is not grand; its events are poised between tableau and anecdote. Except for the narrator, characters don't emerge very far past the proscenium arch of the prose. Of course, it's the prose and the corresponding isolation of the narrator/hero that give the novel grandeur.

One is always guided back to the surface. For example, White abandons the conventional timeline of a story about a boy's education. We don't travel with this boy into his future. He is fifteen when the book begins. He spends the summer with dad at a beach resort and has an affair with twelve-year-old Kevin. In the second section, during the previous summer, the boy is fourteen and working for his father. In an impressive display of realpolitik he negotiates his failed plan to run away into the purchase of a hustler.

He's seven in the third section; we learn about his parent's divorce, his life with mother. Then we go forward to his eleventh year, and the family drama extends to include eccentrics at home and at camp, where the boy has sex with a dysfunctional camper. In the fifth section, the boy, now thirteen years old, rises to the call of popularity and falls in love with a girl. In the last section he's fourteen: he encounters more eccentrics at a pseudo-Anglo prep school, and he stages the betrayal of a teacher that heralds the onset of adulthood.

This manipulation of forward momentum sends us into the thematics of the story; it provides the leisure for these thematics to develop associatively and through figurative language. For example, the father's sexual life is described as follows: "This hint of mystery about a man so cold and methodical fascinated me—as though he, the rounded brown geode, if only cracked open, would nip at the sky with interlocking crystal teeth, the quartz teeth of passion." Two pages later the simile is revamped to include the son, a manipulation of imagery at once subtle and outlandish. "What if I could write about my life exactly as it was? What if I could show it in all its density and tedium and its concealed passion, never divined or expressed, the dull brown geode that eats at itself with quartz teeth?"

The problem set up at the start of *A Boy's Own Story* is, how can I put myself in relation to my dad, who is all powerful? This problem is elaborated throughout the novel by means of a governing trope, the king or sovereign. The novel, you could say, magnifies the education of a boy through images of sovereignty. That a novel of sexual maturation addresses forms and relations power is one reason *A Boy's Own Story* is so un-American, so French.

These images comprise a system or fundamental structure (like Hegel's master-slave dialectic) because they are made to address such a broad spectrum of social relations. Sometimes they are mock epic (home is a fake Norman castle), but mostly they illustrate a continental wisdom: that desire and power are linked, that they are based on a kind of betrayal, a crime against love. These lofty images comprise a "theme and variations" that lend grandeur to the large movements and to the details. Images of sovereignty are brought to the isolation in the nuclear family, racism, male privilege, class privilege—issues that lift the book out of the box of psychology and the overheated nuclear closet. They remind me of Bataille, certainly Nietzsche, who might have written: "I even envied his sovereignty, though the price of freedom—total solitude—seemed more than I could possibly pay."

Many of these images center on the father—a Zeus, a deity, a king—and then they devolve onto the son as he matures.

When he was alone he was "not a boy at all but a principle of power, of absolute power." In a nice twist, in the last of these images our young fag attains full royal stature—as a queen. "Or I felt like someone in history, a queen on her way to the scaffold determined to suppress her usual quips, to give the spectators the high deeds they wanted to see."

A Boy's Own Story appeared in 1982, and I encountered it, as I encountered everything in those years, as a gay man. Its publication was greeted by myself and others both as a literary and cultural event. We were grateful to find incontestable literature that applied to us—an expressive possibility had arrived. In the early eighties, few books offered a reading of our experience, and we approached them with the emphatic interest of looking into mirrors, testing new reflections against expectations. We were alert to every nuance of sexuality and always searching for possibilities of identification.

A Boy's Own Story was published by a trade press and we needed to see our new identities in the national forum. We wondered how this book, which treated our sex in such an offhand manner, got past the guards? It's not enough to say that its ticket was quality because other literary books—those of Genet, Irving Rosenthal's *Sheeper*, John Rechy's *City of Night*, for example— were published by wicked Grove rather than august E. P. Dutton. New Directions published Isherwood's *Berlin Stories*.

The answer, I think, is partly the times and partly the prose. A gay market had been created by small presses, and suddenly editors working at large houses, like Bill Whitehead, could act on their interest in gay fiction. And in *A Boy's Own Story* every sentence tells a story—and that story is, "Look, this is literature." Sentences go to it like trumpets at Jericho: "I say all this by way of hoping that the lies I've made up to get from one poor truth to another may mean something—may even mean something most particular to you, my eccentric, patient, scrupulous reader, willing to make so much of so little, more patient and more respectful of life, of a life, than the author you're allowing for a moment to exist yet again." That is, this writing already comes to you from beyond the grave, a location more grandly French than English or American.

Perhaps this beauty "underwrote" the content, the recognizable (to us) push toward truth in sexuality. Two tykes are on an outing to buy Vaseline in order to ease the Way. "He pulled it off without a trace of guilt, even asked to see the medium-size jar before settling for the small one. Outside, a film of oil opalesced on the water under a great axle of red light rolling across the sky from azimuth to zenith." So their sex is splayed out across sea and sky (before the days of water-solubility). You could say the prose safeguards the experience of being gay.

Still, the book was a bit confusing in 1982. Unapologetic homosexuality was not the only unusual matter it brought to the larger realm of American letters—its portrayal of aggressive child sexuality, its savaging of the nuclear family, its unapologetic love of surface and preoccupation with artifice. *A Boy's Own Story* didn't jibe completely with the smaller realm of gay-community self-description—healthy, moral, natural—or nature that had been victimized. On the cover a boy in a tank top gazes outward, to the sea, to the future; his promise of health and offer of physical beauty were certainly on the movement's agenda. But the boy between the covers is entirely corrupted by self-consciousness and the knowledge of gender roles.

A Boy's Own Story's claim to the largest forum was not only based on its lyrical prose, a feather in our cap, but on its negative vision, its grand homosexual theme of betrayal. Love is not something you give to others, but something you do to them. Sex and friendship are taken from people. It's a description of extreme isolation.

A Boy's Own Story is so amoral. The blurbs promised a cross between J. D. Salinger and Oscar Wilde. I'd keep Wilde for prose that generates at once feelings of precision and incredulity, the great queen's aggression and assertion of surface that foregrounds the relation between writer and reader. But the moral anguish and problems of belief in Salinger are not even close. *A Boy's Own Story* may be a Bildungsroman with a Dickensian enthusiasm for eccentric guides, but at heart it has more in common with Machiavelli's "The Prince" than with *The Catcher in the Rye.*

If *A Boy's Own Story* does resemble *Catcher*, it's because both books ask, what constitutes maturity? Certainly every adult is an unacceptable model, and that is the joke of *A Boy's Own Story.* So, why not take revenge and betray one of these adults into revealing his false relation to life? That is, if your sex is viewed as a weakness, why not weaken an adult with it?

The hero has a lack of naïveté that he loathes in himself; in fact, he is the manipulator that many of us felt ourselves to be. I am reminded of another wonderfully chilling child portrait, that of baby Sartre in *The Words.* The hero of *A Boy's Own Story* is made unlovely because he is frozen on the grid of natural/unnatural. He wonders, as we had, whether he is estranged by his sexuality, or whether his sexuality is just another symptom of deeper isolation. He can't take people for granted because his secret poisons every attempt to belong with them.

After reading *The Beautiful Room Is Empty,* I think I see an overall thematics in these memoirs. *Beautiful Room* ends with the Stonewall Riots, the beginning of the present gay move-ment. White seems to be saying, you can't have love or moral life in a void—in a void you are just trying to survive. Moral life can't exist outside the context of a community.

A Boy's Own Story could be taken both as a model for the crossover novels of its period *and* as the novel that subverts the genre. Crossover novels tended to be family novels, tails of growing up and coming out, like Robert Ferro's *The Family of Max Desir.* The family remains our national forum, so it's no surprise that the family romance would fall to us just as we were claiming space on the national stage. Entrance into the mainstream would have to be a battle for public existence in the family.

But the family value White describes is lust for power: the indifference and brutality of those who have it, the craven self-loathing of those who don't, and the internecine battles to acquire some. And sex destroys families rather than binds them together. Hatred of the family and the assertion of child sexuality seem to go hand in hand. Dad is a philanderer; our hero mimes his father's sexual exploitation of Alice, the class evil made explicit: "I'd used and discarded him—just as my dad had mistreated Alice, the Addressograph operator."

As earlier forms are swallowed by later ones, I wonder if the theme of betrayal is domesticated here, its existential consequence replaced by a social one. The gay self (whatever it is) is extremely aware of itself as the product of historical and familial tensions. In *A Boy's Own Story*, the existential terror remains, along with the sense of isolation—why should they be eliminated? But they are framed and "flattened" by an awareness of the self as a construct as they undergo a series of middle-class remedies: prep school, camp, therapy, imported religion.

This awareness of the self as a construct is mirrored in *A Boy's Own Story* by attention to surface and by obsession with manners and mores, the nuances and ins and outs of communication. The message is always membership and status rather than specific content. Any society thus examined becomes every society. The outsider puts everything on a single plane, that of artifice. That is the wisdom of the closet: the anthropologist or imposter sees the extent to which everyone is playing a role, with degrees of self-awareness based inversely on degrees of success.

Examining nuances that signal status and affiliation has been a practice of White's since *Forgetting Elena*. That this examination is first the study and imitation of heterosexuality by a little fag will be immediately recognizable to all gay people. So here we have the poles of *A Boy's Own Story*. On the one hand, conversance is perfected. The outsider's imitations gain meaning through his struggle for self-preservation and his risk of being unmasked. Conversance becomes a strategy for safety even when it's expressed as a highly ornamented surface. "Somehow—but at what precise moment?—I had shown I was a sissy; I replayed a moment here, a moment there of the past days, in an attempt to locate the exact instant when I'd betrayed myself." On the other hand, this passage leads into an historical awareness, an identification with (his idea of) black people who were "exiled, dispersed into the alien population," and a wish for their community life. "I really believed I, too, was exuberant and merry by nature, had I the chance to show it."

But White does not conclude by giving the boy's suffering a pious moral value, because it is also linked to the will to dominate, to seize power. In the next paragraph White says, "I was desolate . . . I wanted power so badly that I had convinced myself I already had too much of it . . . I was appalled by my own majesty. I wanted someone to betray."

"A Boy's Own Story" was published in "Edmund White / Samuel R. Delany," *Review of Contemporary Fiction* 16, no. 3 (Fall 1996). It was reprinted in *Fifty Gay and Lesbian Books Everybody Must Read*, ed. Richard Canning (New York: Alyson Books, 2009).

AFTERWORD FOR BRUCE BOONE'S

MY WALK WITH BOB

In 1978 two friends, Bruce Boone and I, published companion books to launch our small press, Black Star Series. Bruce contributed an afterword to *Family Poems*, and now, twenty-seven years later, I am doing the same for the republication of *My Walk with Bob*.

Bruce's stories are examples of what can be done. They are excavations of the incidental and even the threadbare offered as stories, and yet informed in tone and sometimes in structure by essays from the Frankfurt School and by critical theory generally. A passing thought about a film or newspaper article counts as action. When action is slight, the story becomes an example of story. These stories wanted to jumpstart a discourse of intimate confession and intellectual questing in order to exalt a humanness that is almost too common and too glorious to be put into words. They convey a feeling of grandeur and maybe even a few "divine sparks" of messianic Marxism.

The beginning of modernism is a man (Baudelaire) walking through a city. Bruce experiences his own version of the fragment in a walk with me through a part of San Francisco that reminds him of earlier eras both in his life and in the life of our culture. Now the city is a stage of public and private memory. That is, Bruce returns the fragment to its place of origin. His story is told in language that notes its own distortions and deformations. It is written with a drawl that seems amused to combine the leisurely and pressured. Wonder and dread, faith and bad faith reel through Judgment, Final Things, Loss, and Language into a kind of boundlessness.

It is one of my life's pleasures that the writing here is part of a long conversation between Bruce and me that takes place on and off the page. Bruce declines to make a distinction between life on or off the page, between author and friend, between friend Bob and character Bob. He achieves this by combining essay and gossip—an essay speaks directly to us about the world we share, and gossip conveys the local reports of a community. Somehow together they direct the writing outward into a real time/space, as opposed to the mirror world of fiction.

Our writing and ideas grew out of our friendship, the texture of which Bruce lovingly conveys. We were both studious, so our friendship studied itself: how we were the same and how we were not the same, the mystery that one person is different from another, which is the mystery of form. Bruce and I put our trust in our friendship through the intervening decades. Like the complicated knots that Marie Antoinette and the Princesse de Lamballe wove from their hair to commemorate their love, Bruce and I knot ourselves together in our writing. Friendship itself is an idealized collaboration, an exalted messenger pigeon bearing affection along with the latest gossip through the mediums of telephone, literature, coffee dates, and of course walks.

"Afterword for Bruce Boone's *My Walk with Bob*" is the afterword to *My Walk with Bob* by Bruce Boone (San Francisco: Ithuriel's Spear, 2006), written to celebrate the book's republication.

DONALD ALLEN

TRIBUTE

One afternoon in 1981, Donald Allen introduced himself to me on the phone and asked if I had a manuscript he could publish in his Four Seasons Foundation series. Robert Duncan had shown him some of the stories that would become part of my first prose book, *Elements of a Coffee Service*. It was one of the happiest days of my life. Don's *New American Poetry* had been my Bible—my copy was so worn that it had come apart and I read it in smaller and smaller sections. The backlist of Four Seasons was a roll call of sorts, and Don was the literary executor of Frank O'Hara, another god. Later on, as though Proust wrote my story, Don and I would become buddies, and then later still I would be one of the people who took care of him in his old age.

When Don and I worked on my book, we had our troubles. I was driven, obsessive (still am), and Don was imperious, incommunicative. Every few days I sent him pages of, say, sixty comma changes. I expected wisdom from on high, but the few assertions he made baffled me. No, we could not put a Caravaggio on the cover because the book was not about boys. (?) In one story he wanted me to change "garden path" to "allée." Allée!— as though I were a swish New York fag, blind to the class aspiration behind word choice! Had my own deity misunderstood me? Of course it was simply the correct word, though it still seems a little dressy. When my book was done, he knocked on my door, handed me a copy, and turned away—and he attended the book party long enough to shake my hand. On the other hand, Don was absolutely meticulous, and he produced a book with no errors in it, a miracle I could not appreciate at the time. With the trauma of publication behind us, we became friends. It took me a while to realize that his abruptness had no particular emotional valence. Like Robert Duncan, when he was done talking, he hung up without complimentary close—click.

Don famously did not like crowds. Very occasionally we would attend a reading by an old friend—Barbara Guest, for example—but there was no telling how long he would put up with the social occasion, and we always left before the end. The question was, how long would he last? Later he became deaf and that naturally increased his disinclination. When Small Press Traffic gathered poets who had appeared in the *New American Poetry* for a reading honoring its republication, I somehow convinced Don to attend, though he equivocated until the last moment. "Is that Ebbe Borregaard?" Don marveled, "He looks like Santa Claus!"

Like others who are engaged with the present as they grow old, Don always had young friends. At one point he asked me to go to Spain with him, and we made plans, looked at maps, discussed cities, made arrangements. I got a passport. Then a week before we were supposed to leave, Don mentioned in passing that he had cancelled our trip. That is a Don Allen story, and most of his old friends have one to laugh about in retrospect: the cancelled trip, or, say, the dinner in his honor that he didn't attend. In his late seventies, he bought a sports car, a red Porsche, and that was a surprise.

Don avoided crowds, but he did enjoy people one at a time and in small groups. Often he asked me to make a third when his friends came to town, perhaps to deflect the burden of conversation. And yet he was ready to be amused by it all; he would sit back, taking it in with a smile. I think Don's leading characteristic as a friend was loyalty. Every year we traveled across the Bay to fête Sam Steward with lunch on his birthday. Sam was dear to Don. In fact, they were both gentleman of the old school, courtly, cultivated—they dressed in suits, vests, ties, even during the summer. Sam had been a tattoo artist, a pornographer, and a member of Gertrude Stein's circle in Paris. He told us about going on picnics with Gertrude and Alice (Gertrude pissed standing up). Don also took me to tea with James Schuyler and to lunch with John Ashbery at the Grand Café. It was amazing for a young writer. John mentioned that he had just met Aaron Shurin and that he was a fan of Aaron's poetry. I said that one of the sad things in my life is that I will always be the same age as Aaron. They knew exactly what I meant. "Oh Bob, don't be silly, you look fine—how old ARE you?" "Forty-three." "AARON IS FORTY-THREE???" When I relayed this to Aaron, he turned the knife one increment farther by saying, "But Bob, your boyfriends are so cute."

Don told me about dinner parties he gave in the fifties for his artist and poet friends. He served asparagus with soft-boiled eggs in egg cups—the guest dipped the spear into the yolk. During one era of our friendship we went to Berkeley every few months to look at Japanese art and eat at Ginger Island. We were interested in Yoshitoshi, a late nineteenth-century wood-block artist. Don had lived in Japan and China; his interest in Asian culture helped to shape Grove Press in its early days, and so the counterculture.

Don talked about Frank O'Hara and the other great poets who had been his buddies, but not so much as one might expect. He told me one day that O'Hara read "Hôtel Transylvanie" to him in a cab on their way to a party, and the poet had wept as he read. Once Don asked, "Did you get to know Jack?" "Jack Spicer? No I came into the scene years after Jack had died." "Oh?" Jack's supporter and publisher said in his blandest manner. "You were lucky." I think Charles Olson was Don's favorite poet, and one of his last projects was Olson's *Collected Prose* for UC Press, which appeared in 1997.

Don always had a number of projects going—as recently as two or three years ago he was considering a publishing arrangement with City Lights. He never seemed to be in a quandary about what he wanted to do. He did as he pleased. He continued editing for UC Press into his late eighties. Writing about Don, I realize that few people know what he was like, and I would not want to torque my description. At the same time, I find I am reluctant to intrude on a privacy that was closely guarded. He would start off a conversation by saying, "Say Bob, do you like—?" And then he would make a gift of whatever it was: a certain Scotch, a certain book, a copper saucepan, lunch at a certain restaurant. When I kissed him on the cheek, he murmured thank you. He ended his frequent notes drolly with *Onwards* (was this from Olson?) or *Later*.

This tribute was published in *Jacket*, no. 25 (February 2004).

STEVE ABBOTT

LIVES OF THE POETS

I met Steve in 1974, shortly after he came to town. He wanted to meet me and it seemed to me that he was welcoming me into the local community, rather than the reverse. We sat at my kitchen table and I understood at once that Steve was a real writer and that he was automatically part of the little overheated community I belonged to, as well as some larger communities that I did not. I bummed the first of hundreds of his horrid Carlton's, which he always relinquished with a sigh. We realized that we would not be having sex (always a consideration in those years).

Steve joined my workshops at Small Press Traffic, and so I saw him every week at least. I suppose we knew pretty much everything about each other's lives, because that's what we talked about and wrote about and then showed each other. Steve had the gift of knowing what the next thing was—he was a great reader.

Sometimes Steve complained about the stress of being a single parent. That was many years before I became a parent myself, and I have to admit I was not very sympathetic. After listening to Steve for a while, I would take his arm and say very earnestly, "Steve, sell her!"

Bruce Boone and I published *Lives of the Poets* in 1987 in our Black Star Series. I was more involved with *Lives*—both the writing and design of the book—than with any of Steve's other books, possibly with the exception of *Holy Terror*, which he wrote in my workshops. He dedicated *Lives* to Bruce, Kevin, Dodie, and myself.

I think Steve was the exemplary New Narrative writer, maybe because his Buddhism allowed him to empty without violence both fiction and lived experience so that they could freely interpenetrate, and this undertaking was supported by the most disinterested friendliness—a Buddhist friendliness—toward all of creation and also all kinds of creation, with our terrors and desires.

For me that book is essential Steve. In it he riffs on the tawdry glamour of the writing life, and gives us a glimpse of a further glamour, because the writing life for Steve was a kind of saint's life—he was ambitious for literature in that way—and so he retains the wonder that writing and life do come together. He sees in the act of writing a kind of divinity that interrupts mortal existence.

Those existences are diverse. Writing is a strange thing to do and it makes strange the people who do it. Steve recounts the lives with the zeal of an anthropologist—or a zoologist. The book ends with a picture of chimps and Jane Goodall looking at each other in harmony across voids of difference.

But at heart I think Steve was making a community—and Steve was the community builder par excellence, so here he summons a writing community of the living and the dead. Mostly the writers' names are subtracted from their stories, so the lives are unframed, more easily interpenetrating, with the spotlight trained on the activity of living and writing, and so the book becomes an autobiography of writing itself.

This tribute was read at an event celebrating Steve's work held at Small Press Traffic, San Francisco, November 6, 2011. I was out of town, so Alysia Abbott read it.

CHRIS TYSH

PREFACE FOR *OUR LADY*

Reading Chris Tysh's poem, *Our Lady of the Flowers, Echoic*, I am reminded of the days—my own days—when homosexuality was a sickness and a crime, and my flesh was dense with disease and guilt. Tysh's poem inevitably tests the difference between those days and these days. In fact, of the many translations that occur in this work, I wonder if translating the present into the past isn't foremost?

Next comes translating a novel into a poem, or more specifically, into stanzas. In the first place: a novel. In the first place: written inside a prison on brown paper used to make bags for occupational therapy. In the first place: an aid to masturbation, "For the enchantment of my cell"—the goal of many novels but few (if any) poems. Georges Bataille, ever the pedagogue, complained that Genet's writing was indifferent to communication, but what exactly does one ask of an aid to masturbation? Sade, Genet—powerful masturbators, dead stars of the self who swallow the beams they emit. Those beams are a monstrance, glorying in divinity's presence. "Thus I live with the mystery / Of infinite holes in the shape of men."

Perhaps the only fully realized character in Genet's *Our Lady* is his "voice," and the isolation of that voice is the most profound experience of reading Genet. Tysh's poem translates that isolation. Tysh's "voice" is more porous, it conveys affinity and a confusing intimacy. She confuses the personal pronoun, and it's impossible (in a good way) to know how to take this couplet: "I could without changing much / Speak of my life right here and now." Let's say she proposes a self that comes to equal an uncertain reading. But like Genet, Tysh is something of a snake charmer, or the snake itself?—lyricism unfolding kaleidoscopically, extending emotions and meanings, fastening this mouse/reader to the spot.

Duality's pluses and minuses make a battery that powers Genet's novels. He turns hidden and visible on their heads, pure and impure, dirty and proper, loyalty and betrayal, *and so on*. What concerns Tysh most, I think, are the endlessly shifting relations of the original that seem to lift out of the text (maybe this is what Bataille meant by uncommunicative). The poem further detaches these relations from narrative consequence, suppressing the difference between figure and ground, and revealing instead overall patterns of gesture. Gestures become patterns that, taken together, are a continuous exchange that manufactures structures of gender and sexuality.

Tysh's poem adds a chapter to the practice of appropriation in that it conflates reading and writing, the way a cover (of a song) conflates listening to the original and making one's version. Tysh does not answer the plot but plays it again on her own instrument, which is her poetry—or more particularly, her stanza. The writer-audience dynamics organized around the performance of self that characterize appropriation are replaced by a sense of vertigo before the act of creation. In that sense, I would call this project conceptual.

The great queen's mighty transformation into a woman must fail a little to allow the art to be witnessed. Homosexuals perfected the art of controlling our own invisibility. I long for the days when such stage effects really did make a performance. I would say that Tysh enlarges this proposition: artifice extends to the self, which controls its invisibility. The great queen exerts her revenge on time and space. Artifice leads to the truth of the self, and the truth is murder and guilt, "The astounding story where / A fake murder leads to a real / One."

"Preface for Our Lady" is my preface to *Our Lady of the Flowers, Echoic* by Chris Tysh (Los Angeles: Les Figues, 2013).

ISHERWOOD AND BACHARDY

Christopher Isherwood and Don Bachardy lived together near the top of Santa Monica Canyon in California. One sunny afternoon twenty years ago, I parked above, and Don led me down to their house with Spanish tile floors, views of the Pacific, and a tree growing through the deck. No harm could come to me in such a setting. Don was lanky, with a shock of white hair. He spoke with a trumpeting English accent, more English than mild Christopher. Don was born in Los Angeles, but apparently his relation to Christopher made him British. Christopher was thirty years older than Don, and I wondered how that worked. They were both so kind—they said they had read the manuscript of *Jack the Modernist* aloud to each other before bed. It was clear that over the years they had received generations of young writers, performing their lovely marriage with identical graciousness.

A tour of Don's studio was part of the program. He wanted to draw me. I sat in a chair while he sketched, cutting back and forth like a golden retriever, like an artist in a movie, rushing back to gain perspective, holding out his thumb to gauge relation, then hurtling to the easel to place a mark. The result was shocking to me because I was vain. In fact, it was merely accurate with a tart comic realism that could have been British—more Stanley Spencer than Lucian Freud.

Later, Christopher and I had lunch on the deck. Here was the short man with the famous eyes. His memories had happy endings and the polish of many retellings. "We laughed, we cried." In fact, I had already heard two or three at his public lectures. I was not put off. Could he construct a new life for every young writer who marched through his door? But I wondered how he experienced a past that was not private or messy. He kept saying he was lucky. "I'm lucky," he said with an air of simplicity. He was seventy-seven, and I thought being old was not lucky at all. Still, his assertion seemed to disown his own part in his achievement, and why do that? To make me comfortable, as though the difference between us was only a matter of chance? To make himself comfortable, disowning power but not really—like a master who instructs his servants to address him by his first name (very Californian)? Is achievement intrinsically lucky? A surprise inheritance of genius or will? Should you acknowledge the luck and forget the effort?

I thought Christopher was lucky to have a mate like Don, who seemed to love Christopher with accuracy. As Christopher said, "Loved for what you are, not what you pretend to be"—or what your mate pretends you are, I will add. Now I find myself saying "I'm lucky to have a good teaching job," to the young woman who may never find one, and "I'm lucky to own a house in San Francisco," to the young man who can barely afford his horrid rent. It makes me feel less awkward. Sometimes I even feel lucky to be aging, now that I clearly grasp the alternative. As for the steady love of a Don Bachardy—no such luck.

"Isherwood and Bachardy" was published as "Pas de Chance" in *Les Lettres Françaises*, the literary pages of *l'Humanité* (Paris), nouvelle série, no. 2, April 27, 2004.

JUAN GOYTISOLO

THE GARDEN OF SECRETS

Kathy Acker once said that Juan Goytisolo is the writer she wished to be (if she were no longer herself). Maybe she was drawn to the great Catalan novelist's wild lyricism, ambition for literature, and ability to balance the world against each sentence. Goytisolo was born in Barcelona in 1931; an enemy of Franco, he went into exile when he was twenty-five, first to Paris, then to Marrakech. With his Mendiola Trilogy—*Marks of Identity*, *Count Julian*, and *Juan the Landless*—he secured a place in world literature alongside Thomas Bernhard and Samuel Beckett, those other innovative despisers of their homeland. In Goytisolo's case, he was also exercising a Catalan contempt for Castilian central power.

The Garden of Secrets tells the life of Eusebio, a poet arrested by Fascists in 1936 during the Spanish Civil War. Eusebio makes an easy target since he has a taste for burly guys, "Mohammeds and laborers." As usual, the powers that be conflate sexual non-conformity with insurrection: Eusebio shares guilt with those "who wish to undermine the foundations of family and nation, encourage bestial erotic groping, foment depravation and confusion of sexes, pawns in the grip of Moscow International." (If only homosexuality *could* destroy the state!)

Twenty-eight people, one for each letter of the Arabic alphabet, meet in a "delightfully cultivated garden" over the course of three weeks to narrate possible versions of Eusebio's life from the time of his arrest. They give themselves "the task of unraveling through their own explorations the destiny of a poet engulfed by the whirlpool of our merciless civil war." Their stories play out the experience of exile: Eusebio betrayed his fascist protectors to save his own skin; he was "rehabilitated" with shock treatments and torture; he escaped to North Africa; he was a black marketer in Tangiers. He's a martyr, a double agent, a reclusive Moslem saint who mourns the love of his male servant, or a phony Polish count murdered by his own double.

The story collection is an elegant, courtly form that harkens back to *The Decameron* or *One Thousand and One Nights*. Inside this sturdy framework, nothing holds. A story may build on the previous one, refute it, or begin along entirely different lines. Some narrators appear in their stories, some are characterized by their stories, others vanish into what appear to be official documents and transcripts of interrogations. Some narrators invent random tales hardly connected to Eusebio. There's a send-up magic-realism version of his life. Another narrator claims to be peeking into someone else's journal. Still another presents a filmic version using Visconti's *The Damned*. So Eusebio undergoes continual reframing, not only in content, but in the way his story is told. The way a story is told determines how experience is understood. A story is a kind of contact that carries its alienations, its vertigo of otherness. The fictional authors of this book are united in their desire to "put an end to the oppressive, pervasive notion of the Author."

If *The Garden of Secrets* is elegant and parodic, it also rages against "the reality of a stubborn, viscous, cruel, blood-thirsty country." It is spare and pressured, it never lets the fiction become transparent; instead, it asserts the fiction of public memory. We accept Eusebio's life, which refracts into so many stories, as if the meeting of his fictional body with the historical scandal of the Spanish Civil War—the currents of "therapeutic" electricity; the doctors, torturers, and interrogators; the fake good health that equals repressive politics—fragmented Eusebio till consciousness itself escaped in all directions at once. If fiction and history are opposites, they come to appear very much the same by novel's end.

"The Garden of Secrets" was published in *Bookforum*, Winter 2000.

EDITH JENKINS

TRIBUTE

I met Edith Jenkins when she entered one of my workshops at Small Press Traffic in 1978, when she was sixty-five. Her mother Flora Arnstein was a poet, and Edith had been living inside poetry since her teenage years at least, when she was an Edna St. Vincent Millay groupie, finding her way to different cities to attend readings by that first poetry superstar. At UC Berkeley she was involved with *Occident*, the campus literary magazine. One friend who was a Berkeley student at that time recalled her to me: "She was the most *elegant* communist."

By living inside poetry, I mean that she saw the world through the lens of poetry. She had tons of it memorized, and these poems were markers for her. Poetry was not emotion recollected in tranquility, as Wordsworth said, because where was tranquility to be found? Poetry was part of an urgent grappling, understanding, and struggling. Edith had a great faith in poetry, she felt that poetry could travel everywhere, and it did go everywhere for her—to bawdy limericks; to varieties of love and indignation, affectionate comedy, searing contempt, and elegant lament; to the conundrums of time and the mystery of form.

Over the years she took an occasional workshop, most disastrously from Robert Duncan. (Robert believed Edith had rejected his poems from *Occident* back in their UC Berkeley days—but Edith had never been on staff.) It was not until the seventies, when she took a workshop with Kathleen Fraser, that Edith really came into her own, and then Kathleen sent her my way to join my group at Small Press Traffic. Although I had a superb older-writers' group, Edith declined to recognize herself in that demographic and joined the general workshop. That workshop was life-changing for many of us—by us, I mean Camille Roy, John Norton, Francesca Rosa, Dodie Bellamy, Kevin Killian, Richard Schwarzenberger, Steve Abbott, Mike Amnasan, and others. Edith attended for ten years. Out of those years came most of her first book of poems, *Divisions on a Ground*, which I edited for Lapis Press, and her book of memoirs, *Against a Field Sinister*, published by City Lights, in which, perhaps most famously, she wrote about her friends Robert Oppenheimer and Jean Tatlock, as well as the flood in Florence and her experience with the House Un-American Activities Committee. She went on to publish two more books of poetry, *The Width of a Vibrato* and *Selected Poems*.

Sometimes Edith kiddingly introduced herself as my protégée; actually, she invited me into a grander San Francisco than I had known. On one hand, she was descended from the merchant Jews who formed a kind of nineteenth-century aristocracy. On the other hand, she and her husband Dave Jenkins had been members of the Communist Party and they were active especially in the labor movement at a time when that movement equaled the history and vitality of the city. They were involved in the life of the city on every level, from the election of mayors to supporting the opera and small, literary nonprofits.

Edith was earthy, effective, elegant, solitary, and deeply engaged. I had the pleasure of bringing her onto The Poetry Center's board of directors and Small Press Traffic's board of directors when I was director of those literary-arts organizations. In 1995, when Small Press Traffic was failing, Edith was instrumental in relocating it to the shelter of a college, thereby saving the organization.

I'm making a point of Edith's engaged life because her writing is elegiac and contemplative. She wrote with a high degree of analysis combined with a high degree of lyricism. It seems to me she owes a debt to the metaphysical poets, who also tried to bring absence and presence together. Often her poems begin with a pang of loss, a pang dwelled on until it passes into the affirmation that expression can provide—not conclusion or resolution (she is at home in the fragment), but the assertion of a deep engagement with language, form, and the world; an engagement which is, after all, the real solace that writing can offer. She makes a strict accounting that takes pleasure in discarding what may be comfortable in favor of what is incontestable.

Edith was my dear and loyal friend. We dealt with our thirty-four-year age difference by simply ignoring it, which gave our friendship a kind of liberty since each could abandon the expectations of our age group. We gossiped freely and we enjoyed a trust that allowed us to speak about the most intimate things. She was not one of those friends who hesitate to give advice, and her advice could be bracing. Once when I was making a long baroque complaint about some distress in my current relationship, Edith took my hand and said, "Bob, don't fuck it up." She was a magnificent friend in every sense. I especially miss our late-night calls that usually were initiated because she wanted me to help her identify a line of poetry that had stuck in her head like a persistent tune. I will miss hearing her read her poems, how she rushed through them, the opposite of declaiming—to get them out, it seemed, so as not to get in the way of the emotion they were building toward.

I'm going to read a poem by Edith, one about Santa Margherita, which was a place she and Dave kept returning to over the years—it was a kind of heaven on earth to them.

Poem

> Scimitar curve of the coast,
> the bright lights of Hotel Helios
> at night blue on the Tigullian,
> houses in Liguria, how above the café
> awnings, a palimpsest of colors—apricot
> and ochre, the huddled Italian pines,
> red roofs with curved repetitive tiles,
> the church of Santa Margherita a Montici
> where Galileo went for comfort.

These things I store
against the dying of friends, blackouts,
My own death parched and miniscule,
the heart beating out its defiance.

I want to sing, *Where e're you walk*, my voice
rising, *cool gales shall fan the glade.*
I want to sing, *I attempt from love's sickness
to fly in vain.* I want to sing, *Blow, blow,
thou winter wind.* I want to sing, *Lullay,
lullay, the faulcon hath bourne my love away.*

This tribute was read at Edith Jenkins's memorial service at the Unitarian Center, San Francisco, January 2006. I expanded my introduction to *The Width of a Vibrato.*

BARBARA GUEST

TRIBUTE

I've selected *Stripped Tales* to read from. Kelsey Street published it in 1995. Barbara sent me a copy, and I like to imagine she saw in this poem some overlap in our interests. If so, she was right. *Stripped Tales* is a narrative that seems to come from the other side, a narrative of negative space. It walks on air, the steps of the story are in air. Instead of midair, I could say silence; the steps of the story are in silence, and if the narrative gestures she distributes throughout the poem are taken from the fables and gossip of court poetry (from the poetry of our court), then the poem's porous silence surely belongs to us as well, and is also recognizably Barbara's. Often she breaks an italicized phrase with a small block of story. The broken phrase creates a counternarrative with its own suspense, as the phrase is suspended by the story, or over the story, or the story is suspended from the two halves of the phrase.

This tribute was read at the UC Berkeley Art Museum, June 29, 2003.

JOHN WIENERS

TRIBUTE

John Wieners was without defenses; his imagination did not protect him from the world and he described that openness (in conversation with Robert Duncan) as a condition of personal danger. He transmuted that vulnerability into a sweet and heartbroken poetry whose fragmentations can be comic but are painful at heart, like those in the world. Who has written such beautiful love poetry? "I beg I bring you closer / with each word I write/I hope / your loveliness, despite jealousy / plays beauty upon my head / upon your breast. I exist / for your kiss." His work is an "event" in language because of its sweetness and dissonance.

This tribute was published in "The Man from Joy Street: John Wieners, 1934–2002," *James White Review* 19, no 2/3, ed. Christopher Hennessy (Spring/Summer 2002).

PHILIP WHALEN

TRIBUTE

To place Philip Whalen, first there's his West Coast genealogy, which goes back to Robinson Jeffers through Rexroth. In that regard, he should be cited as one of the West Coast nature poets, an asserter of West Coast localness—for example, his writing of the little towns of Washington, Oregon, the Cascades. He overlaps with Snyder in this West Coast colorism.

In another genealogy, he has the primary colors and childlike qualities of Blake. He's an eccentric—with a vision that is unsystematic in principle. A good comparison in the visual arts would be Philip Guston. In both there is suffering and play, with the bullshit pruned away.

Whalen is the gentlest of the Beat writers, and in general he has a larger scale of reference in his work. This larger scale of reference is joined to a lack of agenda not found in the other Beats. Another way of saying that: Whalen most fully explores the dictum "First thought, best thought," and the "nonself" self that lies behind this idea.

He shapes his presence as a writer through observation—a sense of Be Here Now—a look at what is happening instead of imposing a prevision. His message would be: the point of writing, and existence, is staying in the present. His poetry is more ephemeral and playful than others', and at the same time he most fully brings these Eastern, and specifically Zen, ideas into an American, West Coast idiom.

Steve Abbott told me that Philip used to call me the "Shy Pornographer." When I was running The Poetry Center, I brought John Wieners to read, and he wanted to see Philip, so I brought John to the zendo on Hartford St. where Philip was the abbott. Philip was almost blind and he had grown very large. He said to John, who was a wreck, "You look just the same." "So do you," said John, "I guess that's the important thing."

Actually, I can't remember what this tribute to Philip Whalen was written for . . ."

GAIL SCOTT

MY PARIS

My Paris, a novel in 120 sections plus a coda, recounts the 120 days Gail Scott lived on ritzy Boulevard Raspail in the "leisure lottery studio" she won in a Quebec artists competition. In Scott's previous novels, *Heroine* (1987) and *Main Brides* (1993), her narrators are emphatically stationary during the entire story—the first soaking in the tub, the second drinking in a café—yet both emit a soulful phantasmagoria of city, culture, and desire. In the first scene of *My Paris*, the narrator is reclining on a divan, but she is also traveling. *Her* Paris is a city in which the country mouse returns to the master narrative and the avant-gardist returns to the Mecca of her tradition.

In Scott's earlier books, her palette is the sentence, and it takes a few pages of *My Paris* for the reader to register the telegraphic elegance of this novel in sentence fragments.

Dodging little Saabs and Renaults. Loving walking here. Sun alternately streaming. Obliterating physiognomies. No longer nouns. But movement. Disappearing. Now heavily raining. Sitting out anyway. Over drain smelling of beer. Cold air blowing up. Under chair. From labyrinthine grottoes. Metro. Sewers. Fetid breath of Paris. Two cold coffees. Watching shadows lengthening. On la Gaite opposite. Where Colette once performing. Having walked in old boots across city. Drawing mole on upper lip. Rice-powdering delicious arms. Paris a drug. P saying on phone. Yes Paris a drug. A woman. And I waking this a.m. Thinking there must be some way. Of staying. Now my love's silhouette of rooftops eclipsing. Into night. Cold heinous breath. Blowing on privates. Through grill underneath.

These participles are deprived of tense, so cumulatively the prose conveys a grand stasis along with a headlong rush. The riches of the moment can be noted—nineteenth-century architecture, revolution, a stylish nape—and she can swiftly alter the mood and scale of an intimate scene merely by reporting, "Raining in Bosnia." Scott has found a new way to make lyricism out of fragmentation and juncture. Like line breaks, her periods bring us to attention. Paris and participles invoke Gertrude Stein, but Stein's sentences, as she observed, move across the landscape like automobiles, while Scott's fragments travel on bumpy roads that take the reader everywhere at once.

In a foreign culture, it is difficult to fathom the usual, the ordinary things the natives take for granted, and so for the visitor figure and ground continually shift. Thus the narrator finds herself trying to decode the position of the curtains of her scary concierge, or the "Glazed look of waiter. Saying outfit doesn't pass. Unless it's my anglo-quebecois accent. Putting sheen on his face." Self-consciousness blossoms into paranoia; the narrator sees meaning everywhere, which in Paris is an especially fruitful condition. She reads the "face in the crowd." That object of brief meditation includes both the faces on TV and the stylish Parisiennes she cruises.

The narrator enjoys *la douce France*—attending to hair, posture, shoes, cuisine—but guilt draws her to the legitimate dilemma of those from "the south." The colonial tide that carried France past its borders now returns with its postcolonial refugees—a new France, "Conjuring up mint in the margins." The narrator's identification takes the form of anxiety about her visa. Her friends laugh at her and correct her toward the realities of race and class, adding that of course if she were North African or African American . . .

The narrator reads Paris ferociously through the eyes of Balzac, Stein, Breton, Proust, Baudelaire, Colette. She finds Walter Benjamin's *Arcades Project*. Cast as "B," he becomes her

Virgil, leading her through a theater of public memory and montage. "Today might try and find one of those old 19th-century passages. B likening to ghost stepping right through city blocks." The subject of melancholy is also taken up through Benjamin. "Slipping into nothingness. Therefore bottling up what B calling tedium vitae. Supposedly reflecting increasingly alienating division of labor. In 19th. Now leading to useless pathos. Like: 'I not coping very well with life.'"

Influenced by Benjamin's exploration of early commercial space, the narrator obsesses on the window displays of an exclusive men's shop across Raspail. It's life inside the commodity, and her friends show her the Way: "Tres cher I telling P later. She saying stop fetishizing price tags. Value here measured otherwise." In fact, the narrator makes filigrees of positive and negative value. "Walking up Raspail in pinkness of dusk. I musing whether all ends of centuries requiring—resume of surfaces."

My Paris ends with "le Sexe de l'art," where Paris is obliterated by a fog of gratified desire. Scott and her lover "Pink-lips" fly through the city in fast-forward lust (periods become dashes) and so the adventure ends with a kiss. What is it about Paris? When I return from that city I fall into a panic—*must* get back, *must* get back. But if I can't have *my* Paris, I'll take Scott's book of fragments, a new kind of novel that sets both Paris and the genre on their ears.

"*My Paris*" was published in *Bookforum*, Winter 2003.

MATTHEW STADLER

THE DISSOLUTION OF NICHOLAS DEE

Matthew Stadler's first novel, *Landscape: Memory* (1990), was a rich, quiet book with an Edwardian patina, an amorous friendship between two college boys set before World War I. Stadler's second novel is much bolder, a supernatural tale in which his themes of dream and waking, history and the present, subvert and amplify each other. There are plenty of surprises.

Nicholas Dee is a thirty-three-year-old historian who asks, "Is it possible to insure against personal loss?" His own fear of loss prompts him to research and write *The History of Insurance*, beginning with Alton Motley's opera house, built in the 1670s in a remote northeastern corner of Holland. Dee's subject becomes wildly inclusive—he discovers that modern math, in fact all forms of modernity, were developed to support the needs of insurance companies. Democracy equals an actuarial table. But his quest becomes an awakening more "rich and strange" as he learns to welcome his own disintegration.

The novel is set in two locales so lovingly described they become characters in their own right. Dee lives in an American city controlled by brutal systems of surveillance. The sky is always studded with choppers. To escape the police and to pursue his research/fate, he flees with the dwarf Amelia Weathered, her son, and the beautiful Oscar Vega to a mythic Holland that embodies Dee's metaphors of inundation and sleep: "Stained pages in the archives; the unbordered spillage of my dreams . . . I was engulfed."

The story belongs to Dee, comically opaque, a hero from Kafka or Canetti. His fastidious, antiquated prose rings absolutely true and lends credibility to the lush romance. His observations are solemnly strange. At the house of his superior, he says, "My tongue was dry from the tea, and I kept lapping at a pool of cream I'd poured into my cup to relieve it." His disinterested stance weds such matters as music, scholarship, alchemy, modernity, magic, and surveillance into a fable, but also keeps them discrete enough to convey a sense of the incommensurate.

The police, history, clocks and heartbeats, the city, and the university stand on the side of order and legibility. The university is "strictly military in origin and intent." Its agenda is social control, in partnership with the police, who observe—"Useful information is the policeman's most powerful tool." The city reads "like a fractured sentence," and scholarship is entirely commodified, involving double-deals for "a hard/soft bio into three figures and a film option."

Order is based on confessions of guilt and complicity, and it can't allow an exception. In fact, Inspector Clausewitz, his droll, menacing police, and history itself all want to protect Nicholas, but from what? At what cost?

On the other side, a glimmering beauty beacons. Dee's growing awareness of submersion, naps, boys, orgasms, water in all forms (from oceans to urine), states outside chronology and control, and dissolution of self, all governed by a Prospero who has been shrunk by his place in history—a history of reason and force—into an extremely small woman. Amelia asks, "Could there ever be an art, again, conjured from the wisdom, the faith, of a magus? An art that was wise about power and magic?" Her son Francis is her Ariel.

The world can be read like a book, and that knowledge strengthens the powers that be—how can we subvert that legibility? Amelia says, "Facts and figures are doors, Nicholas, hard and flat. And the university pays for you to fit them neatly in their frame and keep them closed. You're capable of more. Real researches upset a certain social order . . . It's like napping or sleep, you see, when we really give in to a complete reading . . . It's a dissolution that muddies the order of things."

Stadler's book provides one answer with its tracery of plots: Dee's search for his father, who had a gift for "dissolution"; excerpts from Dee's *History of Insurance*; pieces of a musical score from *The Tempest*, a seventeenth-century "operatic prayer to the water gods"; the construction of Motley's opera house and the loves and contentions of the players of that early venture, wildly lyrical and heavily insured. These stories are dovetailed in a "flickering erasure" that mimes a kind of ideal state for Stadler— an aching, Keatsian stasis.

In all, *The Dissolution of Nicholas Dee* is an exalted romance that wanders in space and time while it adheres to a tight thematics. For example, at one point Oscar Vega fucks Dee in the heart, bringing together heart/clock/legibility with illegibility/orgasm. This gorgeously fateful story inflicts an extra pang by inviting us to contemplate the loss of youth, a loss that comes "irreversibly, from the inside." It is, in part, the unreadable body of fifteen-year-old Oscar Vega that pulls the hero into "deep water." Dee's desire for Oscar supports both the novel's subversive program as well as its love of the curious and antique. Love of boys and a painful nostalgia do seem to go hand in hand.

"*The Dissolution of Nicholas Dee*" was published in the *Stranger* (Seattle), September 28, 1993.

1985

NOTES ON AARON SHURIN'S *THE GRACES*

San Francisco is known for it's avant-garde writing. More than that, there is a gay tradition in twentieth-century experimental literature (being gay is something of a twentieth-century experiment!), and while it's fun to claim Gertrude Stein, Ronald Firbank, and Jean Genet as our own, our newest writing can seem forbidding. Somehow it lacks a context. When the dust settles (when we are history) the relation of our own writing to our period will be clear, but that's for the English Depts. of Christmas Yet to Come. Meanwhile, I want to thank Ron Bluestein for the seriousness he brought to Aaron Shurin's book of poems, *The Graces*. I thought I would contribute my own appreciation of these poems . . .

> quite a difference between the freedom you feel and the freedom they gave you, they gave you for DEAD, their flower, over grave. This time was different—the clifftop & reef, wind blowing pelicans eye-level, in consequence of sight unplanned. Man, this boy is quite a woman. See time, and that with aquatic ballet seconds . . .

If I ask, "what does this mean?" my response will not be entirely appropriate, because Aaron does not use meaning in the traditional sense. As in much current writing, meaning is developed between the reader and writer; it's a sort of play between a verbal code provided by the poet and a set of experiences each reader provides. Is this poem about gender, adulthood, repression, time? Its meaning is evocative, connotative. Look at the double meaning of "See time" and *sea time*. I think of Land's End. But this poetry wants to be extremely open, flexible; it argues against closure and the rigors of correct interpretation; it abandons syntax in favor of speed and song; it's exciting; it mimes the pluses and minuses of late capitalism; it wants to be capable of endless substitutions.

Here's how Aaron's book starts:

> the water flows sweetly where the earth cowers
> calls up a jug, an urn, a jig, a kilt
> An Irish poet ponders a Greek vase
> the water tumbles   falls

> Anyway I always liked the corner drugstore
> & especially penny candies, the bigger the better
> Big Time with a purply wrapper, peanuts out of place
> in the flat nougat, the chocolate thin & crackled

> advance to house,   advance to big time
> the celestial idea of navigation by stars
> Movies of course, the big pull of the myth to be
> what want to be most
> with moist lips filling the screen
> & that is all

First I enjoy this as a collage of verbal "nuggets" placed side by side. When I read it again, I see the first stanza is about the elements, old mortality, contemplation of Time. The second stanza focuses on temporal life, personal history, and time in the small, penny-candy sense ("Big Time"). In the third stanza Aaron combines these two notions of time: we are somewhere between the celestial stars (on a ship?) and movie stars (in a theater?). Little time and big time—individual and myth. So timelessness and time are not incompatible, at least when they become art.

Now that's my reading; you will have another. What we share is the pleasure of discovery and the surprises in imagery and rhythm—I especially like the drugstore candy and the big

Hollywood kiss that ends the poem. All this is organized by Aaron; he patterns this material with a number of overall motifs. I've mentioned his preoccupation with time. In *The Graces* he also give us nuggets of America:

> "Mary," said Beth, "call up Peggy & see if Joline wants to come."

> Then we all go to the Dairy Queen, I'm sorry, & we eat fried clams & have cones of vanilla softy

> this could be seen as a sign for good crops
> or it could be painted in the American style
> eating corn in between two plastic/metal prongs that look like corn

And love and sex:

> How stabbed he was, for me, because my master called me slave. How thoroughly, I said, deliciously, I slave to master.
> [. . .]
> I leap upon you on the bed right now, pull up the page. Darling is gross, and darling is tall, and all intimations of mortality centered between your teeny breast which do not blink but stare relentless immortal throughout the flesh and land of senses slaver, silver luscious core.
> [. . .]
> So that and how it was, along lines of sight only possibly described as endearing, a head cradles in arms, a head on a breast, & all the surreptitious delicious dialogue of eyelashes. For that, & because of it, the nausea of unstoppable giving, the rectitude of the blood organ's unflapping lift.

And flashes of perception:

> A platitude on which the whole of loving rests (chopped head)
> [. . .]

The best becomes better only with care, implicit in the infolding of tongues, and the one who goes knowingly down the desire is the one who knows better in the end.

And a high song rooted in the work of Robert Duncan, Aaron's "Master of Rime":

> O that river song green came through again body bountiful, that lay back in the arms of water I also called breast, beautiful to merely look, mere looking raised to real sight, floating without acceleration or goal, baking little cookie of self in shell evaporation—tender thing.

Aaron brings these themes to bear on what is perhaps his main theme: the mystery of words—what they communicate and what they withhold. "Bend down & show yourself, you nasty sentence." *The Graces* is a tapestry; its language has a bite, a tension that I look for in poetry I enjoy, read, and reread.

This was written for the *Bay Area Reporter*; it wasn't published.

EDNA ST. VINCENT MILLAY AND I

If you come from Northern California, as I do, the East Coast summer seems tropical, even ferocious. At Millay the light is silver—because of the pollen? In San Francisco the light is golden. At Millay, at dawn, there is an uproar of birds. I step into the day from my barn/bedroom and gasp, "What a beautiful planet!" There are native rhododendron in the forest, and you can take a little path to Edna's grave. At night, fireflies. I'm grateful that I have to climb a hill to get to the Internet—I wish I could install such an incline in my apartment. The cell phones work (sometimes!) in the meadow above the barn, and that can be challenging. During the record-setting heat wave, I wished for a little air conditioner on days too scalding to enter my studio, where I would fry like an egg under the barn roof.

Edna and I have a sort of history. I had the classic wonderful high school English teacher, Marjorie Bruce, who started me writing and reading poetry in 1963, and guess who her favorite poet was? So Edna St. Vincent Millay was a presence in the long, chaotic night of Taft High in the West Valley in Los Angeles. Mrs. Bruce recited for the class her own sonnet on the death of President Kennedy. It was spoken by Jacqueline, comforting the infant John, "My tender baby houseled at my breast." *Houseled?* Receiving a sacred meal? So the first poet I came to know was Millay, and I bought and read and copied her poetry. For the senior English final, Mrs. Bruce had the class analyze one of my sonnets along with one of Millay's sonnets, certainly my purest triumph as a writer, and a strange moment for Edna and me.

Thirty-four years later, in 1997, I first visited the Millay Colony. I had been a fiction judge; in that era judges were rewarded with a residency. It felt like a transitional period in the colony's life; moreover, a mouse had died under the barn stairs, asserting its presence ever more emphatically. I got to wander through Steepletop, which I had already read about. Edith Jenkins, a poet friend much older than I, had been a Millay groupie when she was a teenager, following the superstar from city to city. Edith described a green medieval gown, couture fashion from the twenties, and there it was, in one of the closets at Steepletop, the very gown Edith had described: jewled, green velveteen, with long dagget sleeves.

"Edna St. Vincent Millay and I" was published in *The Barn Swallow*, no. 10 (Winter/Spring 2011), the newsletter for the Millay Colony for the Arts.

GEORGE STAMBOLIAN

TRIBUTE

I belong to a community of writers in San Francisco that interested George. Kevin Killian and Dodie Bellamy, two other writer friends from California, are also here tonight.

I met George in 1985 in New York. We had been corresponding for a while; he had just completed a review of my book *Jack the Modernist* for the *Advocate* and, amidst all his praise, just between us, he went on to point out a few of the book's defects. I recognized George immediately. The humor, the love of talk, the expansive gestures, the intense loyalties and causes, the desire for connection, even the grievances—in George those traits may have been Armenian, but he so resembled my soulful Jewish relatives that we pretty much skipped the getting-to-know-you phase of friendship.

George was a born missionary. He wrote me this in 1985 about his book *Homosexualities and French Literature*: "Elaine Marks and I did this book so that graduate students could write about the subject and not be discouraged by the 'experts,' so that scholars could write without fear of being disdained or of losing their jobs. Personally, it was my revenge for a terrible purge that took place at the University of Wisconsin in 1962 when I was a graduate student there. Friends were kicked out, professors I loved were destroyed. We tried to say something about this in the introduction, but Cornell would not hear of it. As a compromise they allowed us to keep 'that word' in the title."

George was of the Violet Quill school of gay manhood, and he loved that elegance and romance—he loved making a million calls and speeding things up and being in the center of at least one known universe. In that vein, I want to mention his book *Male Fantasies/Gay Realities*, which was published in 1984 by Felice Picano's Seahorse Press. It is a collection of ten interviews George conducted—the first was in 1980, when he interviewed a masochist for *Christopher Street*. The book is a time capsule. A black man explores racism pre- and post-Stonewall. A generic handsome man talks about, well, that. A French professor talks about being a famous drag queen. The book is a trove of observations. The subjects are various, but taken together they self-consciously form a travelogue through the complexities of gay identity, the book itself elegantly poised in its year and culture. It performs the kind of cultural anthropology and self-scrutiny that is the best part of an intellectual life outside the academy. Today the collection might be published by a university press with a focus on gender studies, a less interesting context. The book communicates a warm sense of "the sexual humanity of strangers."

Certainly if George had a life project, it was to nurture writers and to validate the activity of telling stories. He went on to read thousands for his *Men on Men* anthologies—everyone I know who submitted work got a personal reply.

Men on Men was dreamed up by Dudley Fraser, Elaine Koster, and Arnold Dohlen at Plume. They wanted to generate a gay list, and to be in touch with gay writers. They invited George based on his essays for *Christopher Street* and he went on to edit four volumes. The forth is to appear this spring. The impact of George's anthologies can't be overestimated. Although he published many established writers, his real love was discovering a new voice. For many writers, like Robert Hule, it was their first time in print. Writers like Lev Raphael, Allen Barnett, Melvin Dixon, C. F. Borgman, William Haywood Henderson, and Greg Johnson went on to publish novels or collections of stories. For those of us who had been publishing with small presses, it was our first opportunity to reach a wider audience. In fact, I like to think one of the reasons I was asked to talk about George's influence as an editor is because I am an example of his missionary efforts. Perhaps his French studies gave George access to writing whose roots are more European than English. At any rate, he was one of the first East Coast editors to pay attention to West Coast and nonmainstream types like Dennis Cooper, Kevin Killian, and San D'Allesandro, and he was among the first who brought our work to colleges and universities.

The success of those anthologies surprised Plume, and even surprised George. The first volume sold thirty-two thousand copies and still sells four hundred copies a month. Those numbers changed the course of gay publishing. George made the major presses aware of an audience that had been created by a few major literary figures like Christopher Isherwood and Edmund White, and by many small presses over the preceding decade. He brought that audience into the larger marketplace, and he enlarged and educated that audience. In an interview in the *Bay Area Reporter* in 1990, he said, "The object is always the same—it's one of the few things I really believe in as a political and literary act, which is to be sure that never again will a gay writer not have an outlet for his work or be afraid to write that work."

We owe a debt of gratitude to George and to people like him who have such strong faith in the value of experience. George loved his life. He gave unstintingly of himself and loved to share his tremendous energy and enthusiasm. He beamed me so much confidence over the years that I had come to think him a force of nature.

This tribute was read in New York City, 1992.

LYNNE TILLMAN

HAUNTED HOUSES

Lynne Tillman is a citizen of the New York art world. She directed a film based on the life of Frances Farmer; her chapbooks *Living with Contradictions* and *Madame Realism* show a wry and loving familiarity with the tenets of feminism and the avant-garde; and under the nom de plume Madame Realism she publishes criticism in *Art in America* and other journals. Now she has written a novel, *Haunted Houses*, which could serve as a primer for postmodern prose. Each sentence carries the book forward, incidents are illumined more than narrated, and there is a wealth of cultural reference, from Bruce Conner to Martha and the Vandellas.

Tillman follows her heroines, Emily, Jane and Grace, from childhood to their midtwenties in (about) 1970. Jane's father is "her boyfriend at three." She grows up trying to sort out what to accept and what to reject. At one point she declines to have sex with her boyfriend and to communicate with her dad, but accepts her uncle and the fairytale past he purveys of glamorous mobsters and family harmony. She loves Jimmy, sheds her virginity, feels like an actor. "Someone is deceiving a husband, a wife. They're walked in on. The woman pulls the sheet to her naked breasts, the man grabs for his pants—Jane sees the scenes as set pieces with all the actors knowing their parts." Like Jane Bowles, who is, I think, her governing figure, Jane "walks a fine line invisible to anyone but herself."

In a tour de force of concision, Tillman creates Emily's childhood, and the childhoods of her friends, through their relations to Hilda, their lesbian piano teacher. Emily (Dickinson?) goes by intuition, a cautious spirit: she is humiliated by feelings, preferring to read about them. "She assumed she was not ready for many things which was why she didn't feel exactly what she thought she should." She resists friendship, sexuality, and the assumptions of language; and in turn she is "occupied" by them as though by invading armies.

Grace (Edgar Allan Poe!) looks for the uncanny, for her dolls to start breathing. She threatens Ruth with a knife: "What punishment could fit the crime of attempted matricide? These weren't Greek queens and kings—these were middle-class white people with problems."

Grace goes to art school, enters a fallen angel stage, befriends Mark (Oscar Wilde): "His Bible, his comfort, was 'Notes on Camp,' which he insisted Grace read as a way to know him. He told her some people would call her a fag hag. She said, 'They can go fuck themselves.' He said, 'I love you when you're brutal.'" Grace submerges in transgressive sex, "to violate that which is Law, merely because we understand it to be such," she explains, quoting Poe.

We are led to wonder—in an Oscar Wilde play they mount at a bar—whether a certain character has to die, while a serial murderer in the "real" world is killing women. Tillman's writing seems to coextend with the world, rather than close in on itself, so when Grace goes off with the murder suspect, we wonder about probabilities, statistics, rather than the "symbolic necessity" of her death. At all points, fields of possibilities open, though choices emphasize the disjunction between what we are taught and the world that confronts us.

Haunted Houses has a film-noir quality, not because the characters lead perilous lives, but because their lives are scrutinized with such precision. Personality itself appears to be a confining genre, an inadequate form. "Grace's idea of herself was a kind of box of odds and ends, signifying nothing . . . She has inherited nothing that she wanted to make use of. No, was carrying qualities she had learned like a disease she didn't yet have."

Tillman's book is patterned more than narrated, and one of its main themes is wisdom received as a hodgepodge of discrete units. "Dead is dead, as Ruth would say, and homilies rushed into Grace's mind and out her mouth, so that after saying one she wanted to slap her hand over that mouth, but even that gesture may have been borrowed or stolen from her mother."

Culture figures add to the pool of possible ways of being, combining the desire for fame with the desire to embody the times as a way of understanding them: "Right after Jimmy woke up, when his face hadn't set yet, and he'd been up all night on speed, he thought he saw a trace of Bob Dylan." Beneath this pessimism is the constantly reiterated theme: reality is founded on variables, irreconcilable differences, vagaries. The characters are always observing, as Grace does, "It adds up, it doesn't add up."

Jane, Emily, and Grace never meet. At first this seems to mime "real life," where people don't necessarily know each other. Tillman resisted the novelist's (and daydreamer's) temptation to make characters touch each other in every combination. But the people who interest us usually do meet, and I kept waiting for the chance encounters, like those of Pierre and Andrei in *War and Peace*, the two "depths" meeting only superficially. Depth of character submitting to nonrecognition of that depth is something novels often portray.

I think this lack of meeting asserts the bookness of the book—that the characters are contained in a novel and that their proximity is one of literary geography, of themes, prose rhythms. Tillman floats us between characters' associations and her own. Emily is reading Austen's *Mansfield Park*: "People argued about whether or not acting was a corrupting influence, particularly on young women, because lines that were not true were spoken from their lips. They dissembled. When Emily applied cream to her face and hands she studied her skin, which didn't yet have any lines. She wanted to have great deep lines when she was old but she hoped her cheekbones would hold the skin up, much as a clothesline holds up clothes. When I have lines they'll be my part, like an actor's part."

Haunted Houses mostly proceeds by increments of one incident per paragraph, the length of the personal anecdotes we exchange all day long. This balances the moral of shifting realities against a voice welcoming and familiar. Tillman portrays life as an accretion of stories. "Grace told Mark that she hadn't slept at all and that she felt she was filling up, and one day she might spill over. She was a story. There was hers, Mark's, Lisa's, the play, the people at the bar, hundreds of stories. Mark asked her to concentrate on her role, forget everything but it for just a few days, until D-day, when he said he could talk to her about how she was in a story and so was he. Not in one, she said, we are them."

"*Haunted Houses*" was published as "A Post Modern World" in the *San Francisco Chronicle*, 1987.

FIVE

———

TALKS

THE MODERN POET IN HIS DAY

Browning's influence worked in two contrary directions at least, and it is my intention to explore them, and to take a look at some ideas Browning might have entertained.

The dramatic monologue becomes "academic poetry" during the course of the twentieth century, an expression of sensibility and psychological nuance. The poet-speaker relates a story that has dramatic unity and telling details that generalize it. My example is the confessional school, Robert Lowell. But most poetry conforms to this model.

The irony here is double. Rather than its embodiment, the dramatic monologue was a departure from the norm in the mid-nineteenth century. And Browning developed the form in order to escape from writing about himself. It represented a self-disappearance.

Pauline: A Fragment of a Confession was published in 1833, when Browning was only twenty-one. It was reviewed by John Stuart Mill, who said the poem paraded a "morbid state of self-worship . . . A more intense and morbid self-consciousness than I ever knew in any sane human being." *Pauline* was modeled on Shelley's poetry; it is rather gushy without the fire and ice that Shelley somehow infused even in his most ostentatious gush. Browning resolved to avoid autobiography, and in fact he wrote plays for the following ten years. He cultivated a quality that he came to call objective.

Browning's second lineage of influence is of course his endlessly discussed relation to Ezra Pound and the use of personae. Perhaps this take on Browning was closer to Browning's spirit, since Pound was making something new. The dramatic monologue puts distance of various kinds into the poem, and resituates the reader as a reader of character—as a therapist, you could say. And experience becomes a case history. Mid-nineteenth-century poets seemed rather empty handed; they were searching for a ground of authority, for authentic subject matter. Matthew Arnold was "Wandering between two worlds, one dead, The other powerless to be born." That poem ("Stanzas from the Grande Chartreuse") was published the same year as Browning's *Men and Women*, 1855. Arnold wrote long, tedious lists and one short, thrilling list ("Dover Beach") about what could no longer be known and written about.

I suppose writers get to the new paradigm—in this case psychology—before the scientists. Look at Renaissance poets like Pierre de Ronsard, who created images of infinite space before scientists like Bruno advanced the idea. Like the contemporary novelists, Browning replaced the old Christian problem of free will with the new problems of social role, self-image, and underlying truth. Perhaps a certain kind of compassion or empathy was created or revealed by fiction, a feeling that will vanish from the world when fiction does. Surely no other art puts us so emphatically in an experience different from our own.

What made Browning's dramatic monologues different? Others did them—think of Walter Savage Landor's *Heroes and Heroines*, a crowd of speakers. Or the neoclassical form of the letter. Pope wrote them and he even took the voice of others—in "Eloisa to Abelard," for example. But these are public statements on the whole—morality tales of the struggle between reason and passion. For Browning's confederates we need to look elsewhere.

I'm going to invoke two writers from Browning's era, who articulated the same kinds of problems. Their names are never linked to Browning's. I hope that you will agree that they should be. In fact, these writers invented three forms that heralded modernism. I think these forms generated modernism in writing in the same way that new technologies generate new social relations. The writers are Edgar Allan Poe and Charles Baudelaire. Poe was creating the short story and Baudelaire was creating the prose poem. Why did these forms appear at this time? All forms of literature (and in fact all artistic forms) are influenced by the dominant art practice of their period. Twentieth-century writing would look very different if film did not exist. The language of film saturates our sense of what makes an image and scene, as well as the way we look and talk and move. Some people write novels with the idea that they will be made into films and of course literature has been the great source material for film. (D. W. Griffith filmed *Pippa Passes* in 1909 and *A Blot in the 'Scutcheon* in 1912.)

In the mid-nineteenth century, poetry sales remained constant while novel sales exploded. When Baudelaire published his book of prose poems in 1862, he hoped to tap into that market. He was ambitious for poetry and wanted to infuse it with the new. What was the new in the 1850s? "Which of us has not, in his ambitious days, dreamed of the miracle of a poetic prose, musical without rhythm and without rhyme, supple enough and choppy enough to fit the soul's lyrical movements, the undulations of reverie, the jolts of consciousness? This obsessive ideal came to life above all by frequenting enormous cities, in the intersection of their count-less relationships" (Baudelaire's "Appendix" to *Paris Spleen*). Modernism is in the first place a walk in a city. The aesthetics of chance begins when I turn a corner, along with the unstable point of view. (In Jane Austen, for example, one stranger enters a tight-knit society and by the novel's end he is integrated into it. By the time of Dickens people are having chance meetings—impossible if you have grown up in the presence of everyone you know in your little valley.) We can deduce two things from Baudelaire's "Appendix." First, he wanted to create a form in which the reader follows mental processes (that is, psychological processes); second, he wanted to create a crowd. Another way of saying this is that he relinquished the desire for a comprehensive point of view and settled instead for the truth of the many, of social role and self-image, of the problem of free will worked out as a psychological drama. In "Fra Lippo Lippi" the painter says he wants to portray things "just as they are" and counts it a crime to let "a truth slip." To these novelistic attributes Baudelaire wanted to add the speed and flexibility of poetry.

Being a purist, Edgar Allan Poe wanted to save for poetry what was essential to it—that is, its lyrical nature. So he said a poem could not be more than a hundred lines, and he recommended that its subject be the most beautiful because the most sad, the death of a beautiful maiden. No *The Ring and the Book*-length poems for Poe, though in *The Ring and the Book*, as in much of Browning, we can also read about the death of a beautiful maiden.

Poe was interested in science—as was Browning. Poe regarded his little stories as case studies, examples of the mind's dark workings. Could Poe have written Browning's "Porphyria's Lover"?

> She put my arm about her waist,
> And made her smooth white shoulder bare,
> And all her yellow hair displaced,
> And, stooping, made my cheek lie there,
> And spread o'er all her yellow hair,
> Murmuring how she loved me; she
> Too weak, for all her heart's endeavour,
> To set its struggling passion free
> From pride, and vainer ties dissever,
> And give herself to me for ever:
> [. . .]
> That moment she was mine, mine, fair,
> Perfectly pure and good: I found
> A thing to do, and all her hair
> In one long yellow string I wound
> Three times her little throat around,
> And strangled her. No pain felt she;
> I am quite sure she felt no pain.
> As a shut bud that holds a bee
> I warily oped her lids; again
> Laughed the blue eyes without a stain.

Browning invites us into the mind of the criminally insane and demonstrates that the whirlpool of a character's mental ruin (combined with the death of yet another maiden) is sufficient for a literary work. The criminal and the insane are the first objects of the new field of psychology, because the extreme is easier to see than the normal. G. K. Chesterton said of Browning that "he took a pleasure in retelling and interpreting actual events of a sinister and criminal type." He took an interest in court cases and criminal records.

Of course Browning didn't confine himself to demented narrators entirely, but we do love them—these black villains like the Duke of Ferrara and even the battleship-gray villains like the Spanish monk. In general Browning sought to reveal the devious ways our minds work and the complexity of our motives. Browning himself understood the struggle in many of his poems as the conflict between the Objective and the Subjective—positions that describe a psychological makeup. Is it surprising that Browning was nearsighted in one eye and farsighted in the other? This battle between subjective and objective tendencies in a personality is the central struggle in *Sordello*.

I want to look for a moment at that quality of subjectivity. Since she is so famous, let's look at the Duchess. Surely she is the granddaughter of romantic heroines—Lucy of the "Lucy Poems," for example. Or even Dorothy as she is depicted in "Tintern Abbey."

The difference between Dorothy and the Duchess is that Dorothy's spontaneity was approached through her union with the Imagination. The concept of subjectivity was new in the early nineteenth century. I would like to propose that this romantic interest in spontaneity was passed on to future generations, but not only in content. Poets used freer lines, then free verse, and then verse freer than free to bring play and spontaneity into the realm of poetry. When Pound breaks his line into clusters, or Charles Olson constructs lines out of breath units, they are both in some measure descended from the poor Duchess, who was put to death for just such validations of the moment.

Browning was thinking about novels. His work contains the kind of grotesques loved by Baudelaire and Poe, and also by Charles Dickens and Thomas Carlyle; the kind that can be found in John Ruskin's aesthetic-movement theories. In fact, the first time Browning encountered the story that became *The Ring and the Book*, he tried to interest a novelist in the project. Years later, he made it into his own sort of novel, conflating the epistolary (*Clarissa, Dracula*) with the modernist relativity of many points of view (*Nostromo, Ulysses*). This was certainly observed by Browning's contemporaries. Swinburne said of Browning's long poem *The Inn Album*, "I see the *Anthenaeum* gives high praise to Browning's new 'sensation novel.' It is a fine study in the later manner of Balzac, and I always think the great English analyst greatest as he comes nearest in manner and procedure to the still greater Frenchman" *The Inn Album* is about two love triangles, villainy, and suicide. I could mention any number of such pieces. "Red Cotton Nightcap Country" was also taken from life—a sordid history involving illicit love, self-maiming (the hero burns his hands off in a fire), religious fanaticism, insanity, and suicide, which occurred in Caen, France in 1870. Browning visited the scene of the mayhem two years later, gathering data from legal documents and newspaper accounts, and he even interviewed the scandal's femme fatale.

Like Poe and Baudelaire, Browning was attentive to the new in his period. As he wrote at the end of book 3 of *Sordello*, "The greater poet, like the sailor, willingly describes his voyages, but, at the first opportunity, departs on new explorations. These, not describing them, constitute his life."

Note on the Browning Society: I have spoken a number of times over the years to the San Francisco Browning Society. The organization began in 1902 and it is still going strong more than a century later. I love intellectual life that takes place off campus, so the Brownings always interested me. They sponsor a dramatic-mono-logue contest for students at San Francisco State University, that I won in 1972. After my reading, they instituted one of their own to judge along with a judge from The Poetry Center—I think it was the sex in my poems that fueled the change.

I attended the Browning Society's award readings and the lunches (tuna on wilted lettuce, carried by ancient waiters on silver trays, and butter cookies) at the threadbare but grand Women's Athletic Club while I was working at The Poetry Center, and I was struck by the Brownings' attitude. After a young prize-winner read her poem, one of the Brownings might say, "No, that's not how I see it"—and read the poem her way. Another might offer still another interpretation. I have been schooled in the tradition of "the grain of the voice," so this was something new to me. It was something old, actually, a kind of time capsule. Before Dylan Thomas and the other moderns put their stamp on the performance of their works, a poem was considered a script to interpret. An evening celebrating a poet might begin with the master himself reading a poem or two, a few friends reading a few poems, and then a hired actor taking over.

CENSORSHIP

One

Censorship is an unyielding topic; it invites positions that are either hopelessly absolute or lost in a sea of relativity. Moreover, freedom of speech is claimed by all sides to give ballast to their positions: President Bush, in his State of the Union address on January 30th, 1990, said, "But the fact that all voices have the right to speak out is one of the reasons we've been united in purpose and principle for 200 years."

There is hardly any way to approach censorship except through the ideology of rights, which is based on a certain concept of the individual and the possibility of an open forum. But that individual and forum may not exist. The individual is a free agent who watches from the observatory of a discrete and continuous consciousness. The art this individual produces finds its value in a forum on the outside, or to the side, of its culture. But what happens to the idea of freedom when such topographies are remapped? I may be free, whatever that means, but I am also influenced and channeled—for better and worse—by my various cultures and communities and languages. Parts of myself, like my gay identity, are such recent inventions that their historical armatures are still visible. When the self becomes relative, so does freedom of speech.

Instead of the Utopian forum where free speech takes place, our forums are developed and influenced by the marketplace: by art dealers, publishers, film companies, TV corporations, newspaper corporations, the Trilateral Commission, and so on. When you pay for speech, how can it be free? Can we experience our right to free speech on prime-time TV? Responding to Desert Storm protests, Bush said, "There is no antiwar movement. There may be a few voices, but they can't be heard." The concept of democratic rights may be already on the trash heap of history, and on some more personal trash heap.

Two

Of all the Utopian ideas, freedom of speech appears to be most possible because it seems to mean we can say what we want, which we already do in the little forums of our kitchens and bedrooms. Yet the world of articulation is divided between what we endlessly think to ourselves, what we endlessly say to others, and what we keep ourselves from thinking and saying.

Possibly art is closer to our thoughts, with a dash of what we keep ourselves from thinking. Certainly we test freedom of speech with worst-case scenarios. I turn on the TV and there's a beautifully assembled documentary on the death camps, with all their terrible heaps of corpses, and then I see the program's expert commentators are rejoicing in Germany's efficient solution. I can't tolerate anti-Semitism at eight o'clock on channel 2. Except for *The Simpsons*, I don't like what appears there now. Perhaps the only course of action is to seize control of the state and make all programming decisions myself. Here an enormous portrait of Stalin descends behind me, or an enormous portrait of Bob.

So we are thrown back on "normal community values." The idea of fighting for community values is less exciting than fighting for the rights of the individual; community values put us in a relative position. Each version of art can be seen as an alternate form of jurisprudence, another system of law, another judgment. The values of one community contend with the values of another. That contention puts a different light on the public forum of a museum.

It's unlikely that Robert Mapplethorpe would have appeared in museums at all without a gay movement, gay economic power, gay taste, gay voters. His S/M photos first appeared in alternative galleries where they were understood as tokens of friendship toward his particular slice of gay life. In that community the badge of sex elicits recognition and solidarity, like the pilgrim's scallop shell. We correctly understood that Jesse Helms's attack on Mapplethorpe was gay bashing. The problem of censorship becomes more interesting in the light of movement politics.

Remember the free-speech movement of the late 60s? That movement was linked to student demands for Black, Asian, Chicano, and Women's studies on campus. These courses, departments, and disciplines grew out of questions posed by students: Who gets to be part of history? Who decides what constitutes history? Who gets to participate in the public forum?

When someone attacks you, you should consider his grievance. That is, Helms thinks I would like to destroy some things he holds dear—that I represent a tendency in society that endeavors to demolish those things. He is right, that is correct. For example, I want people to have sex in public places. I don't want the family to be our only public forum. I want images of gay people to claim recognition from the "general" audience, and then enlarge that identification as a real possibility. We may assert the difference between representation and life, but images do restage themselves in our minds, and so call us into existence, and they gain power if they represent tendencies latent in ourselves and in the culture. Otherwise art would have no kick.

That's why I like the broad accusation of obscenity. It connects Helms with nineteenth-century social hygienists who didn't describe specific acts, but were able to contain homosexuality, female dominance, and certain art practices inside the term *degeneracy*. The Right uses obscenity in the same way. A person might not see the point of uniting under the banner "stop fistfucking"—or even "stop gays"—but might take part in an antiobscenity movement to safeguard society as a whole from the changes I have in mind, changes already occurring in the form of my existence.

Three

I'd like to relate a few personal examples of censorship.

1. Writing by myself and other gay writers was seized at the beginning of Thatcher's England. Shipments from America were not allowed into the country—the books were destroyed. It is curious that the border of a country can have its own laws, which do not necessarily resemble the laws of the country it surrounds.

2. A pressman in the Midwest would not print one of the photos I had collected for illustrations to my book, *Jack the Modernist*. I'd spent six hours in a used porn store looking for the exact right image to fit the lines: "There's Bob gazing at his hard cock with the irresistible lust (yearning) of Ulysses being lured by the Sirens." So now there's an empty page in the volume.

3. In the early eighties a friend asked to see the response to his writing from the NEA fiction panel; he thought it would help him when he reapplied. The letter to him blandly recorded the remarks of one panelist who said, "We find this to be very well written until we see that the story is about gay men, and so we lose interest." This year, I asked to see the panelists' comments: they said that the writing was of high quality, but the characters didn't interest them. Can I have discovered a code? Could a panelist say that about a well-written story by a black or Latino? I'm not saying that the characters *were* interesting (whatever that means), especially since the main character was myself, Bob. The story they rejected, "Denny Smith," was published in *The Faber Anthology of Gay Short Fiction*.

Four

I'd like to return to the idea of obscenity. In my job as director of The Poetry Center, I sent letters to our mailing list about the controversy surrounding the NEA reauthorization in 1989, and the politicians to contact regarding it. Allan Ild of San Mateo wrote back, saying he took the opposite view. He had complained to the UC Berkeley Art Museum, where Mapplethorpe photos were shown, and Jacquelynn Baas, the museum's director, wrote to him that, in her opinion, the photos were not obscene. In his letter to me, Ild threw up his hands in exasperation: "If one man urinating into another's mouth, another, a close-up of the mid-section of a fellow dressed in a well-pressed suit with his genitals hanging fully out, a third of a chap with his hand and wrist inserted into another's lower intestinal tract, if these don't measure up to your standard of what is obscene . . . what does?" I applaud Ild's enthusiastic description and I join in his frustration.

Possibly the director was protecting herself on legal grounds, but what is an artist to do? Certainly those photos were intended to be obscene, to register in the viewer as obscene, and yet they could not be described as such by their presenter, a hero in the censorship story. How strange for that bugbear *obscenity* to back her into a corner. So I have to ask, why shouldn't obscenity be part of the public forum? Does the high-art status of an image wash the obscenity out of it? Does the same status eliminate other political content as well? Does adding redeeming social value to the work, even as a frame, help obscenity fulfill itself as subject matter and field of investigation?

"Censorship" was delivered at the Outwrite Conference, San Francisco, February 1991. Outwrite was an annual gay/lesbian literature conference.

QUEER

In deep sadness there is no place for sentimentality. It is as final as the mountains: a fact. There it is. When you realize it, you cannot complain.

—William S. Burroughs, Queer

Indiscriminate Image Hunger

Queer is Burroughs's second book. It tells the story of Lee, a man in his midthirties. Lee is also the hero of *Junkie*, Burroughs's first book, published in 1953, whose author was William Lee. In *Queer*, Lee is casting about for someone to fall in love with; he passes on a few, settles on the reluctant Allerton, a much younger man, who either puts up with Lee's attentions or doesn't. On a deeper level, Allerton "did not like to feel that anybody expected anything from him. He wanted, so far as possible, to live without external pressure." Lee is a junkie, more or less, and he suffers withdrawal. Midway through the book, they travel from Mexico City to Ecuador looking for yage, a hallucinogen that fosters telepathy.

In a complex and beautiful introduction to this book, written when *Queer* was first published in 1985, Burroughs's guiding idea is that the novel is haunted by the death of Joan. As you must already know, Burroughs shot his wife in a drunken game of William Tell. He claims that her death, and the routines he began to transcribe in this book, led him to become a writer. Becoming a writer means manipulating images. What is an image? What is it for? What does it do?

We could aim this idea at our present image overload, and the siren call of the Internet that distracts me even as I am writing this. In *Junkie*, Lee is "covered"—he's on junk, so he has no sex drive or emotional need. Coming off junk, the sex drive returns full force. He says, "Men of sixty experience wet dreams and spontaneous orgasms (an extremely unpleasant experience, *agaçant* as the French say, putting the teeth on edge)." In *Queer*, Lee is "disintegrating, desperately in need of contact, completely unsure of himself and of his purpose." Burroughs concludes, "While it was I who wrote *Junky*, I feel that I was being written in *Queer*." That is, he is merely equal to *Queer*'s images. If he is being written, later on he will find himself difficult to read, and he uses the same expression—"sets the teeth on edge" —to describe reading every "word and gesture" of this book. Why?—because the character Lee is trying to escape from the events of Burroughs's life. Why? Because they led to the murder of Joan. With these routines, Lee escapes into flights of fancy. For the third time, Burroughs uses the expression, "sets the teeth on edge," because of the thick pall of menace that surrounds the routines. In the first place, the routines exist to escape the knowledge of Joan's death. Guilt is destabilizing, and the self escapes that condition by furiously manufacturing images to feed an "indiscriminate image hunger."

But Burroughs goes further. He says that Joan's death made him a writer, that he was trying to escape from possession, from Control. The host itself makes images—then, like any virus, it makes copies of itself. So, you could say the writer's destiny is to *be* this battle of images. The Control is screaming in Burroughs's ear, "YOU DON'T BELONG HERE"—which it could say to the writer, the homosexual, or the murderer.

Lee becomes more and more depressed. Finally, he is grasping for images. When he sees a handsome young man: "He felt the tearing ache of limitless desire . . . He could feel himself in the body of the boy. Fragmentary memories . . . the smell of cocoa beans drying in the sun, bamboo tenements, the warm dirty river . . . A boy sat down by Lee and reached over between his legs. Lee felt the orgasm blackout in the hot sun . . . Now he was in a bamboo tenement. An oil lamp lit a woman's body. Lee could feel desire for the woman through the other's body. 'I'm not queer,' he thought. 'I'm disembodied.'" Later, "They have maleness, of course. So have I. I want myself the same way I want others. I'm disembodied. I can't use my own body for some reason.'"

At his lowest point: "An iron bedstead painted light pink, a shirt out to dry . . . scraps of life. Lee snapped at them hungrily, like a predatory fish cut off from his prey by a glass wall."

Queer

It was an odd experience, reading *Queer* again. I suppose I respond to a book like this, a book that describes a gay milieu in the early 1950s, fewer than twenty years before I entered gay life, as too close for comfort and too distant for comfort—the toxic social relations and the complex oppression founded on living inside a secret.

I remember the days when I had to somehow discover if my love interest was queer, or at least receptive, or not going to take a punch at me, or murder me. I hoped he somehow understood that I was queer (unless he was not queer), and if he did not understand, how was I going to break the news? Now I know in advance his cock size, the distribution of his body hair, whether he's a member of the "underwear community," his identity as top or bottom. His desire for a nonfeminine, masculine, and even "straight" gay man sadly persists. "'Oh yes. Well, Maurice is as queer as I am . . . As a matter of fact, he's so queer I've lost interest in him.'"

Lee feels uncomfortable in "something I have to tell you" routines and he knows from bad experience the difficulty of a casual come-on: "'I'm queer, you know, by the way.' Sometimes they don't hear it right and yell, 'What?'" Here *routine* means communication, dealing with the risk and static that is obstructing it. In fact, the first full-fledged routine in the book is about Lee's homo identity in a pulp parody: "I shall never forget the unspeakable horror that froze the lymph in my glands—the lymph glands that is, of course—when the baneful word seared my reeling brain: I was a homosexual . . . It was a wise old queen—Bobo, we called her—who taught me that I had a duty to live and to bear my burden proudly for all to see . . . Poor Bobo came to a sticky end. He was riding in the Duc de Ventre's Hispano-Suiza when his falling piles blew out of the car and wrapped around the rear wheel." A parody of the death of Isadora Duncan.

Robert Duncan made a first public stand for homosexuality in *Partisan Review* in 1944, with his essay "The Homosexual in Society." A modernist through and through, Duncan makes a public announcement of his homosexuality, and at the same time comes out against camp, the cult of homosexuality and its contempt for "jam," along with the Beat contempt for the square, the Jewish contempt for the goy—in favor of a common humanity. He sees an allowing and disallowing secret homosexual elite. He reminds me of the young Karl Marx writing about the Jews's lack of integration, and blaming the Jews for it. Here is a first meeting of Lee and Allerton: "As Lee stood aside to bow in his dignified old-world greeting, there emerged instead a leer of naked lust, wrenched in the pain and hate of his deprived body and, in simultaneous double exposure, a sweet child's smile of liking and trust, shockingly out of time and out of place, mutilated and hopeless." The meeting occurs in a milieu that is not exactly elite. "Dume belonged to a small clique of queers who made their headquarters in a beer joint on the Campeche called The Green Lantern. Dume himself was not an obvious queer, but the other Green Lantern boys were screaming fags who would not have been welcome at the Ship Ahoy."

Need

In Burroughs, Need exists without explanation or judgment. In fact, one need is equal to any other. At various points, a need for sex is described in the same terms as the need for heroin: "Every cell aching with deprivation," and, "When Lee was hungry, when he wanted a drink or a shot of morphine, delay was unbearable."

Some of these passages are so beautiful, I want to read them to you:

> Lee watched the thin hands, the beautiful violet eyes, the flush of excitement on the boy's face. An imaginary hand projected with

such force it seemed Allerton must feel the touch of ectoplasmic fingers caressing his ear, phantom thumbs smoothing his eyebrows, pushing the hair back from his face. Now Lee's hands were fanning down over his ribs, the stomach. Lee felt the aching pain of desire in his lungs. His mouth was a little open, showing his teeth in the half snarl of a baffled animal. He licked his lips.

And:

In the dark theater Lee could feel his body pull towards Allerton, an amoeboid protoplasmic projection, straining with a blind worm hunger to enter the other's body, to breathe with his lungs, see with his eyes, learn the feel of his viscera and genitals. Allerton shifted in his seat. Lee felt a sharp twinge, a strain or dislocation of the spirit.

And: "Lee pressed against him, convulsed by the adolescent lust of junk sickness." So junk and lust are explicitly connected, and both lead to nothingness: "He saw himself desperately rummaging through bodies and rooms and closets in a frenzied search, a recurrent nightmare. At the end of the search was an empty room. He shivered in the cold wind."

Routine

If for no other reason, *Queer* would be important because it is the first book in which Burroughs consciously uses routines—little stories told in voices borrowed from the folksy cracker barrel and the hard-boiled detective. They are existential riffs where Burroughs's sarcasm, indignation, humor, and lyricism come together. These routines resemble early stand-up improvisations—say, by Lenny Bruce—and that is what the comedians called them. Routines are the heart of Burroughs's work. His first writing was to transfer these performances from spoken to written word.

Routines come to him, he says, "like dictation"—echoes of Jack Spicer. A.J. and Doctor Benway are the descendants of Chess Players, Texas Oilmen, and Corn Hole Gus. In the first place, the audience for these routines is Allerton. So, being a writer and being a gay man are equal. The routines themselves mirror or extend the action, a series of allegories.

The first tentative routine begins with a newspaper account of the murder of a wife. "There was a story about a man who murdered his wife and children. Cochan looked about for a means to escape, but every time he made a move to go, Lee pinned him down with 'Get a load of this . . . When his wife came home from market . . .'"

To cover his disintegration, Lee starts making up routines to command Allerton's attention that both mask and reveal himself. Here is a second reason for the routines. Lee wants Allerton to be the world in the form of an audience. What do we want from the world? For it to acknowledge us and return our love.

In the first days of their relationship, Allerton looks forward to spending time with Lee, and the explanation is that he has never heard some of Lee's routines. At the same time, he feels oppressed by Lee, "as though Lee's presence shut off everything else."

Before long, in a quiet way, Lee is giving Allerton gifts of money to forge a connection. During a routine, Allerton leaves, but the routine continues in his absence. So, Lee is on his own now, and the routine riffs into buying and selling boys. "I figured the boy would get me as far as Timbuktu, maybe all the way to Dakar. But the Lulu-Effendi was showing signs of wear even before I hit Timbuktu, and I decided to trade him in on a straight Bedouin model . . . In Timbuktu I went to Corn Hole Gus's Used-Slave Lot to see what he could do for me on a trade-in." After this, Lee more or less tries to buy Allerton. He buys Allerton out of his job by paying two weeks of his salary and then he makes a deal for sex two times a week in exchange for traveling together to South America. "I'm not a difficult man to get along with. We could reach a satisfactory arrangement."

In the final pages of the novel, a routine is also a dream. Lee is a finder of missing persons. The Missing Person's Office internalizes the search for the Missing Person (Allerton? any lover? any audience? Joan?). Perhaps the attempt to exchange love for money is resolved. Lee's name is Skip Tracer and he is searching for Allerton—"We don't like to say 'Pay up or else.' It's not a friendly thing to say. I wonder if you have ever read the contract *all the way through?*" So, need is married to money and threat. Lee says, "No hiding place down there. Not when the old Skip Tracer goes out on a job." "Down there" being the unconscious? "Every now and then some popcorn citizen walks in the office and tries to pay Friendly Finance with *this* shit." He flashes a roll of $1,000 bills. So in the end money can't appease. Lee starts rotting, "There was mildew under the lapels and in the trouser cuffs." He finishes, "We'll come to some kind of an agreement."

The rhythms of this and other routines in *Queer* seem to lead to the cut-ups in later books. First a narrative, then the cut-up version—disjunct, lyrical—in which phrases from the narrative jump out.

Yage and Telepathy

"Think of it: thought control. Take anyone apart and rebuild to your taste. Anything about somebody bugs you, you say, 'Yage! I want that routine took clear out of his mind.' I could think of a few changes I might make in you, doll." He looked at Allerton and licked his lips. "You'd be so much *nicer* after a few alterations. You're nice now, of course, but you do have those irritating little peculiarities. I mean, you won't do exactly what I want you to do all the time."

Lee knew that he could not find what he wanted with Allerton. The court of fact had rejected his petition. But Lee could not give up. "Perhaps I can discover a way to change fact," he thought . . . Like a saint or a wanted criminal with nothing to lose, Lee had stepped beyond the claims of his nagging, cautious, aging, frightened flesh.

Lee's aging flesh is about thirty-five years old.

Burroughs runs away from Control (literally, to escape a criminal trial in Louisiana). Yet control is also what he seeks. He riffs on Russian and American bureaucrats—they "want the same thing: Control. The superego, the controlling agency, gone cancerous and berserk."

In his introduction, Burroughs describes being possessed, that the killing of Joan is enacted by the entity possessing him. But he wants to find yage to be able to possess, to enter the mind of Allerton, to alter the world so that it will love him. There is no release at the end. The story is not one of need satisfied. Allerton takes his place in Lee's unconscious as the Missing Person.

Burroughs's last bit of writing is a journal from 1997, the year of his death. Among the entries, during the last months of his life, one simply reads, "Last night sex dream of Marker. Ran my hands down a lean young male body. Woke up feeling good."

Here is the obituary of the man who became Allerton:

> MARKER—Adelbert Lewis Marker, a longtime resident of Jacksonville, passed away Saturday, April 25, 1998 at the age of 67. Mr. Marker was born May 5, 1930 in Gate, Oklahoma and had honorably served his country in the U.S. Army in Germany. He traveled worldwide and worked as an accountant supervisor for Philco-Ford Corporation in Vietnam and Bell Helicopter International in Iran. He was the retired owner of a small business in Jacksonville. He was a sailing enthusiast and enjoyed many hours on the water. He is survived by his wife, Mimi Marker; two sons, Anh and Be; daughter-in-law, Muoi; two grandsons, Khanh and Philip; and his sister, Gayle M. Farber. A private memorial service will be held 12 Noon Saturday, May 9, in Jacksonville. For information call 743-7303.

"Queer" was delivered at Fort Mason, San Francisco, May 21, 2011, to celebrate the revival of Erling Wold's opera Queer; my fellow panelists were V. Vale and Kevin Killian.

Sources: William S. Burroughs, *Queer* (New York: Viking Penguin, Inc., 1985).

William S. Burroughs, *Last Words: The Final Journals of William S. Burroughs*, ed. James Grauerholz (New York: Grove Press, 2001).

WRITING AND NUCLEAR HOLOCAUST

According to Helen Caldicott, before the first nuclear test by the Manhattan Project in New Mexico, Oppenheimer and the rest worried that the world could "go critical" and explode. They reworked their calculations; the probabilities remained the same. They blew it up anyway—from lack of imagination? Nuclear destruction is hard to believe because we are not accustomed to believing in the world in the first place, and we have been trained to regard nuclear war as "unthinkable." The inability to think about nuclear conclusions spills over into the arms race itself.

> They asked me what I thought of the atomic bomb. I said I had not been able to take any interest in it.
>
> I like to read detective and mystery stories, I never get enough of them but whenever one of them is or was about death rays and atomic bombs I never could read them. What is the use, if they are really as destructive as all that there is nothing left and if there is nothing there nobody to be interested and nothing to be interested about.

That was from "Reflection on the Atomic Bomb," written in 1946 by Gertrude Stein, the first to say everything. "If there is nothing there nobody to be interested." Nuclear war was termed unthinkable even by the exact politicians who were thinking about it all the time. This is odd, considering to what degree the USA was *devoted* to the arms race, even predicated on it. Edward Thompson says it's evasive for us to say we have a "military-industrial" complex—we *are* that complex. One-half of all physicists, mathematicians, and engineers work in arms-race production. Thompson observes that "Increasingly, what is being produced by both the United States and the USSR is the means of war, just as, increasingly, what is being exported, with competitive rivalry, by both powers to the Third World are war materials and attendant militarist systems, infra-structures and technologies." Thompson describes the MX missile project as the greatest artifact of any civilization. So it isn't surprising that our national personality reflects an increasing militarism, and that distinctions between civilian and military should blur.

It would be naïve to blame the major poets of the 50s and 60s for not dealing with the arms race to the degree that it preoc-cupied our national life. Certainly we find in their work a trove of attendant feelings: fear, guilt, anxiety. And of course they took political stances in areas of their lives outside writing. For now, let's simply acknowledge that the subject resisted artistic production.

The problem is obvious: an Auschwitz of meaning without the concrete details for the write-what-you-know of creative-writing workshops. So when a poet like Allen Ginsburg describes nuclear war—

> Sheer matter crackling, disintegrating back to void,
> Sunyatta & Brahma undisturbed, Maya-cities blow up like
>   Chinese firecrackers,
> Samsara tears itself apart—Dusk over Chicago . . .

—he refracts it through religious systems that may be hard to grasp, but easier than nuclear holocaust. Ginsberg and other poets interpret the End from a refuge far from the mainstream, where poetic language and "human scale" can occur. Of course a linguistic refuge is inadequate; it doesn't do justice to the fact that during most of our lives a missile is pointed at us with a delivery speed of—at this time—ten to fifteen minutes. Or have religion and nature become more abstract than the bomb? But that's not the whole story. Subject matter "opens up," becomes accessible to artistic production. Los Angeles was the City of the Future in the 50s and 60s, yet its emptiness defeated most poets—they threw up their hands and moved. Now that very emptiness has become poetic material.

Why was political subject matter generally so unavailable?— with the notable exception of the Beats who, after all, claimed the fringe as their own. Is political poetry is a subgenre? Is political understanding a subgenre? For once I'll refrain from invoking Brecht—I'll invoke Spenser, Shakespeare, Milton, Coleridge, Shelley, Yeats, H.D., Pound. Perhaps during the last three decades political understanding fled to the autonomous movements where a daring leap was made: people's lives equal history. Access to that thought would give Judy Grahn the mobility to write:

> here, general, hold this soldier's bed pan
> for a moment, hold it for a year—
> then we'll promote you to making his bed.
> we believe you wouldn't make such messes
>
> if you had to clean up after them.
>
> that's a fantasy.
> this woman is a lesbian, be careful.

Now that I've generalized, exceptions start to rally. Let me include the major one: science fiction. Obviously, science fiction visualizes what hasn't happened. In the arts, it is the one voice that consistently criticized the irresponsible handling of nuclear materials. Often sci-fi plots resemble the one dismissed by Gertrude Stein: everybody dies. But this plot does interest us because it locates our fear. Not exactly fear. I'm thinking about *The Twilight Zone*: one person (the viewer) survives some mass destruction—not thanks to skill or preparation, it's a fluke. Suspense, horror, fear?—not really: anxiety that blocks emotion. Sometimes the hero ends up alone; sometimes he's in a *society* of dead people. In one episode he's stranded on a mortuary planet where dead earthlings were frozen in their favorite historical Golden Age, the 50s. It's an average American town in which Cheerfulness combats Death. No wonder we feel anxious! An average town one instant before the explosion of light. A man permanently mows his lawn, smiling cheerfully; he's dead. A neighbor permanently waves; he's dead. Kid on a bike; dead. (Last week I dreamed I stopped a man to ask him why everyone in this particular town behaves with such vacant formality. He takes my arm in sympathy and I recoil—his hand is the same temperature as the air, he's dead and so is the town. He clamps down on my arm, knowing in the same instant that I'm alive, his smile becoming fiercer and fiercer until it's a white blaze, and I understand with heavy sadness that a penetrating light is now only secondarily an image of spiritual beauty or truth.)

These stories are helpful, to a point. On the surface they are strongly narrative, but the take-home lesson is that time is over and we lack even a towel to throw in. I began this paper saying a belief in the world is hard to muster—we are encouraged to believe that life happens elsewhere, or that it doesn't exist. The understanding that history equals our lives is a precondition for thinking through the nuclear stakes. To change history we must admit the idea of change; moreover, that *we* can dispel anxiety, divine real emotions, assign causes.

During the 50s and 60s and most of the 70s, nuclear war was billed as unthinkable, with the exception of a few rugged hours in 1962. The USA's and USSR's policies agreed—as a logical deterrent—that nuclear war should be completely devastating. The offensive should be overwhelming and no defense possible. For example, in 1962, Robert McNamara, the US secretary of defense under Kennedy and Johnson, suggested a reciprocal policy of hitting military bases rather than cities. Kruschev called the speech "monstrous" and saw it as a belligerent act. In 1972 both countries signed a treaty restricting antiballistic missile sites, agreeing to leave each country open to attack.

But during these years another kind of war was being planned, a war that was not "unthinkable" but merely secret. The intercontinental ballistic missiles carried such destructive power that they did, in fact, deter, so a new game plan was invented to give the advantage to the side with superior nuclear technology. NATO endorsed a "flexible-response" strategy that includes limited war as early as 1967; new missiles were in advanced development by the mid 70s. On December 12, 1979, NATO decided to "modernize" itself. It required that the US government station these ground-launched cruise missiles in Europe, and at the same time it notified European governments that they were to receive them. So without public vote or even public knowledge, Europe became part of the Pentagon's game plan.

The rush toward nuclear war is not the madness of one president, or even one administration, but a policy we have been committed to for more than a decade—and when I say committed, I'd like to remind you of the extent of our commitment, and the degree of its influence in the life of this country. "A selective target list, improved C3 (Command, Control, Communication), civil defense, better ABM, a distrust of arms control and a strategy for victory all make it possible to think and act in a way that may bring about war," writes Paul Joseph in *Socialist Review*. This is not just "waking up" to a peril that informed our lives for thirty years, but recognition of a policy change with its new idea about the future.

Does this change make nuclear subject matter available to writing in a new way? Antinuke content is part of new wave lyrics and poetry. My writing workshops, which I take as a barometer, handle this subject without the usual compartmentalizing, and without coding it in religion or a borrowed ethnic past. Has the war industry, our country's "leading sector," become available?

During the last few years technical language has become part of poetry, even a necessary part. By technical I mean political, critical, and philosophical vocabularies. Sometimes emotion and interior life appear to be an anthropological exhibit. This is not necessarily objectionable—science should be annexed to poetry, it belongs there along with the other ways we apprehend. It increases the scope of poetry and only one of its effects is to make the arms race a lot more tractable. There's always an explosion of energy when poetry incorporates a new language.

Frustrated aggression "backs up" until it pervades a whole society. Taking a stand means that we are against basic policies and social structures in the USA and the USSR—that is, we align oneself with a number of struggles; and not only public stands like anti-imperialism, but movements that propose a reordering of priorities in society and in our most intimate behavior. Judy Grahn's general and his bedpan do not come from a poem against war, but a poem against sexism. For a peace movement to actually bring peace, progressive movements must make coalitions in our own country and abroad. I am moved by that improbable vision, which runs counter to most of what we have been taught. We don't have many futures to choose from; a collectivity might be our only option. Or do we give up control and step into the Twilight Zone?

Structuralism's chill is that without a future life is meaningless. (The "sad face" of meaningless.) The self becomes chromatic when it lacks a future—time is saturated. "I find the intensity I longed for but I'm stuck at the metaphor's *is*—without a future all forms present themselves but without a future I can't become any of them," I wrote in *Jack the Modernist*. "Baring the device" is one way to end the world, and show the secret constructedness of narrative and self. Moreover, all secrets in all plots presage the end of time when secrets are revealed and the body and meaning are united, as in the *Divine Comedy*. I think that's why the national debt is so thrilling—so awesome and pleasurable in its miniaturized version of the end of the world as a vast numerical void that could provide, just before the explosion, the ultimate generation of difference. Wouldn't we be let down in some way if it started decreasing instead of getting bigger and bigger until . . .

"Writing and Nuclear Holocaust" was delivered at Intersection, San Francisco, 1984. I was part of a panel with Michael Palmer, Norman Fisher, and Barrett Watten.

Sources: Edward Thompson, "Notes on Exterminism, the Last Stage of Civilization," *New Left Review*, no. 121 (May/June 1980).

Paul Joseph, "From MAD to NUTs: The Growing Danger of Nuclear War," *Socialist Review*, no. 61 (January/February 1982).

1997

WRITERS ARE LIARS

When I heard the title for this panel, I thought, "That's strange—only liars?" That's so tepid compared to our other sins: pride, envy, and despair. Could we expand the roster of Deadly Sins to include paranoia, the negative face of the search for meaning? I also wondered why this falsehood-and-truth division falls to writers. No one would say, "Quilters are liars" or even "Filmmakers are liars." How did writing become accountable? What is or isn't a lie when we are writing fiction? What is or isn't a lie when we are merely using language, which will always be guilty of the lie of the partial truth? Are we responsible to our various communities to make recognizable portraits of those communities?

"Writers are thieves" would be more like it—what the highly original poet Robert Duncan would proudly called *derivative*, which meant that he made explicit his debt to other writers (Percy Bysshe Shelley and H.D., for two). If you took Marcel Proust, William Burroughs, Frank O'Hara, Kathy Acker, and Georges Bataille away from my writing, I'd be sitting here in my underwear. Another way to say this is that it takes a library to make a book—or, at any rate, more than a village.

Other writers don't just teach me how to write, they teach me how to be. The self is a collaborative project. In order to make that explicit in my books—so that they can be truer?—I've tried to bring collaboration into them. For example, in my first prose book, *Elements of a Coffee Service*, I wrote about people I knew and used their real names. I thought, why, I thought, why not give the manuscript of my stories to them, and let them correct the portraits I made of them? This worked well. People improved the stories. They would say, "I don't talk that way—here's how I would say it." That was music to my ears, because it meant that there was a real overlap between the way people are represented in my books, and the fictions that we construct as we continually make ourselves up. But one friend used this final cut to hack out erotic sections of a story that had nothing to do with his own presence in order to make a more dignified setting for himself.

Behind all this is the assumption that you can rope experience into language with either more or less violence. Is that true? It's an idea that has life on one side, and art on the other. I am supposed to be dragging life through a battlefield across the border of art, either rescuing life and preserving it, or capturing life and imprisoning it. What is all this art-and-life stuff anyway, as though we all were not swimming in and ingesting and made up of some cultural soup all the time? Who would say that the presidential election is not a fiction, whatever else it is? The facts of life and death are almost too simple to utter. In his book, *Strategies of Deviance*, Earl Jackson says of sex: "Sex is friction applied to a region of the body intended to induce an involuntary muscle spasm . . . Consider how deeply and pervasively human histories, cultures, and every aspect of daily life have been informed with and determined by this urgent friction."

Is writing also determined by this urgent friction? My neighbor across the street dances naked in front of his mirror in front of the window, early in the evening, so he may be getting ready to go out, loosening up. Or he exercises with free weights, wearing a jock strap. I became mildly obsessed. I'd turn out all the lights, then creep into the closet with a pair of binoculars and peer through the venetian blinds. My boyfriend Chris was mildly irritated. "Bob, why sneak around if he's doing it in front of his window? It's a performance." I guess the performance didn't seem complete until I framed it with the guilt of the peeping Tom.

Next time, Chris couldn't help calling out, "Hey Bob, your honey's in the window again." When Chris complained more sincerely, I'd say very piously, "The unexamined life is not worth living!" That is, we live in a soup of ideology. What is there for us to do but look at it—and change it? (One day I happened to be outside my house when this show occurred, and each window of my building held a blandly staring male face.)

For John Keats, life stands here, art stands there. When I was a kid I thought so too. A movie called *The Red Shoes* shaped my development as an artist and fag. I saw it on TV when I was twelve. It's one of those strange allegories by the English team Michael Powell and Emeric Pressburger. It retells the Hans Christian Andersen fairy tale. In the film, life is true, but so is art, an exalted shadow-world founded on excess, obsession, and denial. A young student (Moira Shearer) becomes a great ballerina under the Svengali-spell of an impresario (Anton Walbrook). "You must turn your back on life in order to become a great artist." But when life takes the form of the man she loves, she is no longer able to sustain this duality, and finally she brings these two realms together by dancing into a locomotive and killing herself. What great relief I experienced—I could choose between art and life! Baseball, I felt, was on the side of life. But the moral of *The Red Shoes* is that although art and life may be separate for a while, in the end life can't be denied—and the truth of life is that its defining events are irreversible.

In my own work, fiction and fact interpenetrate. Here is a Bob, he's a writer, he lives in San Francisco. Here is Bob's stupid love life, blow by blow. Here are his friends by name. This sets up a different relation to the reader, since it's apparent that at least some of the matter in the novel takes place in the same world the reader lives in. Maybe it's what the French call *autofiction* when they talk about Genet or Hervé Guibert. Often work that interests me has this performance quality to it. I try to approximate the irreversibility of a performance—something you can't take back, some nakedness, some shame, some detail too intimate, something

I make my body do, something that happens to it. Some propriety gets transgressed, some rule gets broken. And perhaps some part of life changes a little. Here is a really stupid example. On Amazon.com readers can post reviews. I happened to look a few months ago, and found a review of *Margery Kempe* that went something like this: "Who is Robert Glück trying to fool? We saw in *Jack the Modernist* that he is a bottom, and now here he is in *Margery Kempe* trying to pass himself off as a top?" I thought, what a perfect New Narrative critique: extraliterary, accountable to a community.

When I discussed this talk with Eileen Myles, she pointed out all the interest in memoir just now—both exalted by reviewers and treated with contempt. All this anxiety about the truth, and interest in the truth, seems to focus on the truth of abjection. This display of true misery has an element of theater. The heroin of *The Red Shoes* can play the dying swan into infinity, but the locomotive that actually kills her is delivering news from the real world.

"Writers are Liars" was delivered at the Readers and Writers Conference, San Francisco, 1997.

ON THE WAR

Hello everyone,
It's Bob Glück here—Camille Roy has kindly offered to read these few
thoughts of mine, since I am away in Buffalo right now.

After the antiwar protests last month, mostly organized by a group
called International Answer, there were some protests about how
the protests were conducted. People objected that a variety of other
issues were raised, from the treatment of American Indians to the
incarceration of Mumia Abu-Jamal. Michael Lerner complained
about the pro-Palestinian speeches and said, "It feels we are being
manipulated when subjected to mindless speeches and slogans
whose knee-jerk anti-imperialism rarely articulates the deep reasons we should oppose corporate globalization." I remember that
these same issues arose in my antinuke affinity group in the eighties: Should we take on other issues at the risk of blunting our
attack? Should we also organize against apartheid in South Africa?
Sure. Anti-intervention in Central America? Yes, certainly. Should
we bury a crystal at the beach in a peace ritual?

As a writer addressing the issue of war, I am faced with a variety
of problems that are also not new. How to avoid rhetoric?—or
better, what to do with rhetoric? Why trust an antiwar narrative
if I subvert other kinds of narratives? What is our writing able to
accomplish given our circumstances? Who do I convince?

I am interested in writing that explores; it is the exploration of
our situation that interests me. So I say, bring on the other

issues. I would like to know what the relation is between the desire for war in the White House and the most intimate ways that we live. I give Kathy Acker a lot of credit for continually bringing the ways we live and feel, and even the way we understand family and sex, onto the largest political stage, never letting us or herself off the hook, implicating language and desire. That is, she demonstrated that the structures of power and oppression replicate themselves from the top down. I also like that she fought dirty, not trying to convey objectivity, but a volcano of rage.

It's weird being an American, we can't seem to get a grip on how we are thoroughly oppressed and used because it does not tally with our commodity culture's self-description. Actually, we live in a violent stew. At the same time we are so insulated by that culture that we can't relate to the poverty and terror experienced by most of the world, including many who live in this country—that is, many of us.

"On the War" was written for a panel on the pending invasion of Iraq at New Langton Arts, San Francisco, January 31, 2003.

UNCERTAIN READING

We were asked to write a manifesto for this occasion. I began airing my opinions about writing in the late seventies, when New Narrative was taking shape. Some of the battle lines from that era seem rather artificial now. Now we take for granted that narrative and the fragment exist in one work, that they may be the same thing, while earlier there could be a dispute between narrative and what was called nonnarrative. It is possible these battles were more a matter of descriptive terminology; or, of more interest, a way to organize and generate community. So I ask myself, what would I like to do and what am I doing and what do I look for?

During the last twenty-five years a rich discourse evolved in the field of poetry. Has any comparable critical language developed in fiction? I suppose most contemporary fiction, even the edgy and hip, is basically middlebrow (to use an old-fashioned term) enter-tainment that supports the status quo. Despite being trapped in an inflated self-description that would more aptly (and did!) describe novels by F. Scott Fitzgerald and the Bloomsbury group, most fiction is no better or worse than most TV, which, after all, does attract lots of talent. I want to experience the depth of a writer's engagement with language and form, and to witness the struggle to bring new content onto the stage of literature. This engagement and struggle make me feel that life—my own life—has value. I believe this is the consolation that art can give to us.

It seems to me that the loss of human scale is our main event, so I am interested in writing that explores our pervasive sense of marginality, our loss of meaning and value, and the reconstruction of meaning and value. When we address these issues, we face the contradictions that shape our lives—how do we value our experience, what measure or yardstick do we use, what is the meaning of the individual versus the group, how do we deal with difference, what *is* an individual?

My various communities are a kind of narrative: they offer me ways to see myself and forms for my being to flow into. They also offer me ways to lose myself. One of my literary communities says this can be done by displaying the materiality of language, in which operation all meaning collapses, or appears to be made-up, two dimensional, a stage set or false front. I get a glimmer of the flip-side of language, that aware silence that language does not convey, and in fact obstructs.

My gay community says that displaying the materiality of the body, whether through sex or death, can generate awe, and I am brought again to a verge where I experience a sense of wonder. I think it is a writerly task to make us feel wonder, to provide a mirror in which to recognize ourselves (or which forces us to recognize a self), but also to provide a picture of an escape from the confines of the self.

In 1994, Tim Etchells was asked to write a manifesto about performance, and I want to assert some of his assertions, but bring them into the realm of writing. Etchells is a British performance artist who founded the company Forced Entertainment in 1984, and he is also a fiction writer whose book *The Endland Stories* is one of my favorites. He's written other books, and just now a novel is appearing, *Broken World*. I am writing my version of an AIDS memoir, a novel called *About Ed*, and I have been thinking about Etchells. I want to build Ed's tomb but that is the kind of undertaking in which issues of truth and respect come forward. I mean *tomb* in the sense of *tombeau*, a musical form in the sixteenth century, a poetic form in the nineteenth and twentieth—"Le Tombeau de Charles Baudelaire." So Ed's tomb is to be a public monument.

Issues of truth telling are perhaps more pressing here than in the erotic and romantic stories I have written.

But where does the truth exist? Surely not in the facts, surely not in the novel genre, surely not in the memoir genre. Everything I write is autobiography, and yet I have little interest in the difference between fact and fiction. If personality is a fiction—a collaboration between ourselves and the world—then what would the truth of any memoir consist in? In the representation of a fiction? Surely not in our language, which can't be activated without a point of view; surely not in anecdotes that have been rounded off to include the useful and reject the entire world.

Etchells says, "Like all the best performance it (investment) is before us, but not for us . . . This privacy of investment doesn't make a solipsistic work or a brick wall to shut the watcher out. Quite the opposite—investment draws us in. Something is happening—real and therefore risked—something seems to slip across from the private world to the public one—and the performers are 'left open' or 'left exposed.'"

He continues, "To be bound up with what you are doing, to be at risk in it, to be exposed by it. As performers we recognize but cannot always control these moments—they happen, perhaps, in spite of us . . . In the complicity of the performers with their task lies our own complicity—we are watching the people before us, not representing something but going through something. They lay their bodies on the line . . . and we are transformed . . . not audience to a spectacle but witness to an event."

Add the sacred to this passage and it could have been written by Georges Bataille to describe a mass or some other sacrifice. But how can this performance—which is the time-based relationship between performer and audience—be transformed into words on a page? Our bodies are material—how do we put them on the page? Death may be real, but how do we include the inexpressible and the irreversible in our description? An orgasm may be real, but the language to describe it is part of the vast engine of ideology.

It seems to me that every goal in writing is impossible, and for this reason every goal invokes its opposite. George Oppen shows us that the attempt to be clear invokes distortion, and yet it is not possible to write nonsense without some kind of sense entering. The concrete poets showed us that there is no language object that escapes all transparency any more than realism or naturalism can entirely suppress the materiality of language. So a performance-based fiction would reassert the limits of language, though it may be a good idea not to know in advance what form that would take.

Etchells writes, "Does this action, this performance, contain these people (and me) in some strange and perhaps unspeakable way?" If we can't alter a text once it is published, we can create a disturbance in the reading that mirrors the intensities of experience, including the experience of writing, which activate the text each time it is read. This strategy could lead to the creation of an uncertain reading. A reading that is out of control, that makes a problem of reader/writer dynamics, because the goal of the writer is not to organize the psychic life of the reader, but to disorganize it.

Here are ways we might create an uncertain reading.

1. Maintaining the stance of an amateur instead of a professional. (Harkening back to the early modernists.)

2. Sentences with no denotative meaning.

3. Writing as though the work is a translation from a richer language. "A translation, instead of resembling the meaning of the original, must lovingly and in detail incorporate the original's mode of signification, thus making both the original and the translation recognizable as fragments of a greater language" (Walter Benjamin).

4. Elaborating the narrative on many levels.

5. A sentence that is porous; composition by the sentence, in order to translate silence onto the page, to create gaps between sentences, to allow each next sentence its full latitude. The sentence is the palette. To suppress the paragraph and assert the sentence creates a writing at once more global and more fragmentary.

6. Mixing modes of composition—which is the same as mixing temporal units. Fragment to extended narrative.

7. Break the guided daydream that most fiction is. Why confine ourselves to the middle distance, which is part of a chain of regulation that extends inward and outward? Why only know that much about the world or a character? Why not introduce a character by how she experiences her death, her birth, her orgasms, instead of by the appearance of her hat? Close-ups so close they become objective—thirst is taking a drink, desire is fucking. Long shots that take in history—her grandfather's immigration exists in her gestures.

8. To not know. To not have all the answers. To not even have a notion.

9. To address the reader.

An uncertain reading allows the reader to experience risk, wonder, loss of self, nothingness, but that is not the whole story. In a performance, the spectator is isolated and yet his loss and risk are experienced as part of a group. The group creates the occasion for isolation, risk, and loss of self, and that dynamic is important in establishing and maintaining the life of a community, even one that lasts only a few hours. So, how to create the experience of a group in a solitary reader?

So many battles behind us, yet next to me on the plane a suit dominates the armrest and his newspaper covers the sky—and I see that as a gay issue, don't you? By the same token, when I look at the sky, the sky becomes homosexual. The life of a sexual minority is such a public thing, I have often thought that even when we are alone or paired off, our sex itself takes place on the village green. Or the village screen. Perhaps the best model for us to aspire to in our writing is an orgy. How to show the reader that he and she are taking part in an orgy?

"Uncertain Reading" was delivered at the CUNY Graduate Center, New York City, 2009. It was published in *Aufgabe*, no. 10, guest ed. Cole Swenson (2010).

Sources: Tim Etchells, *Certain Fragments: Contemporary Performance and Forced Entertainment* (New York: Routledge, 1999).

A COUNTER LANGUAGE

> In the English novel (by which of course I mean the American
> as well) more than in any other, there is a traditional difference
> between that which people know and that which they agree to
> admit that they know, that which they see and that which they
> speak of, that which they feel to be part of life and that which
> they allow to enter into literature.
>
> —Henry James.

Henry James says some things are known and not articulated, but
he also refrains from saying what they are—he means sex and class,
of course. But our inability to articulate goes beyond prudery and
social convenience. We come up against a certain resistance in language itself if we describe the body. We cannot describe someone
eating an apple as closely as, say, the nuances of a legal or philosophic debate. I want to bring new matter into writing—the long
shot that gives historical scale, the close-up so intense that character disappears and shared biology and gesture become apparent. To
describe someone eating, breathing, having an orgasm, sweating is
an adventure, a journey in dangerous terrain.

My next book, *Denny Smith*, is a collection of stories, some
already published, some new. When I was arranging these stories,
I realized that every one contains one or more descriptions of an
orgasm. I was thinking about adding them up and calling the
book, say, *53 Orgasms*. I worried that the stories would seem
redundant, and my preoccupation with sex would make me look
subnormal. I started arranging the stories so that the orgasms

wouldn't bunch up together, tipping the book at one end or the other—but rather presenting themselves equidistantly, like the gas laws applied to excited molecules.

This orgasm problem is compounded by the fact that most of them belong to me, to Bob. They are Bob's orgasms. And often they are not even honestly come by, but the result of masturbation. So I seem like some postmodern Portnoy, trapped in a neurotic appetite for tension and release, confining the modulation of intensities (that fiction is) to the narrow stage of my genitals. And that situation is compounded by the fact that some of these orgasms are fictional, presented as such, and others actually happened, presented as such, and some are fictional and presented as actual, and of course some actual experiences were deployed in my fictional characters. And they are all fiction, since they exist in the language of fiction, and 99 percent of each actual orgasm *was* fiction—that is, drama, fantasy, history, fields of study, and personal interpretation heaped on what is really just a few involuntary spasms.

Is it enough to say, because sex interests me? These intensities often fall in the stories at intense moments. Is sex shorthand for intensity? —the longed for, impossible meeting of feeling and event?

Burroughs put a Buddhist spin his own preoccupation in *Naked Lunch*, that of hanging boys and girls by the neck while fucking them. "Mark reaches up with one lithe movement and snaps Johnny's neck . . . sound like a stick broken in wet towels. A shudder runs down Johnny's body . . . one foot twitches like a trapped bird . . ." Burroughs said that by repeating these images, by meditating on them, he was using them up, wearing them out. Are those recycling images the wheel of fire that desire is to a Buddhist? One image replaces another, but only with an image that in some way duplicates or reinforces the first. I like the notion that I am wearing out obsessions and ghosts, a process leading finally to health, as long as the process of writing is exalted and the impossibility of a cure is obvious, or as long as the result of that successful treatment is the overwhelming awareness of suffering and the acceptance of suffering incompletion—a poorly constructed puppet.

I wonder if those of us who write about sex never really got over the shock of it. Desire is shocking to me; I am still working out the terrors and physical sensations and loss of self, the control of self in order to find a way into sex, the long distance leap from no touch to touch, the gain in control over another body, the generation of pleasure inside another body, the unimaginable intimacy, the involuntary spasm, the fact of skin, the fact of pleasure, the fact that we have bodies.

For my novel *Margery Kempe*, I asked twenty men and twenty women to give me five observations each about their own relations to their body—death, illness, sex. I was trying to harvest a kind of language from a village commons. I gave these nuggets to shadowy fifteenth-century characters, so the Miller's wife can't have an orgasm unless watched by a third person. To describe a character that way, as opposed to, say, describing her hat, disrupts social distance and fiction's middle distance, one link in the long chain of regulation.

I suppose when one is having homo sex, or any sex off the highroad, or maybe any sex at all, it is as though one were meeting through a third party, speaking and acting through a third party—as though sex itself were acting and speaking a counterlanguage. So these little nuggets of physicality, which are far too personal to actually identify anyone, take the form of a community's expectations, become objective. I wanted to install a contradiction in my book, a community of bodily anarchism—that is, the kind of community we live in. By *community*, I mean the entire ensemble of social interactions—in any given moment—which we shape, which shapes our being, which we recognize and where we find some degree of recognition.

Here's a passage from "Workload," a story about looking at porn. "There's a patch of shine on JT's inner thigh, catching the light just at the shadow made by Larry's cock . . . The grease shine is still inside the controlled daydream the photos monitor; it plays a chance role so it conveys more authority. In these accidents I most exist, most take part . . ." This passage puts a spin on the language of porn. Camille Roy says, "Genre is not about representing experience but producing and organizing feeling . . . Because genre writing deals in something as low as feeling, these forms are relatively easy to use in other contexts for other purposes."

You could say this counterlanguage, the language of physical life, insists on the abnormal even in the face of pleasure, which has the quality of making everything seem normal. That is, inside the experience of pleasure, whatever causes that pleasure is normalized for the sake of the pleasure. So it takes a certain kind of attention to retain a certain kind of strangeness. I recall a long passage about masturbation that Kathy Acker read one night on stage in a club, wearing an Issey Miyake gown, in which she kept warning her cunt not to become ridged. That kind of attention. In "The Glass Mountain," I wrote, "First it was fun to gather myself into the precinct of my groin, and I sort of stood back from this piece of the natural world attached to my front, a thing from Wild Kingdom stuck to a body softened by TV and reading in bed. Or a column of rock candy, it's tasting itself, the flavor is sweet." The body is a foreign terrain.

We all know pleasure can bury history and scale, it can destabilize the self, but any sex act can also take you in a lot of directions. In a story called "Hidden in the Open," I try to chart out as many of those directions as I can. I am masturbating at a woman's clinic to produce sperm in order to have a child. All objects and actions have a history: the straight porn magazines, the gay porn I had found one night on the street, the difference between the straight and gay porn (illusion of intimacy vs. illusion of alienation), the history of the vibrator my friend Susie abandoned at my house, and the romantic loss that finally triggers an orgasm.

An irreversible language. Though what may be irreversible is my own shame or risk in revealing it to you. If I show the reader a cunt or a cock in writing, I may call arousal into being. I may be asking for that. Replacing one feeling with the next causes the reader to be anxious, angry, amused. But when I incite arousal, the reader can't replace that feeling with, say, sadness. At the same time, I can't bring him to consummation. Since pleasure can't fully satisfy unless the self is disrupted, how can masturbation disrupt the self? I look out from the page, inviting the reader to believe my excitement stems from his appetite.

In the olden days of the seventies, the promise of sexual pleasure and the promise of narration was that, against all odds, total presence is possible, attainable. In the former, total presence of my mind and body. In the latter, total unity of the story of my life with my historical moment, total identification with my fate. In both cases, a break in consciousness deprives me of this attainment: in the first place an orgasm, in the second place my death. Now I think we take it for granted that such unities do not exist, which makes them more interesting; perhaps they are merely our latest version of the Garden of Eden.

One image replaces another, and that is probably what heaven is. I like that lack of literary integrity, that destabilization. I imagine selves and bodies breaking apart and rejoining like mercury, pieces of bodies (our own and others', imaginary and real) appearing as they call forth our shifting attention.

But even if that were not the case, and the sex described were not arousing but the opposite, the dynamic stays the same, because repulsion and abjection have their own kinds of vertigo. Sexual extremes create a public performance in which the reader is seeing just how far a writer will go. Most writing is a mirror in which a reader can recognize himself without thinking too much about it, but what if I erect a hall of mirrors in which the reader is both fearful and eager to catch sight of his own reflection?

"A Counter Language" was delivered at Prose Acts, a conference at SUNY-Buffalo, 2001. It was published in *Lipstick Eleven*, no. 3, eds. Robin Temblay- McGaw and Jim Brashier (2004), and revised and reprinted in *Séance*, eds. Christine Wertheim and Matias Viegener (Los Angeles: Make Now Books, 2006).

NARRATION

Most art seems to want to be the final image, where substitution stops, that kind of eternity. To complicate that final image is to complicate narrative expectation. Narrative names the world as if it knew it. We can see it operate in the rhetorical scramble that our nation is making, now that the story it tells itself about its own inviolability has been broken—a break in narrative expectation. I instinctively want to feel complete. Is that the essence of self-preservation? Maybe that is why eternity is usually described as unmoving, unchanging, the final image. Incompletion is a position that cannot be tolerated for long. Even in fragmented writing the self goes back and forth between fragmentation and the allegory that any form makes, so a fragmented self can be reintegrated on the level of form. But I also know that my real condition is one of incompletion. For starters, I am only part of the world.

One way we create a human scale and a sense of who we are and what pertains to us is by sending our being into forms that give our being shape—whether stories our friends tell us, or we tell them, or books, or language itself. This process is what I have come to think of as narration. It is a two-part process, in that in order to be complete a story needs a stage with dramatic footlights, and that stage is the consciousness which the reader or listener lends to the speaker. Lending our psychic life to these stories is what gives them strength. Sometimes the reader also becomes the writer, through interpretation or through participation in open forms; sometimes the writer also becomes the reader, through the use of appropriation or an awareness of the always-already-borrowed nature of language.

Maybe narration is nothing except expectation. Then, to foil narrative expectations makes the reader incomplete. That is, when the plot disappears, the reader is left with an excess of being and no place to put it, no story to give it shape. It is as though that state of incompletion corrects an error in self-understanding. So disjunct writing describes a fragmented self. By *disjunction*, I mean a break in narrative expectation, like switching point-of-view midsentence as Juan Goytisolo does in *Makbara*, mixing of genre, working with the sentence as palette, working below the sentence, working with collage and appropriation, seeing character as an environment, or subtracting in order to create a minimalism.

Then how to reintegrate the reader, with what new matter? Where do we apply that excess of being? And then a laundry list: to convey spiritual states, to describe the porousness of experience, to describe the space between fragments, to represent women's experiences, to make writing know itself, to examine the ways narration makes meaning by obstructing that process, to portray a desolate breakdown of character and society, to celebrate the ployvocal, to collapse categories, to display the self as a fiction, as an "imaginary resolution of a real contradiction" (to quote Jameson).

In *The Madness of the Day*, Maurice Blanchot writes with an "I" that will not stay within the borders of the individual—who partakes of and disintegrates into the universe—to the dismay of those custodians of identity, social workers and mental health professionals. The "I" is a riddle—silence, emptiness—that can't be grasped. "As nobody, I was sovereign"—because Nobody can't be recognized. That is, Blanchot adds emptiness to the narrative of recognition. Camille Roy writes, "I think it is possible to have one identity in your thumb and another in your neck. I think identities can travel between persons who have an unusual mutual sympathy . . . I take it as a given that the well-modulated distance of mainstream fiction is a system that contains and represses social conflict, and that one purpose of experimental work is to break open this system . . . Breaking this long chain of social convention at any link can easily result in personal and literary deformity, another term for experimentation."

A mainstream novel will support our conventional notions of time—a point on a straight line or a point on a circle. Giorgio Agamben writes, "The elements for a different concept of time lie scattered among the folds and shadows of the Western cultural tradition" *(Infancy and History: On the Destruction of Experience).* Maybe Baudelaire was getting to it when he wrote, "How penetrating are the ends of autumn days! Ah! Penetrating to the verge of pain! For there are certain delicious sensations whose vagueness does not exclude intensity; and there is no sharper point than Infinity."

Could those "folds and shadows" include experimental writing, which often complicates narrative time by combining it with the time of its own reading—by bringing the reader to his/her own present through fragmentation? That is, by an experience of time in smaller and smaller units? But what about writing that undermines even that seesaw, by including the time of the writer's life, which may overlap with the time of the reader's life? Could such a deep interruption of narrative be like Gnostic time—which may be represented as a broken line?

"Narration" was delivered at Prose Acts, a conference at SUNY-Buffalo, 2001. It was published in *Lipstick Eleven*, no. 3, eds. Robin Temblay-McGaw and Jim Brashier (2004).

ACKNOWLEDGMENT

My thanks and tender affection to Judith Goldman for her careful readings, to Jocelyn Saidenberg for her support, and to Team Bob. Thanks to the College of Liberal and Creative Arts at San Francisco State University, especially Paul Sherwin and Maxine Chernoff. I am grateful to Robert Dewhurst for his exquisite work on this book, and to Hedi El Kholti and Chris Kraus—thanks and love. To the dear editors of the magazines, blogs, zines, journals, newsletters, newspapers, and anthologies who published these essays, *grateful acknowledgment!*

ABOUT THE AUTHOR

Robert Glück is author of ten books of poetry and fiction. His books include two novels, *Jack the Modernist* and *Margery Kempe*; two books of stories, *Elements* and *Denny Smith*; a book of poems and short prose, *Reader*; and, with Kathleen Fraser, a book of prose poems, *In Commemoration of the Visit*. With Bruce Boone, Glück published Black Star Series and translated La Fontaine for a book of that name. With Camille Roy, Mary Berger, and Gail Scott, he edited *Biting the Error: Writers Explore Narrative*. Glück prefaced *Between Life and Death*, a book of Frank Moore's paintings, and he made a film, *Aliengnosis*, with Dean Smith. Glück was an associate editor at Lapis Press, codirector of Small Press Traffic Literary Center, and director of The Poetry Center at San Francisco State University, where he is an emeritus professor. He lives "high on a hill" in San Francisco and in a love nest by the Baltic in Malmö, Sweden, with his husband, Xavi.